AI and Cloud Native Software Engineering

Building enterprise-scale cloud-native applications with AI-integrated software engineering workflows

Dr. Pethuru Raj Chelliah

Dr. Kavita Saini

Dr. Rani Kumari

www.bpbonline.com

First Edition 2026

ISBN: 978-93-78540-479

LIMITS OF LIABILITY AND DISCLAIMER OF WARRANTY

The information contained in this book is true and correct to the best of author's and publisher's knowledge. The author has made every effort to ensure the accuracy of these publications, but the publisher cannot be held responsible for any loss or damage arising from any information in this book.

All trademarks referred to in the book are acknowledged as properties of their respective owners but BPB Publications cannot guarantee the accuracy of this information.

Distributors:

BPB PUBLICATIONS
20, Ansari Road, Darya Ganj
New Delhi-110002
Ph: 23254990/23254991

DECCAN AGENCIES
4-3-329, Bank Street,
Hyderabad-500195
Ph: 24756967/24756400

MICRO MEDIA
Shop No. 5, Mahendra Chambers,
150 DN Rd. Next to Capital Cinema,
V.T. (C.S.T.) Station, MUMBAI-400 001
Ph: 22078296/22078297

To View Complete BPB Publications Catalogue Scan the QR Code:

Published by Manish Jain for BPB Publications, 20 Ansari Road, Darya Ganj, New Delhi-110002 and Printed by him at Repro India Ltd., Rewari.

www.bpbonline.com

Dedicated to

Our families and friends

About the Authors

- **Dr. Pethuru Raj Chelliah** is a principal AI architect at Infocion Inc., Bangalore. Previously, he worked as the vice president and chief architect at the AI division of Reliance Jio Platforms Ltd., Bangalore, IBM Global Cloud **Centre of Excellence** (**CoE**), **Wipro Consulting Services** (**WCS**), and Robert Bosch **Corporate Research** (**CR**). He has gained over 25 years of experience in the IT industry and nine years of research experience. He has finished the CSIR-sponsored Ph.D at Anna University, Chennai. He continued with UGC-sponsored postdoctoral research in the department of computer science and automation at the **Indian Institute of Science** (**IISc**), Bangalore. After that, he got two international research fellowships (JSPS and JST) to work as a research scientist for 3.5 years in two leading Japanese universities.

  He focuses on emerging technologies, including generative and agentic AI, AI model optimization techniques, **Cloud of Things** (**CoT**), cloud-native and edge computing paradigms, platform engineering, 6G communication, and blockchain technologies, as well as quantum-safe cryptography algorithms. He has authored and edited over 75 technology books, published more than 60 research papers, and contributed to more than 55 book chapters.

- **Dr. Kavita Saini** is presently working as a professor and program chair , School of Computing Science and Engineering, Galgotias University, Delhi NCR, India. She received her Ph.D degree from Banasthali Vidyapeeth, Banasthali. She has 22 years of teaching and research experience supervising masters and Ph.D scholars in emerging technologies.

  She has published more than 130 research papers in national and international journals and conferences. She has published 20 authored books for UG and PG courses for a number of universities, including MD University, Rohtak, and Punjab Technical University, Jallandhar, with national publishers. Kavita Saini has edited more than 20 books with international publishers including Elsevier, IET Publisher , IGI Global and CRC Press , Nova Science Publishers and published 30 book chapters with international publishers. Under her guidance many M.Tech. and Ph.D(CS) scholars are carrying out research work and few have completed under her guidance.

  Kavita Saini has also delivered technical talks on blockchain: an emerging technology, web to deep web and other emerging areas and handled many special sessions in international conferences and special issues in international journals. Her research interests include smart and sustainable agriculture, blockchain technology, Industry 5.0, cloud and edge computing, digital twin, and web-based instructional systems.

- **Dr. Rani Kumari** is currently working as an assistant professor at IILM University, Greater Noida, India. She is pursuing her post-doctoral research in machine learning from Lincoln University College, Malaysia. She completed her Ph.D. in computer science from Galgotias University and has qualified UGC-NET.

  She has over 5 years of experience in the software industry, working as a software engineer and developer, along with more than 1.3 years of teaching experience in higher education. Her industry experience includes end-to-end software development, testing, and web-based application development.

  Rani has published several research papers in reputed national and international journals and conferences. Her research contributions focus on artificial intelligence, machine learning, data mining, and predictive analytics, particularly in the domain of manufacturing and Industry 4.0 applications. She has also filed two patents in the field of IoT-based smart systems and agricultural technologies.

  Her research interests include artificial intelligence, machine learning, predictive analytics, data mining, smart manufacturing, Industry 4.0, and IoT-based systems. She is actively involved in academic research, teaching, and developing innovative solutions for real-world industrial problems.

  She is proficient in programming languages such as Python, C, C++, and web technologies including PHP, HTML, CSS, and JavaScript. Her technical expertise also includes database management systems like Oracle and SQL Server, along with strong knowledge of operating systems, networking, and UNIX.

About the Reviewers

- **Dileep Rai** is a technology and supply-chain transformation leader currently serving as manager of Oracle Technology (Cloud ERP/SCM) at **Hachette Book Group** (**HBG**), USA, where he leads a multi-phase Oracle Fusion Cloud ERP modernization program spanning supply-chain, order-to-cash, and demand planning. His work has driven multimillion-dollar operational efficiencies across the publishing, aerospace, and healthcare sectors. A senior member of IEEE, fellow of the **Institute of Supply Chain Management** (**IoSCM**), and Forbes Technology Council Expert, Dileep contributes thought leadership on AI-enabled forecasting, digital twins, and resilient supply chains. He also serves on advisory boards for CCALS and CILTNA, supporting public-private initiatives on supply-chain innovation. Passionate about mentorship and sustainability, he continues to bridge technology, strategy, and social impact across global networks.

- **Karthic Kumar Eswari Subramanian** is a principal engineer at Walmart Global Tech with expertise in backend architecture, cloud computing, AR/VR platforms, and AI-enabled application development. He specializes in building scalable, high-performance systems that power immersive retail experiences across web, mobile, and emerging platforms. In parallel, he develops AI-driven features focused on enhancing user experiences through intelligent automation, personalization, and emerging technology integrations.

  He has progressed from a Java backend developer to a full-stack engineer and now a backend architect, demonstrating strong technical depth and leadership. He has led the development of end-to-end platforms for sourcing, validating, and delivering 3D assets, while also contributing to innovative AI-powered features as a separate track to drive next-generation user experiences.

  In addition to his technical contributions, Karthic mentors engineers, conducts technical workshops, and collaborates with cross-functional teams. His core strengths include system design, cloud architecture, AI-enabled development, performance optimization, and engineering leadership.

- **Prashanthi Matam** has over seven years of experience as a software engineer, having worked with leading organizations such as Discover, Goldman Sachs, Capgemini, and Enel X. She holds a Master's degree in Computer Systems Engineering from Northeastern University and a Bachelor's degree in Computer Science from GITAM University.

  Her technical background includes expertise in cloud-native development, AI/ML-driven systems, and full-stack engineering. She has hands-on experience with AWS, Python, Kubernetes, Angular, React, and Kafka. Over the years, she has built end-to-end telemetry infrastructures, developed secure credential management tools, and designed real-time diagnostic frameworks to enhance performance and reliability.

Beyond her technical work, Prashanthi has actively contributed in leadership and mentoring capacities. She served as Vice-Chairman of ACM and has mentored students through Mozilla and Red Hat programs. She is also currently serving as Co-VP of Partnerships for the Northwest's premier organization for data professionals, where she helps foster cross-industry collaborations.

She has actively volunteered at several high-impact tech conferences, including Startbootcamp and the Grace Hopper Celebration (GHC), where she supported session coordination and event operations. Most recently, she volunteered at the Women TechTogether Conference in May, assisting with speaker management and attendee engagement. Additionally, she mentors at CodeDay, a global network of student hackathons, where she guides students through technical challenges and promotes collaborative, beginner-friendly learning environments.

- **Tanuj Vishnoi** is a Senior Software Engineer at Intuit with over five years of experience building production-grade AI automation platforms. He specializes in Java, Python, agentic development, and RAG-based orchestration to drive enterprise innovation. A patent holder in cognitive AI , Tanuj has extensive experience designing scalable backend systems and distributed architectures. His current interests focus on the evolution of agentic tools and image generation. When he is notengineering, Tanuj is a multi-instrumentalist who finds harmony playing the guitar, flute, and piano.

Acknowledgements

We want to sincerely thank our families and friends for their unwavering encouragement, tolerance, and support during the writing of this book. We would especially like to express our gratitude to our loved ones, whose encouragement and understanding have been a solid source of support during this trip.

We also want to express our sincere gratitude to BPB Publications for their advice, knowledge, and unwavering assistance in finishing this book. We gratefully thank the reviewers, technical experts, and editors for their helpful advice during the collaborative process of producing and improving this work.

We would like to thank our friends and coworkers in the technology field, whose insights and recommendations have substantially enhanced the content of this book. Lastly, we express our gratitude to our readers for their support and attention. Your support has been incredibly inspiring and has been crucial to the success of this book.

Preface

The rapid advancement of **artificial intelligence** (**AI**) is reshaping the technological landscape and redefining the future of software engineering in the knowledge-driven era. This book has been thoughtfully structured to provide a chapter-wise progression of concepts, enabling Indian students and professionals to systematically understand and apply AI in modern software development and IT ecosystems.

In this book, we have incorporated several chapters linking these two pioneering and trend-setting phenomena of AI and cloud-native software engineering. We have covered many relevant chapters to explain every trend and transition in this field to our esteemed readers. Some of the topics etched in this book include

1. AI for application modernization and migration
2. Generative AI tools for software source code generation
3. AI tools towards DevOps process automation, reliability engineering
4. AI for simplified and Swift platform engineering
5. AI for automated software testing and debugging
6. AI for automated software deployment and cloud infrastructure optimization
7. Agentic AI for next-generation software engineering

Chapter 1: Technical Perspective of AI for Ensuring Knowledge Era — The fundamental and technical perspectives of AI are presented in this chapter, along with its crucial significance in the knowledge era. The chapter talks about how AI is expanding beyond analytical capabilities into generative and conversational areas, enabling deep and automated data analytics

Chapter 2: Empowering Software Engineering with Artificial Intelligence — This chapter explores how the **software development lifecycle** (**SDLC**) is being automated by AI, which is transforming software engineering. It explains the use of machine learning, natural language processing, and automation tools to enhance productivity, improve accuracy, and reduce development time.

Chapter 3: Artificial Intelligence for Application Modernization and Migration — This chapter explores how AI technologies are driving application modernization and migration efforts. deeply into the critical role of AI in the modernization process discussed in the chapter.

The chapter covers AI-driven methods for resource optimization, cloud migration, predictive maintenance, code restructuring, and application evaluation

Chapter 4: Generative and Agentic AI Principles and Practices for Accelerated Software Engineering — This chapter explores into the emerging paradigms of generative AI and agentic AI. It highlights how advancements in AI technologies, frameworks, and tools are accelerating software engineering processes. The chapter talks about the journey from AI generative AI and agentic AI.

Chapter 5: Study on AI Tools That Can Generate Software Source Code — The influence of different AI-powered code generation technologies on developer productivity is examined in this chapter, with a focus on the transition from manual coding to AI-assisted programming. In addition to increasing productivity, AI code generators are changing the way developers approach problem-solving. The chapter explores the critical code-generation tools and their prominent features and capabilities.

Chapter 6: AI-powered Tools to Enhance the Stages of Software Development — The chapter discusses about the AI-powered tools to enhance the stages of software development. To make sure that AI technologies are used safely, best practices like thorough code reviews, security scanning, documentation checks, and following ethical standards should always be used

Chapter 7: AI for IT Infrastructure Resource Optimization — This chapter discusses how AI automates resource allocation in IT infrastructure, helping organizations optimize resources and reduce costs. This chapter examines how AI-driven solutions enhance IT resources and enhance sustainability, and ensure the long-term reliability of their IT ecosystems.

Chapter 8: AI and Workload Infrastructure Optimization — This chapter explores how AI optimizes workloads and infrastructure management through automation and predictive analytics. AI-powered tools and systems. By understanding these applications, readers can see how AI is shaping a more efficient and intelligent future for work.

Chapter 9: Challenges of Using AI in Software Development — AI is a prime technology getting much attention these days. Software engineers are overwhelmingly exploring, experimenting, and expounding the unique contributions of AI in their everyday assignments. However, a few critical challenges must be surmounted to make AI the new normal for the software community.

Chapter 10: Next-generation Developer Experience Enabled by AI — This chapter explains how AI is changing the way developers work, especially in IT infrastructure and operations. AI helps developers write better code faster, fix bugs easily, and manage systems with less effort. It also supports developers by giving smart code suggestions, automating testing, and helping with quick deployment.

Chapter 11: Coding to Prompting an Agentic AI Revolution — Prompt engineering is, therefore, an important field of engineering in the agentic AI era. However, prompt engineering has proven to be a complex process, as crafting highly effective prompts is neither simple nor straightforward. However, well-crafted prompts are indispensable, as they can guide LLMs to generate accurate and appropriate results.

Coloured Images

Please follow the link to download the
Coloured Images of the book:

https://rebrand.ly/97b3d1

We have code bundles from our rich catalogue of books and videos available at https://github.com/bpbpublications. Check them out!

Errata

We take immense pride in our work at BPB Publications and follow best practices to ensure the accuracy of our content to provide an indulging reading experience to our subscribers. Our readers are our mirrors, and we use their inputs to reflect and improve upon human errors, if any, that may have occurred during the publishing processes involved. To let us maintain the quality and help us reach out to any readers who might be having difficulties due to any unforeseen errors, please write to us at:

errata@bpbonline.com

Your support, suggestions and feedback are highly appreciated by the BPB Publications' Family.

Piracy

If you come across any illegal copies of our works in any form on the internet, we would be grateful if you would provide us with the location address or website name. Please contact us at **business@bpbonline.com** with a link to the material.

If you are interested in becoming an author

If there is a topic that you have expertise in, and you are interested in either writing or contributing to a book, please visit **www.bpbonline.com**. We have worked with thousands of developers and tech professionals, just like you, to help them share their insights with the global tech community. You can make a general application, apply for a specific hot topic that we are recruiting an author for, or submit your own idea.

Reviews

Please leave a review. Once you have read and used this book, why not leave a review on the site that you purchased it from? Potential readers can then see and use your unbiased opinion to make purchase decisions. We at BPB can understand what you think about our products, and our authors can see your feedback on their book. Thank you!

For more information about BPB, please visit **www.bpbonline.com**.

Join our Discord space

Join our Discord workspace for latest updates, offers, tech happenings around the world, new releases, and sessions with the authors:

https://discord.bpbonline.com

Table of Contents

Chapter 1
Technical Perspective of AI for Ensuring Knowledge Era

Introduction

In this chapter, we will discuss AI and its role in the knowledge era. As we know, the future of deep and automated data analytics lies in **artificial intelligence** (**AI**), which can quickly produce actionable insights. AI is evolving into generative and conversational in addition to analytical. Other prerequisites include the need for AI to be accountable, transparent, ethical, explainable, trustworthy, and sustainable. These trends and the new standards will be covered in full in this chapter.

Traditional systems work effectively if the problem is clearly defined and its expected solution is known. In this approach, a human programmer manually writes the rules and logic for the program to follow. However, traditional programming lacks the ability to learn or adapt by its own when requirements change. Here comes the role of AI and **machine learning** (**ML**).

AI allows systems to learn, reason, and make decisions using data and algorithms. Combining methods like natural language processing, neural networks, and machine learning, AI enables computers to carry out activities that normally call for human intellect. AI is now widely used in many different fields, such as smart technologies, healthcare, finance, and education. The creation of intelligent systems with the capacity for thought, adaptation, and long-term improvement is the ultimate aim of artificial intelligence. AI as a whole refers to the larger idea of designing robots that can perform jobs that normally require human intelligence.

There are various AI techniques helping machines to learn and to act, depending on the type of input, output, or other parameters.

Structure

In this chapter, we will cover the following topics:

- Understanding AI

- Functioning of AI
- Role of AI for the ensuing knowledge era
- AI integration with emerging technologies

Objectives

AI is being termed a transformative technology. AI elegantly squeezes out hidden patterns in data heaps. AI is the way forward to perform deep and automated data analytics and can emit actionable insights in time. AI, in addition to being analytical, is becoming generative and conversational. There are other requirements, such as AI has to be responsible, explainable, trustworthy, transparent, ethical, and sustainable.

This chapter will deal with these trends and the emerging requirements in detail.

Understanding AI

AI is an emerging technology, transforming all industries by extracting hidden patterns, analysing data, and predicting future decisions. AI is used for decision-making, which further helps in reshaping almost all industries.

As earlier pattern identification and analysis were either a difficult or time-consuming process, AI enables us to discover the patterns in no or very little time, with a lot of innovative and efficient suggestions.

AI basically refers to the ability of machines that have been programmed in such a way that the machine can think like humans, or in other words, a machine can simulate human intellect. It focuses on rationalizing and choosing the best course of action to accomplish a certain objective and is related to characteristics that have historically been identified with the human intellect, such as learning and problem-solving.

Machine learning is a subfield of AI. This is the idea that, in addition to performing tasks, machines may learn knowledge from data and past operations and adjust accordingly without human help. By digesting and absorbing vast volumes of data in the form of text, video, and images, deep learning techniques are employed by AI technologies that offer the framework for ML.

The goal of ML, a branch of AI, is to create methods and algorithms that let computers learn from data and make judgments or predictions without needing to be explicitly programmed for each task. ML systems find patterns in data rather than rigid rules, and they gain expertise over time to perform better.

AI techniques

There are various AI techniques that enable machines to learn, reason, and act intelligently based on the type of input, desired output, or specific parameters involved. These methods define how machines interpret information to make decisions and serve as the cornerstone of intelligent system design.

For example, expert systems improve human decision-making by using preset rules, while ML approaches enable algorithms to discover patterns in data.

Natural language processing (**NLP**) helps machines understand and respond to human language, and neural networks enable pattern recognition similar to the human brain. Fuzzy logic and genetic algorithms help handle uncertainty and optimization problems. When combined, these AI strategies enable machines to carry out intricate tasks, adjust to shifting conditions, and gradually enhance their performance.

The main AI techniques used in developing intelligent systems are as follows:

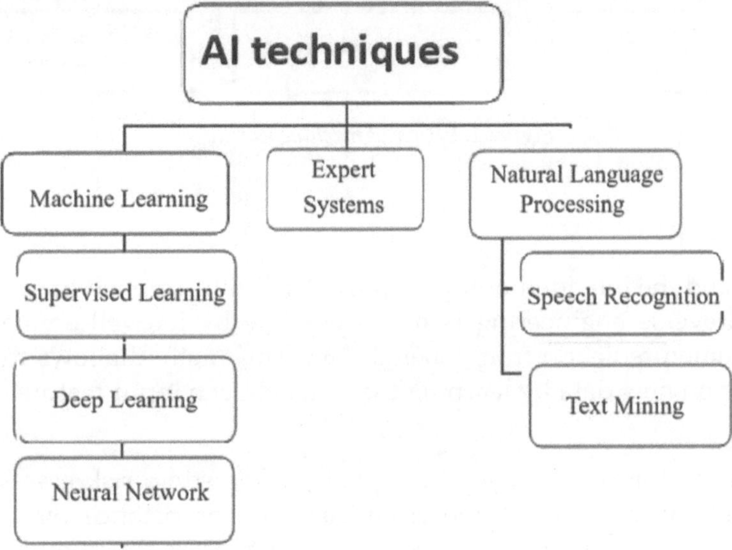

***Figure 1.1**: AI techniques*

ML enables machines to learn patterns from data and make predictions or decisions. It includes *supervised learning, unsupervised learning, and reinforcement learning.* ML systems are flexible, unlike traditional approaches that depend on predetermined parameters. With the help of AI, ML algorithms can recognize patterns in data and predict what is to be done. ML is a branch of AI that focuses on developing systems that can learn from and make decisions based on data. ML involves designing and developing algorithms and techniques that allow computers to learn. It automatically extracts information from an extensive data set by computational and statistical methods. ML is closely related to data mining, statistics, and database systems. In an ML system, a developed model automatically decides without external support.

Types of ML:

- Supervised learning

- Unsupervised learning
- Reinforcement learning

The following figure depicts the same:

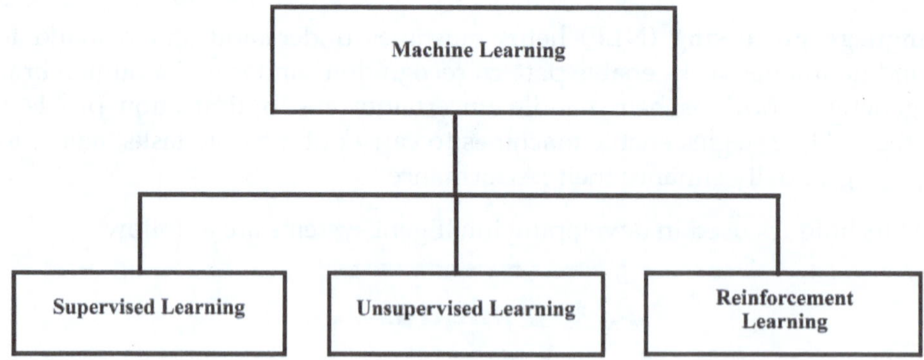

***Figure 1.2**: Type of machine learning*

Supervised learning

The training data and the intended outputs (labels) are both supplied in supervised learning, a subset of ML. Reverse engineering is made possible by its well-defined objectives and emphasis on outcome prediction from labeled data. This method allows the model to make precise predictions on new data by learning the link between input features and their related output labels.

Fraud detection, inventory control, product quality forecasting, risk assessment, and home price estimation are typical uses for supervised learning. For instance, the model can forecast a building's pricing, provided a dataset has labeled details like the number of rooms, dining area, kitchen type, and air conditioning availability. Therefore, when there is historical labeled data available to train predictive models, supervised learning is essential.

Unsupervised learning

Unsupervised learning is a type of machine learning where the system is provided with training data without predefined output labels. With this method, the algorithm examines the data to find hidden structures, correlations, or patterns without being aware of the right answers beforehand. Only the input data is used to decide the output, and the algorithm automatically clusters or segments related data points.

Clustering and segmentation problems are the primary applications for unsupervised learning techniques. Text mining, face recognition, city planning, and targeted marketing are examples of common applications. Unsupervised learning is useful for data exploration and knowledge discovery because of its assistance in finding patterns and effectively organizing big datasets.

Reinforcement learning

Reinforcement learning (**RL**) is a type of ML where both the start state and end state are defined, but the agent must discover the optimal path or relationship between them through trial and error. The system learns by interacting with its environment and receiving feedback in the form of rewards or penalties based on its actions.

In this learning process, the agent aims to maximize the total reward over time by improving its decision-making strategy. RL is widely used in gaming, robotics, and self-driving cars, where the system learns from continuous interaction with its surroundings.

Expert systems are rule-based systems that simulate the decision-making ability of a human expert in a specific field. A major field of AI is expert systems, which aim to replicate human experts' decision-making skills in particular fields. Using a rule-based methodology, these systems encode domain experts' knowledge into a structured format called a knowledge base. Expert-level thinking is represented by the facts and rules (typically expressed as IF-THEN sentences) in the knowledge base. These rules are then applied to the provided data by an inference engine, which then returns findings or suggestions.

For example, in the medical field, an expert system can analyze patient symptoms and suggest possible diagnoses based on its stored rules. Expert systems are used in business to help with strategic planning, investment decisions, and credit risk assessment. These systems are especially useful when it is necessary to make decisions quickly, logically, and consistently. Expert systems eliminate human error, increase productivity, and guarantee well-informed decision-making in a variety of professional domains by mimicking human competence.

NLP is a field of AI that focuses on enabling machines to understand, interpret, and generate human language in a meaningful way. It allows machines to understand, interpret, and generate human language (e.g., chatbots, translation, sentiment analysis).

Tokenization, part-of-speech tagging, syntactic and semantic analysis, and sentiment identification are some of the crucial activities that NLP entails in order to assist machines in understanding the structure and meaning of language.

The following figure shows the input required and possible outputs:

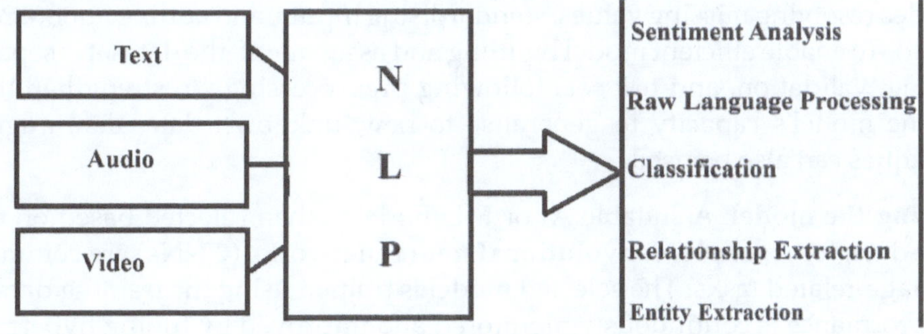

Figure 1.3: *Natural language processing*

Chatbots, virtual assistants, and translation systems can comprehend and process human language thanks to NLP. Particularly in India, it is extensively utilized for sentiment analysis and multilingual communication. All things considered, NLP improves human-computer interaction and increases the accessibility and usability of technology.

Functioning of AI

The following figure will help us understand how AI works:

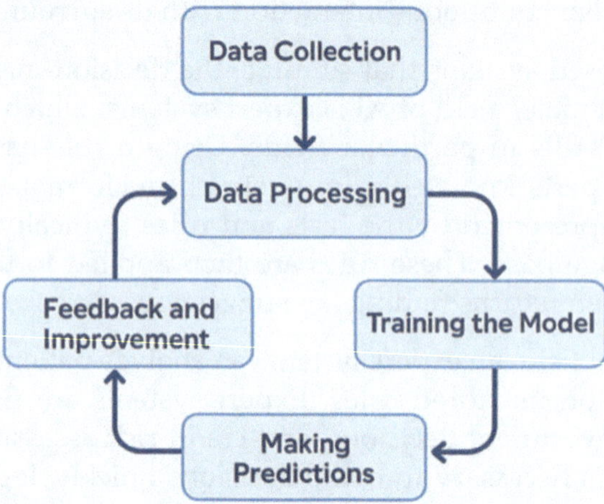

Figure 1.4: Functioning of AI

Let us discuss it in detail:

- **Data collection**: A range of sources, including sensors, databases, and the internet, are used to collect raw data. To enable reliable model training, it is crucial to make sure that the data gathered is pertinent, substantial, and varied. For example, to create a thorough and representative dataset for the diagnosis of diabetic retinopathy, retinal pictures may be gathered from several hospitals.
- **Data processing**: After being gathered, the data is cleaned and pre-processed, which includes resolving missing values, standardising inputs, and adding annotations where needed. To enable efficient model building and assessment, the dataset is separated into training, validation, and test sets following preprocessing. To strengthen the dataset and the model's capacity to generalise to new, unknown data, data augmentation techniques can also be used.
- **Training the model**: A suitable AI or ML model is then selected based on the nature of the data; for example, **convolutional neural networks** (**CNNs**) are commonly used for image-related tasks. The selected model is trained using the training dataset, while its performance is continuously monitored and improved by tuning hyperparameters with the help of validation data.

- **Making predictions**: Once the model is trained, it is used to make predictions on new, unseen data. The output can take various forms, such as class labels, probability scores, or regression values, depending on the specific task. For example, in the context of diabetic retinopathy detection, the model may predict whether a given retinal image shows signs of the disease.
- **Feedback and improvement**: Depending on the application, the model's performance is assessed using a variety of measures, including accuracy, precision, recall, and others. After that, suggestions from users or subject matter experts are taken into account to determine what needs to be improved. The model is routinely retrained with fresh or updated data to guarantee ongoing improvement, enabling it to adjust to shifting trends and sustain high accuracy over time.

Let us look at some of the popular AI tools:

AI tools	Description
Siri	Siri is an AI tool by Apple. It is a virtual assistant and helps in messaging, reminders, and controlling smart home devices. It is integrated across the devices of a user. Siri also makes daily tasks easier by understanding natural voice commands and responding quickly with precise actions. For a number of tasks, including setting alarms, checking the weather, making phone calls, and doing online research, Siri provides a smooth hands-free experience. Since it can sync with the iPhone, iPad, Mac, Apple Watch, and even HomePod, users are assured continuous support across all of their Apple devices. Siri's deep integration and user-friendly design make it a reliable digital companion for easily managing daily tasks.
Cortana	Cortana is Microsoft's virtual assistant integrated into Windows and other services. Cortana also helps customers by offering customized suggestions based on their routine chores, such as setting up calendars, sending reminders, or quickly locating files. Users may effortlessly accomplish tasks without using their hands thanks to voice instructions, particularly when multitasking. Cortana's deep integration into Microsoft services like Outlook, Office 365, and Windows apps enhances productivity and provides a seamless digital experience across devices.

Grammarly	Grammarly is one of the most frequently used AI-enabled writing assistants for grammar checking and style suggestions. Grammarly is one of the most widely used AI-powered writing tools for grammar checks and style suggestions. In addition to correcting basic spelling and grammar errors, Grammarly provides tone recognition, vocabulary expansion, clarity improvements, and plagiarism detection. Professionals, teachers, and students can write with greater confidence because of its real-time recommendations. When writing emails, assignments, or reports, Grammarly ensures that the text is readable, clear, and polished. This is very beneficial for professional and academic communication.
Alexa	Alexa is an AI voice-controlled virtual assistant by Amazon services and is very popular in smart homes. Smart homes frequently use Alexa, Amazon's AI voice-activated virtual assistant. Alexa enables customers to control lights, fans, TVs, and several more connected devices with simple voice queries. Alexa can also play music, set timers, deliver news updates, and quickly respond to frequently asked questions. Because of its wide compatibility with smart home products and user-friendly features, it is a popular tool in many Indian households for creating a modern and useful lifestyle.
Google Assistant	Google's voice-activated AI that helps with information retrieval, smart device control, and more. Google Assistant is well known for its prompt and accurate responses when it comes to directions, information searches, and language translation. It works well on Android phones, smart speakers, and many IoT devices and offers a smooth cross-platform experience. For daily chores like calls, entertainment, smart home control, and reminders, Google Assistant provides consistent support and enhances the user's productivity and convenience.

Table 1.1: *Popular AI tools*

Role of AI for the ensuing knowledge era

AI is revolutionizing knowledge through data analysis, automation, and adaptive learning. It enhances decision-making in industries like healthcare, finance, education, and manufacturing. NLP bridges communication gaps, while edge AI accelerates data processing. Explainable AI builds trust in decision systems.

Apart from these advancements, AI encourages continuous learning through the analysis of user behavior and customization of knowledge delivery. Professionals, researchers, and students benefit from its ability to summarize complex data, generate insights, and predict future trends. AI-driven platforms enable faster innovation because they make it easier for people to obtain the relevant information at the right moment. As companies move toward digital transformation, AI plays a significant part in building a knowledge-driven society where information is not only abundant but also easy to understand and utilize.

The following are a few key points that will help in understanding the role of AI in ensuring knowledge:

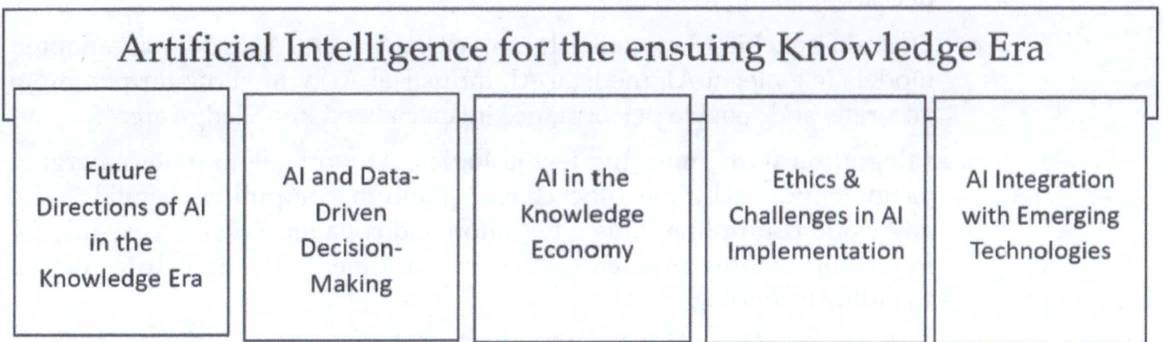

Figure 1.5: AI and the knowledge era

- **Future directions of AI in the knowledge era**: Today, we live in the era of knowledge. AI is one of the biggest tools to be used for knowledge discovery and to automate knowledge discovery, followed by decision-making. An AI system is giving us the freedom to choose one of the best decisions provided as suggestions by such tools by analyzing the results of one suggested model with the other. There are many key directions, including knowledge augmentation, **explainable and responsible AI (XAI)**, and domain-specific AI models, as shown in *Table 1.2*. It also explores the way of AI integration with the other emerging technologies:

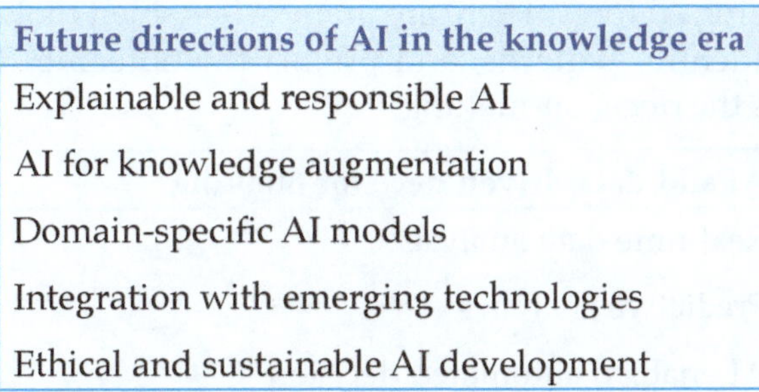

Future directions of AI in the knowledge era
Explainable and responsible AI
AI for knowledge augmentation
Domain-specific AI models
Integration with emerging technologies
Ethical and sustainable AI development

Table 1.2: AI and data-driven decision making

The role of AI in the knowledge era is as follows:

- o **Explainable and responsible AI (XAI)**: At present, AI is helping almost all industries, such as healthcare, automobile, education, finance, and so on.

It is very important that AI systems are understandable and transparent. Future AI will focus on interpretable models that can justify decisions and earn user trust.

- **AI for knowledge augmentation**: AI is introduced not to replace humans but to help them. AI will act as a co-pilot to support humans in better understanding, making decisions, and summarizing information. Further, AI acts as a support system, helping in discovering trends followed by decision-making in no time.
- **Domain-specific AI models**: The move from general AI to domain-adapted models (e.g., legal AI, medical AI, industrial AI) will allow deeper, more accurate, and reliable performance in specialized knowledge areas.
- **Integration with emerging technologies**: AI works with other emerging technologies, including blockchain, quantum computing, Digital Twin, and cloud computing. This integration and collaboration are very helpful in solving real-life problems, even in real-time, with the help of digital twin-like technology.
- **Ethical and sustainable AI development**: Ethical and sustainable AI development should be aligned with AI development to maintain the ethical values, privacy, security, and ensure the minimum impact on the environment. It also means using AI to support sustainable development goals and promoting responsible AI practices. Developing and implementing AI systems that are just, open, responsible, and have as little of an impact on the environment as possible is the goal of ethical and sustainable AI development.

- **AI and data-driven decision-making**: Decision-making is one of the major tasks in any industry. These decisions are driven by data. The use of AI tools has a great impact on decision-making. Not just data, but big data has an impact on various decision-making, even if using AI tools. There are many AI-enabled tools that can handle a huge amount of data, identify patterns, and predict the outcome. The predicted outcome further influences the decision-making.

AI and data-driven decision-making
Real-time data analysis
Predictive analytics
AI-enabled automated decision
Personalization and optimization
Improved accuracy and consistency
Scenario simulation and risk assessment

***Table 1.3**: AI and data analysis*

The role of AI and data-driven decision-making is as follows:

- o **Real-time data analysis**: Streaming data can be analysed by an AI system instantly. It will not just give a quick response but also be faster and more accurate. Cybersecurity, EHR, finance, and media are the core industries where real-time analysis is required, and AI is performing well.
- o **Predictive analytics**: AI is very helpful for predicting future trends and leads to better decision-making. AI-enabled tools are also helpful for businesses to take preventive measures and make well-informed choices.
- o **AI-enabled automated decision**: Automated decision is also possible with the help of AI tools, leading to reduced human efforts and human errors. While making decisions, it also requires more effort for more strategic and creative thinking. It is possible due to learning patterns to automate repetitive decision-making.
- o **Personalization and optimization**: Through the use of ML models, AI helps forecast future trends and behaviors. AI is empowering organizations to take proactive steps and make informed decisions. Other than organizational decisions, individual or personalized decisions are also empowered by AI and help in managing personalized healthcare, personalized communications, commerce, and so on.
- o **Improved accuracy and consistency**: AI eliminates human bias and fatigue, delivering data-backed, consistent decisions across multiple scenarios.

The use of ML models trained on large code repositories allows AI tools to provide accurate recommendations and error detection. It ensures standardization of coding throughout the project and hence improves software readability and maintainability. Further, AI-driven testing and debugging not just reduces manual workload but also increases reliability.

- **Scenario simulation and risk assessment**: AI plays a vital role in strategic planning and resource allocation by simulating multiple real-world scenarios to assess potential risks and outcomes. AI-driven strategies help in planning with the limited or available resources for a given period of time.

  AI involves creating virtual models that mimic real-world systems, processes, or environments to predict outcomes and optimize decisions. These simulations are widely used in sectors like healthcare, agriculture, manufacturing, and urban planning in India to test various scenarios without real-world risks or costs. AI models simulate disease spread and treatment outcomes to improve public health strategies. Urban planning benefits from AI simulations that model traffic flow and resource management for smart cities.

  AI entails building virtual models that replicate actual systems, procedures, or settings. In India, these simulations are extensively utilized to test different scenarios without the hazards or expenses of the actual world in industries including healthcare, agriculture, manufacturing, and urban planning. AI models can be used to improve public health initiatives by simulating the transmission of disease and the results of therapy. AI simulations that simulate resource management and traffic flow in smart cities are useful for urban planning.

- **AI ethics and challenges**: AI presents various benefits but also comes with various ethical issues and implementation hurdles as it gets more and more ingrained in industries, including healthcare, education, finance, and governance. Long-term sustainability, social justice, and public trust all depend on the responsible development and application of AI systems.

AI ethics and challenges
Transparency and explainability
Accountability issue
Data privacy
Autonomy and human control

***Table 1.4**: AI ethics and challenges*

The following are the challenges:

- o **Lack of transparency and explanation**: Many AI systems, especially deep learning models, function as black boxes, which leads to the final decisions and a lack of explanation about the result. If the application is of a high-risk or dealing with critical functions, transparency of taking decisions are far better. Explainable AI solves this problem by explaining the reason behind the scene.

- o **Accountability issue**: In the case of an AI system, this is one of the most problematic things that is accountable in case of incorrect or harmful decisions. It may be the system that learns on its own, a developer, or an organization.

- o **Data privacy**: AI systems depend on large volumes of data available for researchers and academicians, whether public or from any organization. It is sometimes available without taking proper permission from the concerned parties, and breaches privacy. Improper handling of personal data raises serious privacy concerns and risks of misuse or surveillance.

- o **Autonomy and human control**: There is increasing concern about becoming too dependent on AI, highlighting the importance of keeping humans dependent for decision-making. Especially in critical fields like health care and law are the core domains where decisions are AI-dependent.

AI integration with emerging technologies

When AI is combined with other emerging technologies such as IoT, cloud computing, robotics, and many more, it shows the true potential as a whole. This combination is contributing to the development of intelligent systems to cater to day-to-day industrial or even personal work. Electronic healthcare, autonomous vehicles, and Industry 2.0 are just a few examples. By making these technologies more sophisticated, intelligent, and capable of working independently more quickly and accurately, AI plays a significant role.

AI has emerged with various emerging technologies such as blockchain technology, digital twin, AR/VR, and other technologies. These AI with other technologies enhance the overall functionality, security, integrity, visualization, and automation.

The following figure depicts the integration of AI with emerging technologies:

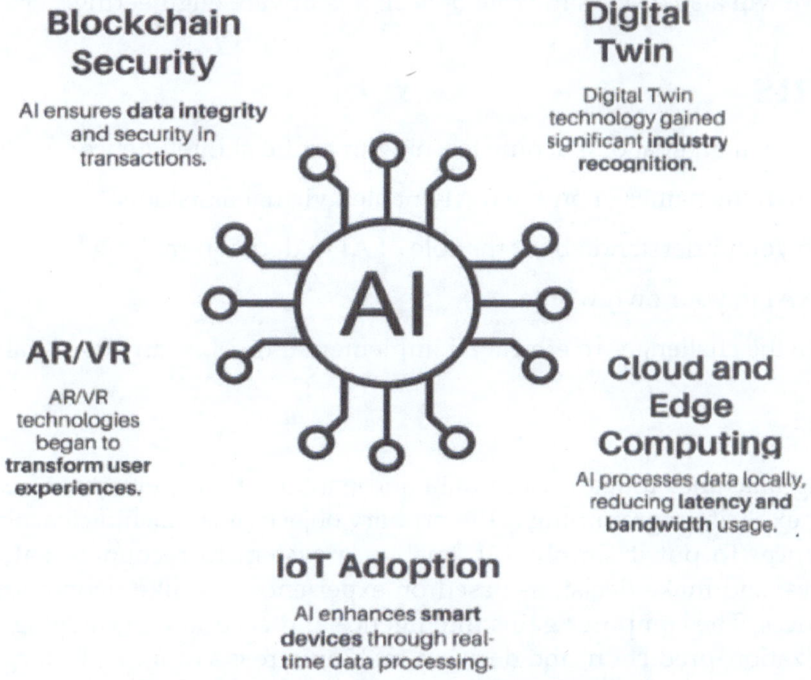

Figure 1.6: AI and emerging technologies integration

The following are a few emerging technologies with which AI is being integrated for different applications:

- **Internet of Things** (IoT) and **Industrial Internet of Things** (IIoT)
- Blockchain
- Cloud and edge computing
- Digital twin

- AR/VR
- Quantum computing

Conclusion

By the end of this chapter, we covered AI and ML and the role of AI in the knowledge era. The chapter discussed various AI techniques, such as expert systems and NLP. Overall, AI functionality is also discussed in the chapter that covers data collection and processing, various training models, prediction, and how popular AI tools contribute to the same. Use of AI in the knowledge era was one of the major discussion topics of the chapter.

In the next chapter, we will discuss AI to empower software engineering and will talk about AI-driven software development, predictive software maintenance, and even software project management. We will also discuss the role of NLP in software engineering.

Questions

1. What is the main goal of machine learning in artificial intelligence?
2. Write down the names of any two AI-enabled virtual assistants.
3. What do you understand about the role of AI in decision-making?
4. Define XAI in your own words.
5. What are the challenges in ethical AI implementation? List any two challenges.

Answers

1. Enabling machines to learn from data and enhance their performance automatically without explicit programming is the primary objective of machine learning in artificial intelligence. To put it simply, ML enables a system to recognize patterns, forecast outcomes, and make decisions based on experience, just like people learn from past experiences. The computer gains intelligence and accuracy in carrying out tasks like categorization, prediction, and decision-making across a range of applications through ongoing training and exposure to additional data.
2. Siri and Alexa are voice-controlled AI assistants.
   a. Siri is an AI-powered virtual assistant and is one of Apple's products. It assists customers in controlling smart home gadgets, sending messages, and setting reminders with voice commands.
   b. Alexa is an AI assistant by Amazon and is being widely used in the Echo and smart home devices. It performs tasks like playing music, providing weather updates, and managing connected smart appliances.

3. AI plays a vital role in helping businesses and systems make smart decisions by analyzing large volumes of data, such as big data.

4. XAI refers to the techniques and methods that make the decisions and workings of artificial intelligence systems understandable to humans. Instead of giving a result like a black box, XAI explains why and how a particular decision was made. This transparency helps users trust AI systems because they can see the logic behind the output.

   Explainable AI is crucial in the modern world, as AI is employed in delicate fields like healthcare, finance, and law. It guarantees equity, prevents prejudice, and assists developers in locating mistakes or hazards inside the system. Overall, by providing users and stakeholders with clarity and confidence, XAI encourages the ethical and responsible application of AI.

5. Data privacy and accountability are two main challenges in the ethical implementation of AI.

   a. **Data privacy**: Protecting personal information from misuse is the biggest challenge. For AI systems to work well, they frequently need a lot of sensitive and personal data. One of the biggest challenges is making sure that this data is gathered, kept, and used in an ethical manner. Serious concerns over privacy rights and trust might arise from improper handling, which can result in confidentiality violations, unlawful surveillance, and abuse of user information.

   b. **Accountability**: Defining who is responsible for AI decisions, especially in critical scenarios. Determining who is accountable when an AI system makes a decision, especially if that decision has unfavourable effects, is one of the most difficult ethical AI problems.

   c. This is especially crucial in urgent situations like:

      i. An accident involving a self-driving vehicle

      ii. An AI-powered medical device that incorrectly diagnoses

      iii. An automated financial system that unjustly denies a loan

Multiple choice questions

1. **In predictive software maintenance, what is the major function of artificial intelligence?**

   a. Manually code debugging

   b. Identifying potential failures

   c. Taking the place of human software developers

   d. Ignoring minor software issues

2. **Which of the following is a subfield of artificial intelligence?**
   a. Quantum computing
   b. Data structures
   c. Machine learning
   d. Digital marketing
3. **Which AI tool is known for grammar checking and writing assistance?**
   a. Alexa
   b. Siri
   c. Grammarly
   d. Cortana
4. **What is the first step in building an AI model?**
   a. Making predictions
   b. Data collection
   c. Feedback collection
   d. Training the model
5. **Which of these is a challenge in implementing AI ethically?**
   a. Faster processing
   b. Accountability issue
   c. Decision automation
   d. Data visualization
6. **Which emerging technology is often integrated with AI to simulate real-world environments?**
   a. Blockchain
   b. AR/VR
   c. Cloud storage
   d. Excel

Answers

1	c
2	c
3	b
4	b
5	b
6	b

Join our Discord space

Join our Discord workspace for latest updates, offers, tech happenings around the world, new releases, and sessions with the authors:

https://discord.bpbonline.com

CHAPTER 2

Empowering Software Engineering with Artificial Intelligence

Introduction

Software developers are increasingly leveraging the game-changing capabilities of **artificial intelligence** (**AI**). AI is particularly useful in code generation, requirements elicitation, and engineering; for example, Watson AI is effective for requirements management. AI reduces the need to go through lots of paper and digital documentation manually. Based on the gathered requirements, AI is more efficient in tasks that require calculations, such as estimating costs and scheduling deadlines. It can also determine the development team setup and the number of specialists needed to meet deadlines within the set budget.

AI enables software engineering in different phases. These phases include software development, software maintenance, and software project management. We will go over these phases in this chapter.

Structure

The chapter covers the following topics:

- Role of AI in software engineering
- Future of AI in software engineering

Objectives

The objective of this chapter is to explore the role of AI in empowering software engineering. AI has become a game-changer for software developers due to its advanced AI capabilities. Wherever code generation is the requirement, identification is the primary area of software engineering, and AI is helping a lot. Instead of working manually, digital documents are being managed for the purpose of requirement gathering, cost estimation, scheduling, code generation, and so on. AI reduces the need to manually go through lots of paper and digital documentation. The chapter discusses AI-driven software development, predictive maintenance, and overall project management.

Role of AI in software engineering

AI can improve software testing by automatically generating test cases, simulating user behavior, and identifying edge cases. **Machine learning** (**ML**) models can predict which areas of the application are most likely to have defects, optimizing the testing process and ensuring better software performance. AI helps in maintaining the task within the allocated budget.

AI-based testing systems can also continuously learn from past mistakes and project experiences, which helps to enhance the testing methodology over time. These solutions ensure faster testing cycles and reduce manual labor by automatically adapting to new codebase alterations. This improves the program's overall quality while assisting teams in meeting strict project deadlines. Ultimately, by reducing rework and avoiding unnecessary testing procedures, AI helps projects function more smoothly and make better use of resources.

The role of AI in software engineering includes:

- AI-driven software development
- AI for predictive software maintenance
- AI in software project management
- **Natural language processing** (**NLP**) in software engineering
- Enhancing testing and quality assurance

The following figure depicts the role of AI in software engineering:

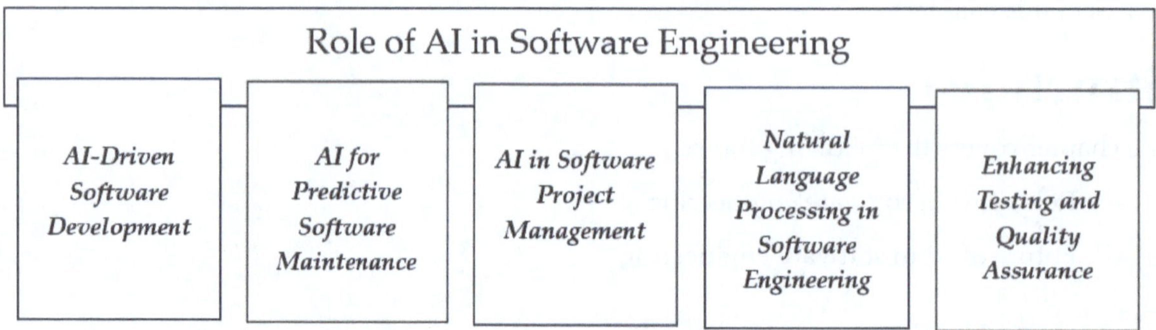

***Figure 2.1**: Role of AI in software engineering*

AI-driven software development

AI has a significant impact on the software development process. It is possible to automate tasks or phases of software development during the software development life cycle, which includes development, testing, and maintenance. Where traditional software development models involve manual tasks, which can be a time-consuming process, AI-driven software development utilizes ML, NLP, and automation tools to enhance the overall software development cycle. The use of AI in software development not only reduces the overall time to complete various tasks but also improves accuracy and productivity.

One of the main phases in software development is coding. Using AI-driven coding tools will automate error-free coding, which will lead to less time required for coding and significantly reduce human errors. Starting from code generation, debugging, and optimization, AI is playing a vital role in software development.

Role of AI software development

Let us learn more about the role of AI software development:

- **Automated code generation and assistance**: Code auto-completion and refactoring tools are two examples of automated code generation tools. Such tools help developers by providing intelligent suggestions based on the training to build such tools. Automated code generation tools improve the developers' productivity. There are many online tools available to practice and to write code, including GitHub Copilot, which is an AI-enabled tool that suggests code to developers and learners while writing a program, a small function, or a procedure.

- **Reduced cost and time in development**: AI is significantly transforming software development by reducing both cost and time with automated code generation with the help of tools like ChatGPT, GitHub, and Copilot.

  In addition to reducing development costs, AI solutions help teams save time by speeding up tedious and complicated coding tasks. Developers can focus more on creative problem-solving while AI handles routine duties like code recommendations, debugging support, and documentation support. As a result, project delays are reduced, and overall productivity is raised. It is because AI makes it possible for businesses to create high-quality software more rapidly, with fewer errors, and within budget, it is a potent enabler of effective software development.

- **Intelligent bug detection and debugging**: There are many AI-enabled tools available that are trained on huge datasets to detect bugs. Such tools can analyze large code and then predict bugs by identifying patterns. Finding bugs and debugging is a crucial phase, and AI-assisted tools are now helping developers to debug the code easily.

  AI-powered debugging tools not only swiftly identify faults but also provide intelligent suggestions to address the problems, minimizing the amount of human labor that developers must perform. Over time, these tools get more precise because they are always learning from past mistakes and advancements. They can even identify possible weaknesses before they become serious issues, guaranteeing improved software security and dependability. Development teams may maintain cleaner code, decrease downtime, and produce stable applications more quickly with such intelligent help.

- **Code optimization**: Once the code is generated, it is also important to optimize it. AI also helps in code optimization by using various ML algorithms. Code optimization helps in making the code more efficient, where AI can support by automating code optimization. AI-enabled code optimization systems can recommend changes where such optimization may help in saving the computational overhead, memory requirements, improve scalability, and many more. AI recommends the enhancement of code in various areas, including execution speed, reducing memory requirements, and reliability of code by using ML techniques and advanced analytics, which is a time-consuming process when optimizing the code manually.
- **Scheduling deadlines**: Scheduling the task throughout the entire software development process is as important as finding the correct requirements. It is important to deliver the project on time, and in this matter, scheduling all the tasks and keeping an eye on whether the tasks are being completed on time or not is important. AI can significantly improve the scheduling of all the related tasks by automating tasks, predicting delays, and optimizing resource allocation. AI-powered tools analyze data, learn from historical patterns, and adapt to changing priorities, ultimately helping projects meet deadlines more reliably and efficiently.

AI helps in analyzing the patterns in large code and suggests improvements in the final code.

AI tools for automated code generation

Some AI tools for automated code generation:

- **Devika AI**: Devika is an open-source AI coding platform from India that aims to transform the development process by using AI to comprehend high-level instructions and convert them into usable code. The innovative open-source AI coding platform Devika was developed in India with the intention of modernizing and optimizing the software development process. High-level natural language commands can be automatically translated into useful code. As a result, it is very useful for both beginners and specialists who wish to accelerate their development efforts. Because Devika connects with external tools and makes multi-step task execution easier, it is a potential step toward India's contribution to AI-driven coding.
- **GitHub Copilot**: AI-powered code completion and generation tool integrated into IDEs like VS Code. GitHub Copilot is a powerful AI-based coding assistant that provides real-time code generation and completion within popular IDEs like VS Code and JetBrains. By learning from billions of lines of open-source code, it assists engineers in building functions, writing boilerplate code, fixing mistakes, and speeding up overall development. Copilot also reduces the cognitive load on programmers by providing context-aware solutions, which significantly boost productivity.
- **OpenAI Codex**: Powers GitHub Copilot and can generate code based on natural language prompts. GitHub OpenAI Codex, Copilot's advanced language model, is

designed to translate natural language cues into practical code. It supports several programming languages and can generate entire functions, algorithms, or files from simple instructions. Codex is a helpful tool for modern AI-driven programming since it makes it possible for developers to automate time-consuming tasks, prototype more quickly, and get more accurate results with less work.

- **Polycoder**: AI model trained on large code datasets for multi-language support. Large code datasets were used to train Polycoder, an AI code generation model that can accurately support a wide range of programming languages. It offers precise autocompletion, function generation, and debugging help. because Polycoder is specifically trained on code and frequently generates output that is both obvious and syntactically correct, it is a dependable choice for developers working with a range of languages.
- **Cogram**: AI-powered tool for autocompleting and generating code. Cogram is an AI tool that helps developers with intelligent code autocompletion, query generation, and documentation support. Quickly understanding the context of previous work and recommending relevant lines of code can help developers avoid tiresome tasks and save time. Because of its natural language features, Cogram simplifies workflow by enabling developers to create queries or code snippets using simple English instructions.
- **DeepCode**: AI-assisted static analysis and security recommendations. DeepCode is an AI-powered static analysis tool that searches large codebases for potential bugs, security holes, and quality issues. It uses machine learning methods to evaluate code in real-time and provides useful recommendations for improvement. By learning from thousands of open-source projects, it can offer incredibly accurate insights, helping teams maintain secure, organized, and efficient code.

AI for predictive software maintenance

Software maintenance refers to the process of upgrading, modifying, and enhancing software programs after their initial release. The purpose of maintenance is to improve software to ensure efficient functionality. Bug fixing, adding new features, and improving performance in the required environments are part of the maintenance. In traditional maintenance, the issues are addressed after facing the problems, rather than focusing on preventive failures.

Predictive maintenance tools can be integrated into software development, enabling real-time monitoring and insights for ongoing optimization. AI helps in predicting Software maintenance, including identifying software failures, improving system reliability, reducing downtime, and more. Machine learning algorithms and data analytics help in predictive software maintenance. AI models analyze the historical data and performance and, based on that, can identify patterns. These identified patterns allow the maintenance team to be proactive and take corrective measures.

Using AI tools for software maintenance helps organizations minimize disruptions and reduce operational costs. AI can predict which specific components are likely to fail and provide a warning in advance.

Role of AI for predictive software maintenance

Let us learn more about the role of AI for predictive software management:

- **Proactive issue detection**: AI for predictive software maintenance makes use of ML to analyze past data, identify patterns, and predict potential software issues. This prediction also helps the maintenance team identify and resolve problems in advance.

- **Reduced downtime**: As mentioned in the previous section, the prediction of potential software issues helps in fixing the issues and also leads to reduced downtime. AI helps in scheduling maintenance work by checking the time to ensure it does not interfere with production or other related tasks. AI helps scheduling maintenance without interrupting the operation, by forecasting when software components are likely to malfunction or deteriorate.

- **Cost efficiency**: By proactive issue detection, predictive maintenance can be done. This will help lower the maintenance cost by preventing emergency repairs. Additionally, AI-supported predictive maintenance allows enterprises to plan their resources and repair operations well in advance. Instead of squandering money on unforeseen malfunctions or breakdowns, teams may schedule maintenance at the right moment to reduce business interruptions and extra costs. This approach increases financial efficiency and prolongs the life of the software and related systems.

- **Increased system reliability**: AI increases system reliability by continuously monitoring software performance and automating maintenance tasks. This helps in constantly monitoring software performance and ensuring its reliability.

  AI systems can quickly identify unusual trends or performance decreases that human operators might find difficult to spot. By alerting teams in real-time, AI speeds up action and prevents minor issues from turning into major failures. The system's long-term stability, security, and efficacy are ensured by this proactive approach. As a result, companies are able to give users consistent performance and maintain a high level of trust in their software systems.

The following table compares the two major software maintenance types:

Traditional software maintenance	AI-enabled software maintenance
Resource allocation is fixed based on initial estimates, often leading to underutilisation or overload.	AI intelligently adjusts resource allocation in real-time using performance analytics and workload predictions.
Updates are performed manually and periodically, resulting in long deployment cycles and higher downtime.	AI facilitates continuous, automated updates with minimal disruption, ensuring smoother and faster deployments.
Code refactoring and optimisation rely heavily on developers' manual effort and experience.	AI recommends efficient code structures, performs automated refactoring, and enhances overall code quality.
Debugging depends on manual inspection, which is time-consuming and prone to human error.	AI-based debugging tools automatically detect, predict, and even resolve bugs by analysing large code patterns.
Testing is largely manual or follows rigid rule-based automation that needs frequent adjustments.	AI-driven test automation adapts automatically to code changes, generates intelligent test cases, and improves accuracy.
Relies on predefined metrics and human analysis.	AI continuously monitors and predicts system failures in real-time.

***Table 2.1**: Comparison between traditional and AI-enabled software maintenance*

AI tools for predictive software maintenance

Some AI tools for predictive software management are:

- **Siemens predictive maintenance**: Siemens offers AI-based solutions that enable data-driven condition monitoring across entire plants or multiple sites. Organizations can implement AI technologies more easily since they readily connect with current industrial automation systems. Maintenance personnel can react swiftly to possible problems before they worsen thanks to real-time dashboards and automated notifications. By guaranteeing that machines continue to operate at peak efficiency, this not only improves operational reliability but also boosts productivity.

- **SAP predictive maintenance and service**: SAP's cloud-based solution utilizes machine learning and advanced analytics to predict equipment failures by analyzing real-time data. SAP's AI engine continuously learns from ongoing data streams, improving the accuracy of predictions over time. It provides actionable recommendations that help organisations schedule maintenance during low-demand periods, thus avoiding disruptions. This approach ensures reduced costs, higher efficiency, and a more strategic method of managing critical equipment.

- **Oracle's AI for predictive maintenance**: Oracle integrates AI to monitor machinery conditions, detect anomalies, and prioritize maintenance tasks. Their platform enhances maintenance management by predicting equipment failures more accurately and swiftly than traditional methods. Oracle's predictive maintenance solutions offer a thorough understanding of asset health and are made to function well with IoT-enabled devices. Additionally, the platform facilitates automated workflows that allow prompt actions based on insights given by AI. This results in increased machine dependability, lower maintenance expenses, and better long-term asset management decision-making.

AI in software project management

AI tools can analyze historical project data, predict potential risks, and suggest mitigation strategies, helping project managers make informed decisions. By automating routine tasks such as scheduling, progress tracking, and resource management, AI reduces administrative burdens, enabling teams to focus on higher-level tasks. Planning, execution, and monitoring are the keys to project management. AI tools are available to cater to such requirements.

AI tools are trained by historical project data, and further ML helps in analyzing the data, predicting the related risk, if any, and helping in managing the project. AI tools help in suggesting mitigation strategies and help the project manager in making corrective plans and decisions.

Role of AI in software project management

Let us now understand the role of AI in software project management:

- **Task management automation**: AI helps in task management by automating it. These tools help in enhancing the planning, execution, and monitoring of projects by automating these tasks. Routine project scheduling, progress tracking, meetings, resource requirements, and management are automated with the help of AI tools, reducing the overhead of administrative work.
- **Risk prediction and mitigation**: AI tools help in identifying the delays in work progress, projects running out of budget, shortage of resources, and problems in resource allocation. With all such information received through AI-enabled task management, it is easy to focus on the weak areas, and actions can be taken on time.
- **Real-time project monitoring**: A project goes through various phases and needs to be monitored. Project progress tracking becomes easy with the help of AI-enabled tools for monitoring. These tools provide managers with real-time information about the project's state, enabling them to make quick adjustments as needed, such as modifications to schedules, budgets, or resource requirements and allocations.
- **Improved decision making**: AI helps project managers make decisions to predict and forecast accurately and improve the overall effectiveness and success of software

projects by utilising AI-driven information and predictive analytics.

By providing precise forecasts, data-driven insights, and real-time analytics that enhance overall project planning and execution, AI helps project managers. AI-driven forecasting enables managers to more accurately anticipate timetables, identify potential risks, and allocate resources. This improves cooperation, reduces uncertainty, and increases the likelihood of successfully completing the project. AI-enabled insights also aid in the assessment of various tactics, guaranteeing that choices are based on trustworthy data and trends rather than conjecture.

AI tools for software project management

Some AI tools for software project management are as follows:

- **Asana**: Asana integrates AI to provide productivity recommendations, helping teams prioritize tasks and streamline workflows. Asana's AI-powered insights help identify bottlenecks early and provide recommendations for enhancing workflow efficiency. Teams may rely on automated reminders, intelligent work recommendations, and improved visibility into project schedules. By encouraging improved teamwork and a fairer task distribution, this enhances the overall performance of the project.
- **ClickUp**: ClickUp's AI features allow users to query project data, facilitating quick access to information and enhancing project tracking. ClickUp's AI can produce work descriptions, flag possible project dangers, and summarize lengthy project documentation.

  Additionally, it helps teams save time and minimize errors by automating repetitive operations. Project managers have a better understanding of the overall health of their projects thanks to AI-enabled tracking and insights.
- **Forecast**: Forecast offers a unified platform that simplifies project creation, budgeting, resource allocation, task management, invoicing, and reporting through automation and smart insights.

  In order to deliver more accurate estimates and better planning recommendations, the platform also continuously learns from past project data. It helps teams maintain transparency by providing real-time dashboards and performance metrics. Forecast's end-to-end automation and wise counsel enable firms to manage complex projects more successfully and confidently.

Natural language processing in software engineering

NLP in software engineering refers to the application of AI and ML methods to allow computers to comprehend, interpret, and produce human language. It plays a crucial role in enhancing automatic code generation, error detection, documentation analysis, and natural language interfaces, significantly contributing to the improvement of software programs.

It plays a crucial role in improving software applications through features such as automated code generation, error detection, documentation analysis, and natural language interfaces.

Role of NLP in software engineering

Let us now understand the role of NLP in software engineering:

- **Improved user interaction**: NLP enables a program to understand and react to human language, thereby enhancing user interaction. Apple's iPhone Siri, Amazon's Alexa, and chatbots are examples that utilize NLP and are commonly used by users today. Such applications are also known as virtual assistants and can interpret user enquiries in natural language and answer the queries. Such machines not just respond to user enquiries but also learn by themselves and enhance the users' experiences.
- **Code generation and documentation automation**: As mentioned previously, there are many tools that aid in code generation; NLP can be utilized to enhance this process even further. By understanding natural language, inputs can generate and optimize code and suggest improvements. It can also generate documents based on the code. NLP also helps with documentation based on the code. It will be an improved document and will serve the purpose of maintenance and improvement. All the tasks performed help save time for developers and improve the code and document quality.
- **Text mining and sentiment analysis**: In today's scenario, we are not just dealing with simple and structured data but rather with large volumes of unstructured data. The large amount of text data includes social media posts, comments, and reviews. Such data requires frequent analysis to know and understand customer sentiment and extract key insights. Later on, this analysis helps organizations make informed decisions. That way, text mining and sentiment Analysis play a vital role in the world of social media and the business environment.

Tools using NLP in software engineering

Let us now understand the tools using NLP in software engineering:

- **GitHub Copilot**: An AI-powered coding assistant developed by GitHub and OpenAI, Copilot uses NLP to understand natural language prompts and generate code snippets, offering real-time code suggestions

- **Tabnine**: An AI-driven code completion tool that leverages NLP to predict and suggest code completions in real-time, supporting multiple programming languages and integrating seamlessly with various IDEs.
- **DeepCode**: An AI-powered code review tool that uses NLP to analyze codebases, detect potential bugs, and suggest improvements by learning from numerous open-source projects.

Enhancing testing and quality assurance

AI-enabled tools can automate all the tasks related to software testing, including writing test cases, executing test cases, and managing tests. The automation makes it time-saving, and the use of AI makes it faster than the usual time taken in testing the software. Other than reducing testing time, such tools also help in improving and ensuring the software quality.

The overall testing procedure is greatly accelerated by AI's speed and accuracy. By executing numerous tests concurrently across various platforms, devices, and settings, AI-driven systems increase test coverage while decreasing validation time. These tools not only save time but also enhance software quality by detecting hidden defects, performance bottlenecks, and possible failure locations far more efficiently than manual testing methods. Sophisticated features like self-healing scripts ensure that tests instantly adjust to code changes, increasing test reliability and reducing false failures. All things considered, AI not only speeds up testing but also ensures a higher degree of accuracy, stability, and robustness, ultimately producing software of the highest caliber that meets industry standards and user expectations.

Role of AI in enhancing testing and quality assurance

Let us understand the role of AI in enhancing testing and quality assurance:

- **Automated and self-healing tests**: By adjusting to code changes, AI-powered testing solutions minimize faulty tests and eliminate manual labor by automatically creating and updating test cases. Automated and self-healing tests have revolutionized software testing. In order to assure correctness, traditional testing methods required testers to manually update or rewrite test cases anytime developers made changes to the application code.

  This labor-intensive and time-consuming method regularly caused delays in project timelines. AI-powered testing solutions circumvent this issue by automatically changing test scripts and continuously evaluating application activity. Every time a code piece is added, modified, or withdrawn, the AI system detects and updates the pertinent test cases without the need for human intervention. This ensures that the testing framework is dependable and functional even in fast-paced development contexts like agile and DevOps.
- **Improved defect detection and accuracy**: By identifying patterns and irregularities in code, AI enhances bug identification, increasing accuracy and reducing the likelihood

of overlooked flaws. Improved defect detection and accuracy are one of AI's most important contributions to software testing. Instead of relying only on manual checks or predetermined criteria, AI-based testing technologies analyze vast amounts of code and application behavior to uncover abnormalities and hidden mistake patterns that human testers would miss.

By continuously observing system responses and learning from past errors, AI becomes more adept at identifying vulnerabilities early on, even before they lead to evident failures. This reduces the possibility of overlooking significant flaws that could impair system performance or user experience and increases testing accuracy. Using AI-driven insights, development teams may maintain higher code quality, solve issues faster, and deliver more reliable software to end users.

- **Faster and scalable testing**: AI accelerates the product release cycle and enhances test coverage by enabling parallel testing across multiple settings, thereby speeding up test execution. Faster and more scalable testing is one of the key advantages of using AI in modern software development. AI-powered testing technologies allow test cases to run in parallel across many contexts, devices, and settings, greatly speeding up the execution process overall.

  Without needing to wait for sequential testing cycles, teams can validate complex and massive apps more quickly without compromising quality. Additionally, by dynamically selecting critical cases and assigning resources according to testing demands, AI guarantees optimal test coverage even under tight deadlines. Businesses can efficiently manage increasing workloads, shorten release cycles, and generate high-quality products far more quickly because of this scalability.

AI tools for enhancing testing and quality assurance

Tools like Testim and Functionize utilize machine learning to create self-healing tests that automatically adapt to code changes, thereby reducing maintenance efforts. Let us go over them now:

- **Functionize**: Combines AI and machine learning to automate the testing process, allowing for rapid test creation and execution. Functionize entirely automates the software testing lifecycle by utilizing AI and machine learning. Large-scale test suites can be swiftly designed, carried out, and managed by testers without requiring a lot of programming or upkeep. Even when the code changes often, its intelligent system continuously learns from application behavior, speeding up test generation and enhancing the accuracy and reliability of results.
- **Testim**: An AI-driven testing tool that accelerates test creation and maintenance for web and mobile applications. The goal of Testim, an AI-powered testing platform, is to speed up the creation and upkeep of tests for online and mobile applications. It makes test cases resistant to frequent interface alterations by using machine learning

to dynamically identify UI elements. Testim guarantees dependable and scalable test automation, lowers manual labor, and boosts productivity with its quick test authoring and self-healing features.

- **Applitools**: Applitools enhances visual testing using AI to detect UI inconsistencies across devices, while Mabl provides intelligent end-to-end testing with auto-healing capabilities. By detecting even the smallest UI differences between different devices, browsers, and screen resolutions, something that traditional automation tools often miss, Applitools enhances visual testing with advanced AI algorithms. On the other hand, Mabl offers intelligent end-to-end testing with performance tracking, analytics-driven insights, and auto-healing features. Together, these technologies boost the testing process by improving accuracy, visual consistency, and overall software quality.

The following table shows the tools for AI that enable software engineering:

Tools/ Role	AI-driven software development	AI for predictive software maintenance	AI in software project management	NLP in software engineering	Enhaning testing and QA
Tools	Devika AI	Siemens Predictive	Asana	GitHub	Functionize
	GitHub Copilot	Maintenance	ClickUp	Tabnine	Testim
	OpenAI Codex	SAP Predictive	Forecast	DeepCode	Applitools
	Polycoder	Maintenance and Service			
	Cogram DeepCode	Oracle's AI for Predictive			

***Table 2.2**: Tools for AI-enabled software engineering*

Example of automated code generation and assistance

Scenario: A developer needs to create a Python function that sorts a list of numbers. Instead of writing the code manually, they use an AI-powered tool like GitHub Copilot or OpenAI's Codex.

Example interaction with an AI tool:

1. **Developer input (Prompt in IDE or AI tool)**: Write a Python function to sort a list of numbers using quicksort.

2. **AI-generated code suggestion:**

```
def quicksort(arr):
    if len(arr) <= 1:
        return arr
    pivot = arr[len(arr) // 2]
    left = [x for x in arr if x < pivot]
    middle = [x for x in arr if x == pivot]
    right = [x for x in arr if x > pivot]
    return quicksort(left) + middle + quicksort(right)
# Example usage
numbers = [3, 6, 8, 10, 1, 2, 1]
sorted_numbers = quicksort(numbers)
print(sorted_numbers)
```

Future of AI in software engineering

AI has the potential to transform software development. With AI, the overall software development happens without much effort because of increased accuracy. Automation of software development, maintenance, and overall project management is the core futuristic repetitive tasks to be performed by the AI-enabled tools. These tools will support the software industries in all aspects.

AI automates software development, testing, and maintenance, reducing time, improving accuracy, and increasing productivity through ML, NLP, and automation tools. In future code generation, requirement gathering, requirements management, and cost estimation for software will be done using AI-enabled tools only. This will lead to reduced cost and time in development.

Furthermore, the use of AI-enabled tools for software maintenance will improve functionality, fix bugs, add features, and enhance performance, focusing on preventive issues at the same time.

Overall, software project management will become easier and smoother with the use of AI.

AI tools will help project managers in making decisions based on analysis of historical data, predicting risks, and suggesting mitigation strategies while automating routine tasks and reducing administrative burdens.

Conclusion

The predictive capabilities of AI improve the overall software lifecycle and enhance the end user's satisfaction, leading to reliable experiences and a better value for the investment of money and time.

AI significantly impacts software development by automating tasks and phases throughout the life cycle, including development, testing, and maintenance. This approach reduces time, enhances accuracy, and increases productivity by utilizing machine learning, natural language processing, and automation tools.

The chapter also discussed software maintenance, which involves upgrading, changing, and enhancing software programs after release to improve functionality, fix bugs, add features, and enhance performance, with a focus on preventive issues rather than addressing them immediately. The chapter further discussed the use of AI-enabled tools in project management, the use of NLP in various tools, and how it is helpful to interpret human instructions.

Questions

1. How is software development changing as a result of AI?
2. How does AI help in predictive software maintenance?
3. What role does AI play in software project management?
4. How does software engineering employ natural language processing?
5. In what ways does AI enhance quality assurance and software testing?

Answers

1. AI is revolutionizing software development by automating numerous operations that were previously completed by hand. AI technologies are capable of producing code segments, recommending optimized methods, identifying vulnerabilities, and even automatically fixing mistakes. By lowering human error, this significantly accelerates the development process and increases accuracy. Instead of concentrating on repetitive coding tasks, developers may concentrate more on creativity and intricate problem-solving with AI-driven insights. Furthermore, intelligent suggestions based on past design trends and current application behavior aid in the development of software solutions that are quicker, more effective, and scalable.

2. AI reduces downtime and enables proactive maintenance by analyzing historical data to predict potential issues. AI enhances predictive maintenance by analyzing historical performance data, system logs, and usage patterns to identify early signs of problems or performance degradation. AI can anticipate some mistakes well in advance, enabling businesses to take proactive steps instead of reacting to issues after they occur. This proactive approach reduces system downtime, avoids costly repairs, and increases the lifespan and dependability of software systems. Predictive models also help prioritize maintenance tasks according to risk levels, ensuring optimal resource allocation and continuous service delivery.

3. AI helps project managers make better decisions by automating tasks, assessing risks, allocating resources, and more. AI helps software project managers make better decisions by offering real-time data-driven insights. It frees up managers to concentrate on strategic planning by automating repetitive management chores,

including scheduling, task assignment, and progress tracking. To anticipate any delays or bottlenecks, AI algorithms assess a variety of project criteria, including budget, workload, risks, timeframes, and resource availability. This enables managers to address problems before they become more serious. Higher project success rates, better cost control, and more intelligent resource allocation are all made possible by AI-powered analytics.

4. NLP facilitates automatic code production, code documentation, and better human-computer interfaces in software tools. NLP is crucial to software engineering because it helps bridge the gap between computer systems and human language. In development environments, NLP models are used to enhance code documentation, enable intelligent search, and automatically generate code from textual descriptions. With NLP-capable tools, developers may recognize ambiguous remarks, understand legacy codebases, and convert natural language requirements into formal specifications. Additionally, enabling voice-based or conversational programming assistants, it improves human-computer interaction and makes development more accessible and user-friendly.

5. AI ensures greater software reliability by automating the creation of test cases, identifying abnormalities, and improving defect prediction. AI significantly improves software quality assurance by automating the creation, execution, and upkeep of test cases. When it comes to evaluating application behavior, identifying abnormalities, and identifying defects, AI-driven solutions are far more accurate than manual testing alone. Self-healing test systems minimize false failures and eliminate laborious manual updates by automatically fixing failing scripts as code changes. AI further enhances defect prediction by identifying high-risk code segments where flaws are most likely to appear, enabling early corrections. This ensures the delivery of high-quality software in shorter release cycles by making testing faster, more reliable, and highly scalable.

Multiple choice questions

1. **In predictive software maintenance, what is the major function of artificial intelligence?**
   a. Manually code debugging
   b. Identifying potential failures
   c. Taking the place of human software developers
   d. Ignoring minor software issues

2. **Which artificial intelligence method is most frequently applied to predictive software maintenance?**
   a. Decision trees
   b. Neural networks

   c. Machine learning algorithms
   d. All of the above

3. **How can artificial intelligence enhance software testing procedures?**
   a. By automating the creation and execution of test cases
   b. By going over each line of code by hand
   c. By eliminating the necessity for software testing
   d. By making the software more prone to errors

4. **Which of the following is a primary advantage of AI-driven code optimization?**
   a. AI replaces all human programmers.
   b. AI enhances code efficiency and reduces execution time.
   c. AI increases code complexity unnecessarily.
   d. AI ignores software performance metrics.

5. **Which one is not an AI tool for software project management?**
   a. Asana
   b. ClickUp
   c. TensorFlow
   d. Forecast

Answers

1	b
2	d
3	a
4	b
5	c

Join our Discord space

Join our Discord workspace for latest updates, offers, tech happenings around the world, new releases, and sessions with the authors:

https://discord.bpbonline.com

Chapter 3

Artificial Intelligence for Application Modernization and Migration

Introduction

In today's rapidly evolving technological landscape, the pressure on organizations to modernize legacy applications is greater than ever. Traditional systems, while foundational, often become bottlenecks to innovation due to outdated architectures and limited integration capabilities. **Artificial intelligence** (AI) is emerging as a transformative force in this domain, revolutionizing how application modernization and migration are approached. By automating complex processes, enhancing decision-making, and reducing human error, AI is paving the way for faster, smarter, and more efficient modernization strategies. In fact, industry reports indicate that over 90% of Fortune 500 companies are actively modernizing using AI-driven tools to stay competitive in the digital economy.

This chapter explores how AI technologies are driving application modernization and migration efforts. We will explore deeply into the critical role of AI in the modernization process. First, we will look at how AI helps in assessing existing applications and deciding which ones to modernize first. Next, we will examine how AI supports the actual execution of modernization strategies. We will also discuss its impact on important areas like code refactoring, resource allocation, and predictive maintenance.

Additionally, we will cover how AI enables user personalization, supports cloud migration, and helps with ongoing system monitoring.

Structure

The chapter covers the following topics:

- Understanding legacy systems and the need for modernization
- Role of AI in application modernization

- Comparative insights and performance data
- Benefits and best practices
- Real-world case studies

Objectives

The main objective of this chapter is to help readers understand how AI is transforming the way organizations modernize and migrate their applications. Many companies still rely on old or legacy systems that are slow, expensive to maintain, and difficult to update. This chapter explains how AI can make this process easier, faster, and more efficient by automating routine tasks, reducing human error, and offering smart suggestions for improvements.

Another key goal is to introduce the various roles AI plays in modernization activities. From automatically rewriting outdated code to recommending which applications should be updated first, AI tools help businesses make better decisions. The chapter also explores how AI supports cloud migration, ensures data accuracy during transfers, and helps monitor the performance of modernized applications in real-time.

Lastly, the chapter aims to share practical examples, case studies, and best practices that readers can apply in real-world situations. It covers different industries like finance, healthcare, and e-commerce to show how AI-driven modernization works in different contexts. By the end of this chapter, readers will gain clear insights into the benefits, tools, and strategies involved in using AI to upgrade and move applications efficiently. By the end of this chapter, readers will also be able to plan AI-driven modernization strategies that can be applied across multiple industries and domains.

Understanding legacy systems and the need for modernization

Legacy systems (older software applications, computer systems, or technologies) are often deeply integrated into the operational fabric of organizations, but they come with limitations: high maintenance costs, lack of scalability, and incompatibility with modern tools and platforms. Modernizing these systems involves migrating to newer, more flexible environments that support innovation and agility. The process can be complex, resource-intensive, and risky; this is where AI proves invaluable.

The *Figure 3.1* shows the *AI-driven modernization lifecycle*, which explains the main steps for upgrading old software systems using AI. It begins with *Assessment*, where AI studies the current systems and identifies areas for improvement. Next is *Planning*, in which AI suggests the best modernization approach, such as code changes or cloud migration. This is followed by *Execution*, where AI assists in rewriting code, automating processes, and moving systems to modern platforms. After that comes *Testing & Validation*, where AI checks the system's performance and ensures everything works correctly. The *Deployment* stage then launches the updated system for actual use. Finally, in *Continuous Monitoring*, AI keeps tracking the system to detect issues early and make improvements. These stages are arranged in a circular flow, showing that modernization is an ongoing process, and the figure uses clear arrows and text boxes to make the steps easy to understand:

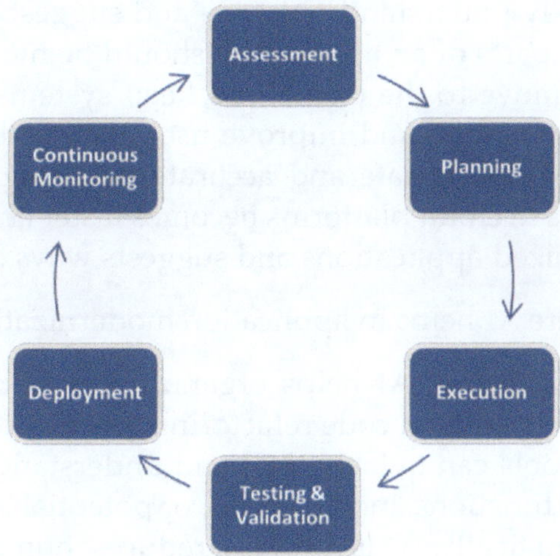

***Figure 3.1:** AI-driven modernization lifecycle*

Figure 3.2 provides a high-level overview of the key areas where AI contributes to application modernization and migration. It highlights the multi-faceted role AI plays, from code updates to cloud transitions and real-time monitoring.

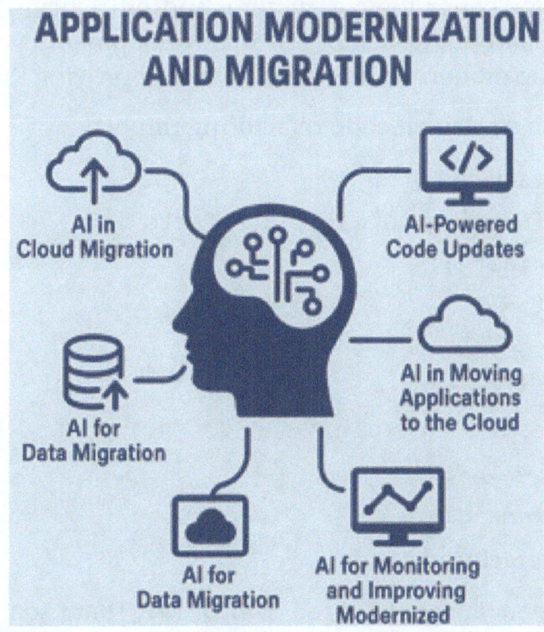

***Figure 3.2:** AI for application modernization and migration*

Role of AI in application modernization

Modernizing old applications is important for making them faster, safer, and easier to use. AI plays a big role in this process. It helps organizations update their systems with less time and effort. AI tools can quickly understand old code and suggest better ways to improve it. They also help decide which parts of an application should be modernized first. AI makes it easier to manage resources, move to the cloud, and keep systems running smoothly. It can predict problems before they happen and improve user experience by making applications more personalized. AI also supports safe and accurate data migration. With AI, updating code and shifting applications to cloud platforms becomes faster and more reliable. Finally, AI continues to monitor modernized applications and suggests ways to make them even better.

Here are some key areas where AI helps in application modernization:

- **Automated code refactoring**: AI helps organizations update old software systems more easily by using automated code refactoring. Instead of manually rewriting large sections of code, AI tools can quickly scan and understand complex code structures. They detect outdated functions, inefficiencies, or potential issues and suggest or apply improvements automatically. This process reduces human error, saves time, and ensures the updated application meets current standards for performance, security, and scalability. AI-based tools also help developers maintain cleaner and more efficient code that integrates smoothly with modern platforms and services.

  Example: Tools like Google's AutoML can analyze code and provide smart recommendations for better logic, structure, and efficiency. This not only makes the code easier to maintain but also shortens the development cycle. Overall, AI-powered refactoring speeds up modernization efforts while improving the quality of the software.

  The following is the AI-driven code refactoring impact:

  - **Before (Legacy code)**:

```
# Legacy function to calculate factorial
def factorial(n):
    result = 1
    i = 1
    while i <= n:
        result = result * i
        i = i + 1
    return result
```

  - **After (AI-refactored code)**:

```
# Refactored and optimized factorial function

from math import prod
```

```
def factorial(n):
    return prod(range(1, n + 1))
```

Impact:

- o Reduced 7 lines to 3 lines.
- o Improved readability and maintainability.
- o Leveraged built-in functions for better performance.
- o Lower chance of errors due to reduced manual looping logic.

Therefore, the AI-driven code refactoring greatly, benefits customers by improving application performance and ensuring faster response times. Simplifying and optimizing the code, it reduces the chances of errors, resulting in a smoother and more reliable user experience. Easier maintenance allows updates and new features to be delivered more quickly, keeping the application fresh and competitive. Additionally, the optimized code uses fewer system resources, which helps maintain high speed and stability even during peak usage. Overall, customers gain access to a more efficient, stable, and user-friendly application that consistently meets their needs and expectations.

- **Prioritization of modernization efforts**: AI plays a crucial role in helping organizations decide which applications or system components should be modernized first. By analyzing data such as system performance, user engagement, business impact, and usage frequency, AI can identify the parts of the software infrastructure that are most in need of improvement. This smart prioritization ensures that modernization efforts are focused on areas that offer the greatest return on investment. Rather than attempting to update all systems at once, which can be costly and inefficient AI guides teams to concentrate on high-impact areas that affect customers, revenue, or daily operations. It also supports better planning and allocation of time, budget, and human resources.

  Example: A banking organization might use AI tools to analyze the performance of its various digital services. Based on user activity and risk data, the AI may highlight that customer-facing mobile applications are underperforming or outdated. As a result, the company can begin modernization with those applications to improve user satisfaction and stay competitive. This data-driven approach not only saves costs but also helps organizations modernize more strategically and effectively.

Criteria	Weight (%)	Application A	Application B	Application C
Business impact	30	8	6	9
User engagement	25	7	5	8
System performance issues	20	9	6	7
Maintenance cost	15	8	7	6

Security risk level	10	9	5	7
Total score	100	8.1	5.9	7.8

Table 3.1*: Application modernization scoring matrix*

In *Table 3.1*, the scoring matrix, each application is evaluated against specific criteria such as business impact, user engagement, system performance issues, maintenance cost, and security risk level. Each criterion is assigned a weight based on its importance to the organization's modernization goals. Applications are then scored on a scale from 1 (lowest) to 10 (highest) for each criterion. The individual scores are multiplied by their respective weights to calculate weighted scores, which are then summed to obtain the total score for each application. Applications with higher total scores are considered higher priority for modernization, ensuring that resources are focused on areas with the greatest potential impact.

- **Intelligent resource allocation**: AI plays a key role in optimizing how resources are allocated during application modernization. Instead of relying on manual planning, AI-driven tools analyze various factors such as system dependencies, real-time performance data, workload trends, and user demand to suggest the most effective use of development and infrastructure resources. These tools help ensure that teams are not overusing or underusing resources, allowing organizations to focus their efforts where they are most needed. By aligning resource distribution with actual business priorities and system needs, AI supports more efficient project planning and execution.

  This intelligent approach helps avoid resource bottlenecks, reduces operational costs, and accelerates the modernization timeline. It also enables IT teams to make informed decisions based on data rather than guesswork, leading to better outcomes and improved productivity.

  Figure 3.3 illustrates the workflow steps involved in AI-driven resource allocation:

  1. **Input data collection**: Gather system performance metrics, workload trends, and user demand data.

  2. **Data analysis by AI models**: AI processes and identifies usage patterns and bottlenecks.

  3. **Priority assessment**: AI assigns priority levels to tasks or systems based on business goals.

  4. **Optimal resource allocation plan**: AI suggests the most efficient allocation of human, hardware, and cloud resources.

  5. **Implementation and monitoring**: Resources are allocated, and AI continues real-time monitoring to adjust as needed.

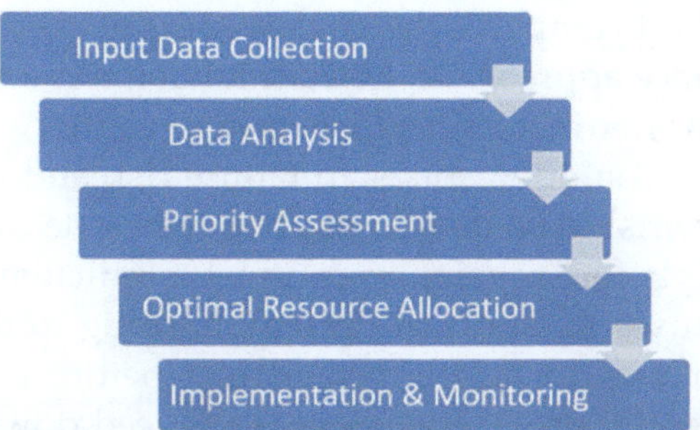

Figure 3.3: Workflow diagram for AI-driven resource distribution

Example: Platforms like Azure Advisor use AI to provide personalized recommendations for resource allocation, cost savings, and performance enhancements. Such tools can analyze usage patterns and suggest how to resize or reconfigure infrastructure components for optimal efficiency. As a result, organizations are better equipped to manage budgets, reduce waste, and ensure that modernization efforts deliver maximum value.

- **Predictive maintenance and failure forecasting**: AI-powered predictive maintenance is transforming the way organizations manage the health and performance of their applications. By using ML algorithms to study historical performance data, usage trends, and error logs, AI can identify patterns that signal potential failures or system issues before they occur. This allows teams to take timely action, such as performing updates or replacing faulty components, before the problem leads to system downtime or disruptions. Such a proactive approach helps maintain the stability and reliability of applications, especially during critical processes like modernization or cloud migration.

  Predictive analytics also reduces the need for emergency repairs, lowering maintenance costs and improving overall operational efficiency. It ensures that modernization efforts continue without interruption and that performance remains consistent post-migration.

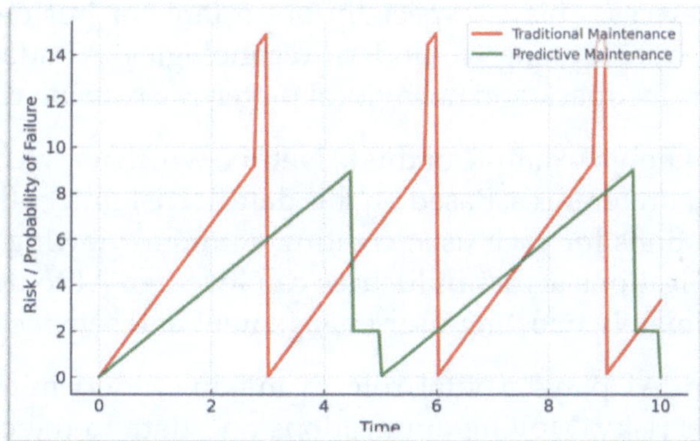

***Figure 3.4**: Cloud failure prediction vs. traditional maintenance timeline chart*

Figure 3.4 timeline chart compares the effectiveness of predictive maintenance against traditional maintenance approaches. In traditional maintenance, work is scheduled at fixed intervals, which often results in either early servicing, wasting resources or delayed intervention, leading to sudden spikes in failure risk and unplanned downtime. The red curve shows how risk repeatedly rises between scheduled checks and sometimes reaches critical levels before repairs. In contrast, predictive maintenance, represented by the green curve, uses AI and real-time monitoring to detect warning signs early. This allows maintenance to be performed just before a failure is likely to occur, keeping risk consistently lower. The result is reduced downtime, optimized resource use, and improved operational efficiency. Overall, the chart highlights how predictive strategies can maintain system stability more effectively than traditional methods

Example: IBM Watson uses advanced AI models to monitor and analyze large-scale systems in industries like manufacturing. It can accurately forecast when a machine or application component is likely to malfunction, enabling companies to fix issues before they affect production or user experience. Similarly, in the context of IT modernization, predictive AI tools help prevent failures in application infrastructure by providing early warnings, ensuring a smoother transition, and reducing risk.

- **Personalization of user experience**: AI significantly enhances user experience by enabling personalized application interfaces and functionalities. By analyzing user behavior, preferences, and interaction history, AI can tailor the way content, features, and services are presented to individual users. This level of customization helps create a more engaging and intuitive experience, making the application feel more responsive to user needs. Studies show that AI-driven personalization can increase user engagement by 25 to 45%, boost customer retention rates by 20 to 30%, and improve conversion rates by 10 to 20% across industries. Personalization not only increases user satisfaction but also encourages longer usage and greater loyalty to the application or service.

  In the context of application modernization, AI ensures that even newly updated systems maintain a consistent yet personalized experience for users across different platforms and devices. This is especially important for businesses aiming to retain customers while transitioning to modern technologies. AI adapts the user interface based on real-time feedback and behavioral patterns, ensuring relevance and usability.

  Example: A well-known example of this is Netflix, which uses AI algorithms to analyze viewer habits and preferences. Based on this data, it customizes the layout, thumbnails, and recommendations for each user, creating a unique viewing experience. Similarly, modernized applications across industries can leverage AI to deliver tailored content and features, ultimately boosting user engagement and satisfaction.

- **Cloud migration**: AI plays a vital role in making cloud migration more efficient, accurate, and less risky. Moving applications and data to the cloud can be complex, especially when dealing with large systems and interdependent components. AI helps simplify this process by analyzing application architectures, system dependencies, performance metrics, and usage patterns. Based on this analysis, AI can suggest the most effective migration paths, helping organizations decide which components should be moved first, how they should be grouped, and which cloud services best match their needs.

Importantly, modern AI tools also support multi-cloud strategies, enabling organizations to distribute workloads across platforms like **Amazon Web Services** (**AWS**), Microsoft Azure, and **Google Cloud Platform** (**GCP**). This flexibility allows businesses to avoid vendor lock-in, optimize costs, and take advantage of the unique strengths of each provider.

This smart analysis reduces the chances of errors, minimizes downtime during the migration, and ensures a smoother transition. AI also assists in cost forecasting and resource planning by recommending configurations that balance performance and budget. Moreover, AI helps identify potential bottlenecks and security concerns before they become critical issues, allowing IT teams to prepare in advance.

Example: AWS Migration Hub, Microsoft Azure Migrate, and Google's Migrate for Compute Engine leverage AI and machine learning to guide users through the cloud transition process. These tools evaluate on-premise workloads and recommend the most suitable services for hosting them, based on factors like performance requirements and application behavior. For multi-cloud deployments, AI can even recommend optimal distribution of workloads across AWS, Azure, and GCP to maximize efficiency and resilience.

By using AI-driven tools for cloud migration, organizations can ensure that their transition to cloud environments is not only faster and more secure but also aligned with business goals. The result is a modern, scalable, and flexible IT infrastructure that supports future growth, as shown:

Figure 3.5*: AI-powered application migration to the cloud*

Figure 3.5 illustrates the AI-assisted journey of migrating applications from on-premise environments to the cloud. It emphasizes how AI orchestrates application transitions, manages configurations, and supports data migration for smoother deployments.

Code updates: AI-powered tools are becoming essential in maintaining and improving software codebases, especially during modernization. One of their key functions is identifying outdated libraries, deprecated methods, and code segments that may pose performance or security risks. These tools analyze large volumes of code to detect weaknesses or inefficiencies that might not be easily noticeable through manual review. Once identified, AI can either suggest updates or automatically apply the necessary changes, ensuring that the application complies with the latest coding standards, industry best practices, and security protocols.

This automation not only speeds up the update process but also reduces the risk of introducing new bugs or errors. AI ensures the code is more efficient, secure, and easier to maintain, which is especially important for applications being modernized to meet current business demands. These updates also help ensure compatibility with newer platforms, frameworks, and technologies.

- **Sample AI suggestion output**: AI Analysis Detected use of deprecated method: `'StringBuffer.append()'` in file: `PaymentProcessor.java`
- **Suggested improvement**: Replace with `'StringBuilder.append()'` for better performance in single-threaded contexts.
  - **Before**:

```
StringBuffer sb = new StringBuffer();
sb.append("Processing Payment...");
```

  - **After**:

```
StringBuilder sb = new StringBuilder();
sb.append("Processing Payment...");
```

Impact: Estimated 15% performance improvement in string concatenation operations.

Example: A great example is GitHub Copilot, an AI-powered code assistant developed by GitHub and OpenAI. It suggests real-time code completions and offers secure alternatives when outdated or risky code patterns are detected. Developers can use it to automatically replace vulnerable or deprecated code with improved, standards-compliant solutions, significantly enhancing software quality.

By integrating AI into the code update process, organizations can maintain a healthier codebase, reduce technical debt, and improve the overall reliability of their modernized applications, without needing extensive manual intervention.

- **Application movement to the cloud**: AI significantly simplifies and enhances the process of moving applications to the cloud. Cloud migration often involves many complex steps, such as configuring environments, managing dependencies, and ensuring that applications run smoothly after the move. AI tools can simulate different deployment scenarios to help organizations understand how their applications will perform in the new cloud environment. These simulations help identify the most suitable configurations and highlight any potential challenges before the actual migration takes place.

AI also automates many of the tasks involved in transitioning workloads, such as setting up cloud resources, adjusting performance settings, and replicating application environments. This reduces manual effort, minimizes errors, and shortens the overall migration timeline. One of the major benefits of using AI is its ability to analyze performance data and suggest the most cost-effective and high-performing cloud setup based on the specific needs of the application.

Example: Google's Migrate for Compute Engine, which uses AI to assess workloads and recommend tailored migration plans. It provides insights into how existing on-premise applications will behave in the cloud and helps optimize resource allocation during the transition.

By leveraging AI in application movement, organizations can ensure a smoother, more reliable migration process that aligns with both technical requirements and business objectives. The result is a well-optimized cloud infrastructure that supports better performance, scalability, and cost-efficiency.

- **Data migration**: Data migration is a critical part of application modernization, and AI greatly improves the speed, accuracy, and reliability of this process. When transferring large volumes of data from legacy systems to modern platforms, challenges such as inconsistent formats, duplicate entries, outdated records, and missing relationships often arise. AI-powered tools help overcome these issues by automatically scanning data for errors and anomalies, identifying duplicates, and cleaning or updating outdated information. This results in higher data quality and better overall system performance after migration.

  Additionally, AI can intelligently map relationships between different datasets, ensuring that data is accurately structured and linked in the new environment. This reduces the risk of data loss, corruption, or misalignment during the migration process. AI also automates many routine tasks involved in data transfer, minimizing the need for manual intervention and reducing the chance of human error.

  Example: An excellent example of this is Informatica's CLAIRE engine, which uses artificial intelligence and machine learning to automate complex data preparation tasks at scale. It identifies data inconsistencies, cleans large datasets, and ensures proper formatting before the data is moved to the target system.

With AI-driven data migration, organizations can transition to new systems more confidently, knowing that their data is clean, consistent, and well-structured. This not only ensures a smooth migration process but also supports more accurate analytics, reporting, and decision-making in the modernized application environment.

- **Monitoring and improving modernized applications**: Once applications have been modernized, the work does not stop there, ongoing monitoring and performance enhancement become essential. This is where AI plays a vital role. AI-powered monitoring tools continuously observe how the application performs, track user interactions, analyze system logs, and detect any unusual behavior in real-time. These platforms help organizations gain deep insights into application health, performance bottlenecks, and potential failures before they impact users.

  By leveraging real-time data, AI enables systems to automatically adjust configurations, allocate resources more efficiently, and fix minor issues without human involvement. This ensures that applications remain stable, secure, and optimized even as usage patterns change or the system scales. Continuous feedback from AI monitoring tools supports long-term improvements and helps development teams refine applications based on actual user behavior and operational needs.

  Example: Dynatrace, an AI-driven observability platform that uses ML for anomaly detection, root cause analysis, and performance tuning. It automatically identifies and resolves issues, ensuring that the application maintains high performance and reliability at all times.

  Through AI-enabled monitoring, organizations can move from reactive to proactive application management. This leads to quicker issue resolution, better user experiences, and continuous optimization of applications long after modernization is complete. In essence, AI helps keep modern applications running at peak performance with minimal manual oversight.

Comparative insights and performance data

To further illustrate the impact of AI on application modernization, the following tables provide useful comparisons and metrics based on industry findings and AI implementation outcomes.

Traditional modernization vs. AI-powered modernization

This table highlights key differences between traditional and AI-driven approaches to modernization:

Aspect	Traditional modernization	AI-powered modernization
Time required	High	Reduced due to automation
Error rate	Moderate to high	Significantly lower
Resource utilization	Manual allocation	AI-optimized distribution
Decision making	Intuition-based	Data-driven insights
User experience personalization	Limited	Highly personalized

***Table 3.2**: Traditional modernization vs. AI-powered modernization*

Table 3.2 highlights key differences between traditional and AI-powered approaches to application modernization. In traditional methods, processes are time-consuming due to heavy reliance on manual labor and decision-making based on experience or intuition. This often results in higher error rates and inefficiencies in resource utilization. On the other hand, AI-driven modernization automates many of these tasks, significantly reducing the time required and minimizing human errors. AI also enhances decision-making by using real-time data analytics and predictive insights, enabling smarter, more efficient strategies. One of the most impactful benefits of AI is its ability to personalize user experiences, offering tailored interfaces and functionalities based on individual user behavior, something not feasible in conventional methods. Overall, the table demonstrates how AI not only streamlines the modernization process but also improves the quality and performance of the resulting applications.

AI tools and their use cases in modernization

This table presents commonly used AI tools and their specific contributions to modernization efforts:

AI tool	Use case	Example platform
Code refactoring AI	Auto-optimizing legacy code	Google AutoML
Migration analyzers	Cloud-readiness and dependency mapping	AWS Migration Hub
Predictive analytics	Forecasting component failures	IBM Watson
Personalization engines	Customizing UI/UX	Adobe Sensei
Data cleansing AI	Enhancing data quality during migration	Informatica CLAIRE

***Table 3.3**: AI tools and their use cases in modernization*

Table 3.3 outlines various types of AI tools and their specific roles in the application modernization process, along with example platforms that implement these functionalities. Code refactoring AI, like Google AutoML, helps improve outdated code automatically, reducing manual coding effort and improving performance. Migration analyzers, such as AWS Migration Hub, evaluate existing systems to determine cloud readiness and identify system dependencies, making cloud transitions smoother and less risky. Predictive analytics tools, such as IBM Watson, forecast failures or maintenance needs in advance, allowing teams to avoid downtime through proactive actions. Personalization engines, like Adobe Sensei, enhance user experience by tailoring application interfaces and content based on user behavior. Lastly, data cleansing AI, exemplified by Informatica CLAIRE, improves data quality by identifying and removing duplicates, errors, and outdated information during migration. Together, these tools demonstrate how AI enables faster, smarter, and more reliable modernization with minimal manual intervention.

Key performance gains from AI integration

This table summarizes measurable improvements organizations have reported after integrating AI into their modernization workflows:

Metric	Improvement range
Application deployment speed	30% – 60% faster
System downtime	Up to 40% reduction
Operational costs	20% – 50% savings
User engagement	25% – 45% increase
Maintenance effort	Reduced by 35% on average

***Table 3.4**: Key performance gains from AI integration*

Table 3.4 highlights measurable improvements seen when AI is integrated into application modernization processes. AI tools accelerate *application deployment speed* by automating repetitive and time-intensive development tasks, resulting in a 30% to 60% faster release cycle. *System downtime* is significantly reduced by up to 40% through predictive maintenance and real-time monitoring, ensuring more reliable operations. In terms of *operational costs*, AI-driven optimization and intelligent resource allocation contribute to substantial savings of 20% to 50%. Additionally, AI enhances *user engagement* by delivering personalized experiences, which can increase interaction by 25% to 45%. Finally, *maintenance effort* is reduced by an average of 35% due to automated issue detection, code refactoring, and performance tuning. Together, these metrics demonstrate the tangible business value and efficiency gains brought by AI-enabled modernization efforts, as shown here:

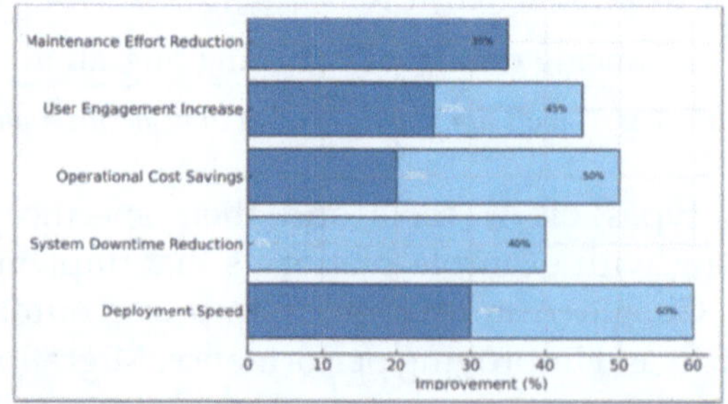

***Figure 3.6**: Visual representation of performance improvements achieved through AI-enabled modernization*

Figure 3.6 visually represents the measurable performance gains achieved through AI integration in application modernization. It highlights improvements across five key areas: deployment speed, system downtime reduction, operational cost savings, user engagement, and maintenance effort reduction. The bars show the percentage improvement range for each metric, illustrating both minimum and maximum potential gains. Deployment speed shows the highest boost (30 to 60%), while downtime is reduced by up to 40% through predictive maintenance. Overall, the visualization makes it easy to compare the impact of AI across different performance dimensions.

Benefits and best practices

The benefits of AI integration in modernization are as follows:

- **Faster development cycles**: Automation of repetitive tasks shortens timelines, with AI reducing modernization time by 30 to 50% on average compared to traditional methods.
- **Improved accuracy**: Reduced human intervention lowers the risk of errors, cutting defect rates by *up to 60%* during migration.
- **Cost efficiency**: Optimized resource use leads to significant cost savings, typically ranging from *20 to 45%* in operational expenses.
- **Scalability**: AI-powered systems adapt better to changing business needs, improving workload handling capacity by *25 to 40%* without major infrastructure changes.
- **Informed decision-making**: AI insights support strategic modernization planning, helping prioritize tasks that deliver *up to 3× ROI* faster than conventional approaches.

The best practices for successful implementation are listed as follows:

- **Start with a comprehensive assessment**: Use AI tools to evaluate the current state of applications.
- **Adopt a phased approach**: Gradual modernization allows for better risk management.
- **Involve cross-functional teams**: Collaboration between IT, data science, and business units ensures alignment.
- **Invest in AI training**: Equip teams with the skills to manage and evolve AI tools.
- **Monitor and adjust continuously**: Use AI analytics to measure success and recalibrate strategies.

Collaboration between AI experts, developers, and business strategists is critical to successful modernization. The following figure captures a typical AI-driven modernization planning session involving multiple stakeholders:

Figure 3.7: Team collaborating on AI application modernization

In the following figure, the AI adoption maturity model illustrates the progressive stages organizations typically follow when integrating AI into modernization initiatives:

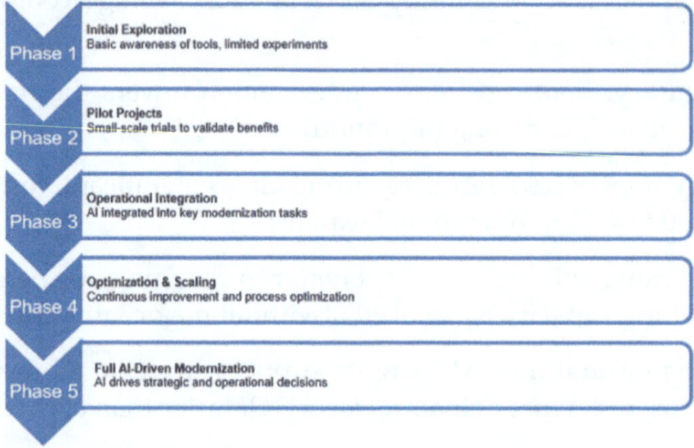

Figure 3.8: AI adoption maturity model illustrating the five phases of integrating AI into modernization workflows

The model begins with *Initial Exploration,* where teams gain awareness of AI tools and conduct limited experiments. In the *Pilot Projects* phase, small-scale trials are used to validate potential benefits before larger investments. *Operational Integration* marks the point where AI becomes embedded in key modernization activities, improving efficiency and accuracy. The *Optimization and Scaling* phase focuses on continuous improvement, expanding AI capabilities across the organization. Finally, *Full AI-Driven Modernization* is achieved when AI informs both strategic and operational decisions, driving sustained innovation and transformation.

Real-world case studies

Let us look at some real-world case studies illustrating AI use in modernization:

- **Financial services firm uses AI for legacy system modernization**: A large financial services organization faced difficulties maintaining its decades-old legacy systems.

By using AI-based code analysis tools, the firm identified redundant code blocks, security vulnerabilities, and outdated libraries. Automated refactoring improved system efficiency by *40%*, while AI recommendations helped prioritize modernization tasks. Migration to a cloud-based infrastructure was completed in *50% less time* than projected, leading to *annual operational cost savings of $3.2 million and a 35% reduction in unplanned downtime.*

- **E-commerce platform migrates to the cloud with AI assistance**: An e-commerce company experiencing rapid growth migrated its applications to the cloud using AI-powered migration analysis tools like AWS Migration Hub. AI assessed dependencies, selected optimal services, and predicted downtime risks. This improved uptime by *25%*, accelerated deployment cycles by *45%*, and reduced operational costs by *30%*, resulting in an estimated *$1.8 million annual saving* while increasing peak season order-processing capacity by *50%*.
- **Healthcare provider implements AI for application monitoring**: A healthcare provider modernized its patient record management system with AI-driven observability platforms for real-time monitoring. The system detected anomalies, optimized resources during high usage, and proactively prevented performance issues. This led to a *20% faster system response time*, a *15% boost in staff productivity*, and *$500,000 annual maintenance savings*, contributing to better patient care delivery and reliability.
- **Government IT modernization using AI (Public sector example)**: A state government modernized its citizen services portal, which ran on outdated mainframes. AI dependency mapping analyzed over 2 million lines of code, automated refactoring, and flagged high-risk components. AI migration planning enabled a smooth shift to a *hybrid multi-cloud environment* (AWS and Azure) with near-zero downtime. The modernization achieved $8 million in annual operational savings, a 55% improvement in service request processing speed, and reduced average citizen complaint response time from 10 days to 48 hours, as shown:

Case study	Key performance gains	Cost savings	Additional impact
Financial services firm	40% improvement in system efficiency; 50% faster modernization timeline; 35% reduction in unplanned downtime	$3.2M annually	More reliable services and faster feature deployment
E-commerce platform	25% improvement in uptime; 45% faster deployments; 50% increase in peak-season processing capacity	$1.8M annually	Greater scalability and improved customer experience

Healthcare provider	20% faster response times; 15% higher staff productivity	$0.5M annually	Improved patient care reliability
Government IT modernization	55% faster service request processing; near-zero downtime during migration; response time reduced from 10 days to 48 hours	$8M annually	Enhanced citizen satisfaction and operational transparency

Table 3.5: *Comparative summary of cost savings and performance gains from AI-enabled modernization projects*

Table 3.5 comparison table summarizes the quantifiable outcomes from four AI-enabled modernization projects across different sectors. It presents key performance gains, cost savings, and additional impacts in a clear, side-by-side format, making it easy to compare results. The data shows that while all sectors benefit, the *Government IT modernization* project achieved the largest annual savings at *$8M* and the highest performance gain at *55%*. The *E-commerce* case demonstrated strong deployment speed improvements (45%) and a notable $1.8M in annual cost reduction.

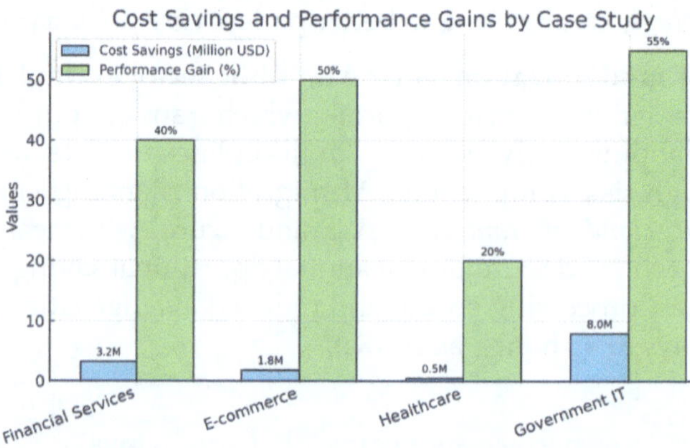

Figure 3.9: *Cost savings (in million USD) and performance gains (%) from AI-enabled modernization projects*

Figure 3.9 bar graph visually reinforces these findings, allowing readers to quickly grasp the relative scale of cost savings and performance improvements for each case. Together, the table and chart provide both numerical precision and visual clarity, making the benefits of AI-driven modernization more compelling and easier to interpret.

Conclusion

AI has emerged as a transformative enabler in application modernization, streamlining processes, improving accuracy, and delivering measurable business value. By automating complex tasks such as code refactoring, migration planning, and real-time monitoring, AI significantly reduces modernization timelines, lowers costs, and enhances system performance. Case studies from multiple industries show that AI's impact extends beyond technical gains, improving customer experience, operational efficiency, and long-term scalability.

Looking ahead, the next wave of innovation will be driven by generative AI and autonomous modernization pipelines. Generative AI models will be capable of automatically rewriting large portions of legacy code into modern architectures, producing optimized, secure, and standards-compliant solutions with minimal human input. Autonomous pipelines, powered by AI-driven orchestration, will manage end-to-end modernization, from dependency analysis to deployment, without requiring manual intervention.

These advancements will make modernization faster, more adaptive, and continuously optimized in real-time, enabling organizations to evolve their digital ecosystems proactively rather than reactively. In this future, modernization will not be a one-time event but a self-improving, AI-managed lifecycle, keeping systems perpetually aligned with emerging technologies and business needs.

Multiple choice questions

1. **What is one of the main advantages of using AI for application modernization?**
   a. Manual code rewriting
   b. Increased downtime
   c. Automated code refactoring
   d. Limited scalability

2. **What does AI use to prioritize which applications to modernize first?**
   a. Developer intuition
   b. Random selection
   c. Usage patterns and data analysis
   d. Cost only

3. **Which AI tool is known for analyzing code and suggesting improvements?**
   a. Watson
   b. AutoML
   c. Dynatrace
   d. TensorFlow

4. **AI reduces which of the following in application modernization?**
   a. Accuracy
   b. Scalability
   c. Human error
   d. Performance

5. **Which AI platform is used for predictive maintenance?**
   a. AWS Lambda
   b. IBM Watson
   c. GitHub
   d. Azure Monitor

6. **Personalization in modern applications is achieved through:**
   a. Code duplication
   b. Generic interfaces
   c. User behavior analysis via AI
   d. Manual design

7. What does AI do during cloud migration?

a. Slows the process
b. Deletes legacy data
c. Recommends migration strategies
d. Prevents migration

8. What benefit does AI provide after modernization is complete?

a. Stops monitoring
b. Continuous real-time performance monitoring
c. Disconnects cloud systems
d. Reverts to legacy state

9. Which AI tool helps detect outdated code?

a. Jenkins
b. GitHub Copilot
c. Slack
d. Tableau

10. Data quality during migration is improved using:

a. Duplicate tables
b. Informatica CLAIRE
c. Cloud functions
d. JSON files

11. What kind of decision-making does AI support in modernization?

a. Instinct-based
b. Trial and error
c. Data-driven
d. User voting

12. A major result of AI-powered modernization is:

a. Increased manual intervention
b. Slower releases
c. Faster development cycles
d. Less user engagement

13. What is a key aspect of intelligent resource allocation?

a. Equal distribution
b. Developer estimates
c. AI-based recommendations
d. Random scheduling

14. AI enables personalization of applications by:

a. Removing user options
b. Cloning legacy systems
c. Learning from user behavior
d. Ignoring preferences

15. **AI for monitoring applications typically**:
    a. Waits for user complaints
    b. Generates error reports monthly
    c. Uses real-time analytics
    d. Disables alert systems

Answers

1	c
2	c
3	b
4	c
5	b
6	c
7	c
8	b
9	b
10	b
11	c
12	c
13	c
14	c
15	c

Join our Discord space

Join our Discord workspace for latest updates, offers, tech happenings around the world, new releases, and sessions with the authors:

https://discord.bpbonline.com

Chapter 4
Generative and Agentic AI Principles and Practices for Accelerated Software Engineering

Introduction

The **artificial intelligence** (**AI**) paradigm is, undoubtedly, growing fast, to gain the stature of principal digital technology capable of artistically tackling various current and future business problems. There is a suite of AI enablers in the form of a dazzling array of breakthrough algorithms, facilitating frameworks, reusable libraries, integrated platforms, application-specific processors, automated toolkits, optimization methods, and so on. AI model engineering, evaluation, optimisation, deployment, observability, and improvement techniques are sagaciously simplified through numerous enablers. AI is decisively impacting several business domains. Several industry verticals are meticulously exploring and experimenting with AI to understand and leverage its strategically sound power. In recent years, AI has inspired the field of software engineering. That is, AI is automating several aspects of the software engineering lifecycle. AI assists software architects and engineers in creating enterprise-grade and environment-friendly software programs. In this chapter, we will focus on how a growing array of advancements in the AI field is propelling and precipitating the software engineering domain.

Software is the most potent and prominent automation technology in human history. Someone wrote that software eats the world. Every personal, professional, and social activity is meticulously and mesmerizingly automated through the distinct power of software products, solutions, and services. All the noteworthy evolutions and revolutions being accomplished and articulated across industry verticals are being precipitated through the exceptional power of software. Without an iota of doubt, software is a pivotal and pertinent entity for humankind. Precisely speaking, software plays an indispensable role in shaping human society. Thus, producing resilient, robust, and versatile software systems is of special significance to businesses and governments worldwide.

Structure

In this chapter, we will go over the following points:

- Technology advancements for next-generation software engineering
- Contribution of AI to software engineering
- Generative AI for software engineering
- Applications and implications of multimodal generative AI
- Agentic AI for software engineering
- Accentuating the architecture of agentic AI systems
- Agentic AI paradigm for software engineering

Objectives

We will start with the widely announced advancements being unearthed in software engineering. Then, we will proceed with how AI will be a game-changer in software engineering. We will also thoroughly explain the hugely popular cloud-native paradigm and how the cloud-native principles will significantly empower the software engineering domain.

Technology advancements for next-generation software engineering

Experts indicate that AI will be closely integrated with software engineering to build intelligent systems. The other popular technologies for producing and sustaining sophisticated software applications include cloud-native computing, **microservices architecture** (**MSA**), containerization, building and management, agile programming, DevOps, low-code/no-code development, **site reliability engineering** (**SRE**), and **value stream management** (**VSM**). Platform engineering is now emerging and evolving with the ready availability of **internal developer platform** (**IDP**) products. Instead of starting from the ground up, the brewing trend is to use the phenomenon of configuring, customizing, and composing software components (microservices) to build, deploy, observe, and improve enterprise-scale, business-critical, process-centric, service-oriented, cloud-hosted, event-driven, knowledge-filled, and context-aware software systems. The faster maturity and stability of the above-mentioned technological paradigms contribute to agile and efficient software development. Software solutions are functionally marvellous and fulfil non-functional requirements such as scalability, availability, reliability, manageability, accessibility, security, and simplicity.

Other technological domains, such as blockchain technology, the **Internet of Things** (**IoT**), edge computing, metaverse (virtual, augmented, mixed, extended realities), and so on, are capturing the attention of many these days. Advanced, artistic, and agile software engineering technologies and tools are mandated to build state-of-the-art software systems to run a variety of IoT devices, wearables, smartphones, wireless and embedded systems, industry machinery, healthcare instruments, head-mounted gears, kitchen utensils, information appliances, defence equipment, wares and utilities, consumer electronics, robots and drones, and so on.

Let us now go over some of these technologies:

- **AI for software engineering**: With the ready availability of generative AI models and agents, software development, testing, optimization, and process excellence are getting accelerated and automated. Many complex software production tasks are insightfully automated and augmented through the smart leverage of noteworthy improvements in the AI field.
- **Cloud-native principles**: This is about building, deploying, running, and managing software applications that leverage cloud infrastructures' unique capabilities. Application scalability is achieved through infrastructure elasticity. The other important requirements, such as continuous availability, manageability, faster and frequent deployment, and reliability, are also readily and rewardingly accomplished through a host of improvisations being unearthed and articulated in the cloud computing space. These principles can bring much-needed improvements in the struggling field of software engineering.
- **Low-code/no-code platforms**: Software developers and engineers increasingly use advanced application development platforms, toolkits, libraries, and accelerators. Even non-expert programmers can use these platforms to create software solutions quickly. These platforms automate many redundant and repetitive activities of software developers, enabling them to arrive at competent software solutions quickly.
- **MSA**: It is the most important principle and practice of cloud-native computing. Software applications are designed, developed, and composed of microservices. MSA applications are innately modular; application design, development, deployment, monitoring, observability, and improvement are simplified and sped up. Microservices can be independently built and deployed, horizontally scalable, publicly discoverable, network-accessible, interoperable, composable, process-aware, API-driven, easily upgradable, and so on.
- **Event-driven architecture** (**EDA**): In the increasingly connected and dynamic world, business-critical applications need to be powered to receive business events, understand what is articulated in the event message unambiguously, and plunge into the correct set of tasks with all the clarity and alacrity. Futuristic microservices, the most optimal building block, must be synchronous and asynchronous in their actions and reactions. Besides conventional microservices, event-driven microservices will flourish in the days to unfold.
- **Compartmentalization (virtualization and containerization)**: Undoubtedly, the concept of virtualization has laid a stimulating and sparkling foundation for the vast success and adoption of cloud computing. Many advanced algorithms and tools have immensely contributed to the mesmerising success of the cloud idea. Containerisation

is quite a recent concept compared with virtualisation. There are containerisation-enabled platforms readily available today. Similarly, container orchestration and lifecycle management platform solutions such as Docker Swarm and Kubernetes are also available. Private and public container image registries and repositories are being made available. The Kubernetes ecosystem is growing rapidly to automate several things connected with container deployment, management, and maintenance. Kubernetes is the leading cluster management platform solution, and today, it plays a vital role in shaping the containerisation movement. Containerization with the support of Kubernetes is destined to streamline and speed up the software delivery process. The portability feature offered by containerization and the horizontal scalability powered by cloud infrastructure modules, in conjunction with Kubernetes' orchestration and automation capabilities, sends a good signal for the software world. Setting up and sustaining hybrid, multi-cloud, and federated cloud environments is enabled through the Kubernetes platform.

- **DevOps**: It eliminates friction between developers and operators to accelerate software deployment in production environments. By preparing data and control pipelines, any application traverses smoothly from the development environment to the deployment environment without any hitch or hurdle. For agile software engineering, DevOps practices and products come in handy. For enhanced security, the new concept of DevSecOps is being recommended. That is, security practices are incorporated throughout the development cycle. Accelerated software delivery is being facilitated through this phenomenon. Continuous integration, delivery, deployment, observability, and improvement are being simplified through DevOps tools.
- **Quantum computing**: It is projected to be the next-generation supercomputing. Fault-tolerant quantum computers can solve many challenging problems that classical computers could not solve within a reasonable time. Some software engineering challenges can be accomplished through the smart leverage of advancements unveiled in the quantum computing space.
- **Edge computing**: This is another futuristic and fabulous computing paradigm. The data processing happens at the edge of devices and environments. There is a gradual rise in migrating applications hosted and run in faraway cloud servers to resource-intensive IoT edge devices. Edge-native applications are being designed, developed, and deployed in edge devices and their clusters to provide real-time data capture and crunching to discover actionable insights in time. Fresh and people-centric real-time and real-world services and applications can be visualised and realised through edge computing. Software engineering techniques ought to go through some optimisations to empower the bustling idea of edge computing or on-device data processing with edge intelligence. Precisely speaking, edge computing insists on real-time software engineering.

Other impactful and influential technologies are yearning for the attention of industry professionals and academic professors. The software engineering domain must be elevated accordingly to produce sophisticated software that activates newer and renowned technology products. For example, the concept of the metaverse is coming up. Software engineering must be advanced to create metaverse applications that run on devices like head-mounted gear and gadgets. Moreover, metaverse applications must be deployed and run on cloud servers. Thus, fresh devices, networks, and server-centric applications are being built and deployed with the emergence of new-generation technologies.

New technologies push software engineering to the next level. Pioneering software engineering methodologies can fast-track the development of competent software solutions that can natively leverage the unique power of new technologies. Software engineering has become the most vital technological domain for all industry verticals. Software profoundly contributes to business automation.

However, it is essential to give the utmost consideration to the quality of the software produced. The implications may be worse if there are any lacunae in software quality. Despite its utility and ubiquity, its quality must be significantly enhanced to keep up with the consistently growing demand. Software products and services should be quickly, affordably developed, and delivered while maintaining quality. Any future technological changes can be easily incorporated into any existing software systems.

Software is critical in modern business, whether integrated into enterprise apps or innovative products. Despite its ubiquity, the ultimate challenge for software engineering organizations has always been to release quality software fast enough to keep up with constantly accelerating demand. Over the years, new methods and technologies have progressively enhanced productivity and quality standards. Agile and continuous product-centric approaches, automation, open-source ecosystems, cloud-native and composable software architectures, DevOps, and low-code/no-code development have all been introduced. Moreover, each has built on the advances of past iterations. However, the demand for quicker time-to-value and better cost efficiency is only accelerating. Software organizations struggle to deliver at the expected pace and with the anticipated quality while controlling technical debt and costs. The industry focus has been on identifying the next significant step in change.

Contribution of AI to software engineering

AI is significantly and positively impacting every industry today. The software engineering industry is no exception. AI is accomplishing many redundant and repetitive tasks in software engineering in an automated manner. Even complex problems are being attempted and addressed through the steadily growing power of AI. Precisely speaking, software engineering is firmly in the saddle with the grandiose contributions of AI. With several advancements in ML, deep learning, and **reinforcement learning** (**RL**), software engineers can improve code quality and create novel applications. The developer productivity is bound to go up significantly. Software engineers, architects, and consultants can surmount challenges with all the AI-inspired confidence and clarity. AI tools, libraries, accelerators, frameworks, and platforms contribute to making adaptive, versatile, resilient, and robust software. Let us now discuss how AI comes in handy for elevating software engineering to tackle its future challenges:

- **Code generation and completion**: Today, many AI-powered tools, like GitHub Copilot, extensively assist software programmers in their everyday assignments. Generating code snippets and completing lines of code are the prominent contributions of AI tools. For example, Google Gemini helps software developers supply correct code when they face errors.
- **Debugging and error detection**: AI tools can analyse codebases and provide workable and valuable suggestions to find and resolve errors. Human errors can be swiftly debugged, and loopholes can be corrected to enhance code quality. Problem identification and resolution can be neatly accelerated.
- **Predictive analytics in software engineering**: AI analyzes a lot of software project management data and can predict project completion timelines, identify potential risks, and help allocate resources. This enables software engineers to use predictive analytics to forecast project timelines, identify potential risks, and allocate resources efficiently.
- **Automated software testing**: AI helps generate and execute multifaceted test cases. This ability ultimately enhances software quality, requiring less human intervention and instruction.
- **Natural language processing (NLP) for software documentation**: AI tools generate, update, and organise software project documents. Team productivity goes up sharply with such standardised documents. With the broader adoption of **large language models (LLM)**, text content generation, summarisation, and translation got a solid boost recently.
- **Intelligent DevOps automation**: DevOps enables continuous integration, delivery, deployment, monitoring, and performance improvement. By integrating AI into DevOps, many everyday things, including software deployment, can be automated. Software performance can be minutely monitored, and potential failures and successful workarounds can be predicted by analyzing the captured system KPIS. In short, software reliability is boosted by synchronising AI with DevOps.
- **Improved security with AI**: Software security is essential; hence, it is vital to make proactive and pre-emptive predictions of any security attacks or loopholes before something serious happens. AI-powered security-enabled tools carefully analyse patterns and pinpoint vulnerabilities and threats in time. In a nutshell, it is all about fulfilling the goal of establishing secure software systems. Data security is realized while in transit, at rest, and usage when AI is fused with software solutions.
- **AI-driven design prototyping**: AI aids in quickly creating prototypes and designs for user interfaces. Interface designers and project sponsors can have an early dialogue to nullify any changes at a later point. The gaps between design and development get closed nicely. At the end of the story, the distance between the required and the

supplied becomes nil.

- **Legacy application modernization**: Banks and other early adopters of legacy software products and solutions are embarking on modernization initiatives and implementations. AI tools do a good job refactoring legacy code, so incorporating the MSA principles becomes more straightforward and quicker. Thus, legacy applications are modernised and migrated to cloud environments to reap all the initially expressed benefits of cloud computing.
- **AI-enhanced collaboration tools**: In recent years, many collaboration tools have emerged and evolved to lessen the workloads of software engineers. These sophisticated tools facilitate collaboration between software development teams (local as well as remote). By blending AI with collaboration tools, software teams' productivity has increased considerably. Fruitful discussions on the task, identifying risks and action items, resolving issues, and mediating conflicting ideas are smoothly and synergistically facilitated through AI-enabled collaboration tools.

In summary, AI has gained the strength to bring about delectable transformations in software engineering. Complicated tasks such as designing, developing, deploying, and delivering software solutions and services are overwhelmingly simplified by incorporating AI models into the software production process. With AI, novel software solutions can be envisaged and implemented. All the complications associated with next-generation software engineering are sagaciously solved by AI methods. AI opens newer opportunities and possibilities in the software engineering field. State-of-the-art software productions will see reality frequently with the fusion of AI. There are innumerable improvisations in the AI space, and these innovations will result in pleasing disruptions in software construction. Cutting-edge AI technologies and tools will take software engineering to the next level to make the world more sophisticated.

Generative AI for software engineering

As indicated previously, AI is a fast track. Initially, AI was expressed and expounded as the most potent predictive and transformative technology. All kinds of prediction needs are elegantly accomplished through AI. With sufficient data and the path-breaking AI-enabled technologies, AI could beautifully deliver on the prediction front. AI has successfully impacted most business domains; every institution, innovator, and individual benefits from AI. In short, AI is termed a transformative phenomenon.

Technical perspective on generative AI techniques

Let us start with **generative adversarial networks** (GANs). Any GAN implementation comprises the two following neural networks:

- **The generator neural network** first learns the patterns in the input data. Such learning enables the generator network to produce realistic data, and the discriminator neural network finds it challenging to distinguish the generated data from accurate data.

- **The discriminator neural network** acts as a timely critic. It evaluates whether the data it receives from the generator neural network is real or fake.

GANs have acquired unprecedented popularity in data augmentation and generation. Data availability is a serious issue in specific verticals such as healthcare, telecommunication, financial services, and so on. With additional yet similar data points, the use case of anomaly detection is seeing the reality. Enough data is required to produce competent AI models for prediction, recommendation, and decision-making in those domains. In such scenarios, synthetic data is generated generously through the meticulous application of the GAN power. With a small amount of input data initially, generating the required data is possible.

Here are the key applications of GANs:

- GANs learn patterns from training and generate images, avatars, and high-quality visuals. Therefore, the scope for GANs has grown, and today, GANs have a solid footprint and foundation in domains such as gaming, art, and design. GANs can transform images without degrading the image quality. For example, sketches can be converted into realistic images. GANs can also create eye-catching images and videos from text descriptions. Low-resolution images can be sharply improved, highly beneficial for medical imaging, satellite imagery, and creative video production domains. The complicated aspects of music, image, and video syntheses are being streamlined and sped up with the enormous generative power of GANs.
- GANs are used to guess and accurately complete some missing information in a dataset (data augmentation). Further, a GAN can be built to generate images of the surface below ground (sub-surface) by understanding the correlation between surface data and underground structures. GAN can generate 3D models from 2D photos or scanned images.
- GANs help developers and testing professionals sharply increase software quality in software engineering. GANs can generate data, a set of relevant test cases, and different input scenarios. GANs can exhibit the power to simulate a wide range of realistic scenarios to analyze system performance under varying conditions critically. Such a setup ultimately pinpoints software bugs. By deeply analysing the generated synthetic data, it is possible to understand the potential areas of software failure.
- As mentioned, GANs can augment datasets by automatically generating synthetic data. **Machine learning** (**ML**) and **deep learning** (**DL**) models can articulate accurate decisions with more correct data. Thus, GANs come in handy in next-generation software engineering. In the same line, GANs can generate images representing multiple visual states of a user interface. This helps identify any visual regressions during updates. GANs can create new data samples that look like an accurate data distribution. GANs can produce different user inputs when checking a web or mobile application.

A **variational autoencoder** (**VAE**) is another powerful generative AI technology capable of producing positive and paradigm shifts in software engineering. VAEs can bring in variations in the existing code to explore various options. VAEs can pinpoint any potential anomalies by learning the underlying patterns. VAEs can generate synthetic code that deviates from the standard code distribution. This is a code anomaly detection. Experts have pointed out the following advantages:

- **Code generation**: VAE networks can be methodically trained on large codebases to empower them to understand the nuances of code structures and untangle functional patterns hidden in the code. This eventually helps VAEs generate new code snippets with similar structure and functionality. **Proof-of-concept** (**PoC**) development gets speeded up, and automated code generation immensely benefits software programming in many ways.
- **Code variation generation**: By creating and manipulating the latent representation of a codebase, a VAE can generate slightly different versions of the existing code. This capability works well in visualising and realising different software testing approaches. It can even explore and exploit different software designs.
- **Code anomaly detection**: By comparing the reconstruction error of a VAE on a given code snippet to a threshold value, developers can identify code sections that deviate significantly from the learned pattern. This helps detect anomalies in code.
- **Code refactoring**: By profoundly analyzing the latent representation, a VAE can identify areas of code that can be refactored or simplified for code rationalisation and optimisation. An encoder neural network takes a code snippet as input and compresses it into a latent representation that is typically lower-dimensional. This representation intricately captures and preserves the essential features of the code. The latent space represents the underlying patterns and any variations in the code. Conversely, the decoder neural network takes a sample from the latent space and tries to reconstruct the original code snippet.

Thus, GANs and VAEs bring forth additional capabilities for next-generation software engineering. For the generative AI domain, besides GANs and VAEs, there are other popular and influential generative technologies such as diffusion models, transformers with multi-head attention, and **state space models (SSM)** such as Mamba.

Generative AI is being touted as the most impactful paradigm for software engineering and its exciting journey. Generative AI has created much buzz amongst multiple industry verticals. Generative AI has the innate strength to fulfil the goal of meeting business and IT challenges head-on. As discussed previously, generative AI significantly influences software engineering, which, in turn, enables more profound and decisive business automation. Generative AI adds new features and functionalities to software solutions. Market analysts, researchers, and watchers say software quality and productivity will increase remarkably. Applying generative AI to software engineering aids in automating and accelerating many **software development lifecycle** (**SDLC**) steps, such as software requirements engineering, software design and architecting, documentation, software coding, testing, deployment, observability, and improvement.

Generative AI for next-generation software engineering

As inscribed, AI is undergoing several strategically sound shifts. AI is gradually transitioning towards generative AI. Then came the concept of multimodal generative AI. We will discuss other disruptions in the latter part of this chapter. In this section, we will concentrate on systematically leveraging the steadily growing power of generative AI to elevate the software engineering field to the next level. Predominantly, generative AI is for code generation. Creating code gets more streamlined. The code generation velocity is also on the higher side. Many time-consuming and troublesome SDLC-related activities get accelerated through generative AI's unique power. The ideals of agile software engineering are easily fulfilled through the thorough leverage of the developments being unearthed in the generative AI landscape. A growing array of ML, deep learning, and RL innovations is painstakingly used to advance critical activities in software engineering. The software industry relies upon the outstanding advancements that simplify all required to achieve a smooth traversal from software ideation to implementation.

Several tasks are termed redundant, repetitive, and routine. Generative AI enables software industry professionals and practitioners to handle these tasks efficiently and swiftly.

Let us discuss requirement elicitation and optimization. Requirements engineering is a top activity in any software development project. This phase is pivotal in unambiguously understanding the functional and non-functional requirements of the software system to be designed, developed, and deployed.

This has been a conventional approach for collecting and finalizing system requirements. Unfortunately, this is a sequential and one-shot process. However, the world is increasingly dynamic, with fresh requirements suddenly arriving. Also, robust technologies and tools are being unearthed and recommended to use to attain more tremendous success in our pursuits. To neatly incorporate these new arrivals in the technology space and a slew of unexpected changes (capacity and capability), pioneers and proponents strongly pitch for rigorously following incremental and iterative approaches. Agility is embedded in coping with the changes around.

Generative AI has the power to generate, verify, and fine-tune system requirements. LLMs, the popular generative AI tools, are extremely good at text summarization, translation, and generation. If there are any overlaps, gaps, and inconsistencies in the system requirements identified, generative AI models can correct and refine requirements accordingly. GenAI also assists in getting timely feedback, well-intended suggestions, and other knowledge to improve the quality of requirements. With details of high-quality requirements, the final software solution will be in good shape to fulfil the project sponsors' objectives. In addition, GenAI aids in facilitating the establishment of communication and collaboration amongst the participating teams to simplify and speed up the process of arriving at competent requirements documents.

Generative AI leverages software engineering principles, best practices, and techniques to create well-intended software that fully complies with the sponsors' requirements. Generative

AI can create sketches to enhance design efficiency. GenAI also analyzes various design patterns and best practices to develop strategically sound recommendations that greatly help developers in their assignments.

As previously mentioned, generative AI is essential in producing software source code. Thereby, the fundamental notion of agility is fulfilled. Humans must get their hands on refining the code generated. Software production has generative AI models, tools, libraries, and accelerators. ChatGPT is built upon the **generative pre-trained transformer** (**GPT**) model. ChatGPT natively leverages GPT's unique capabilities, a popular and promising neural network architecture, to generate human-like text responses. There are GPU-enabled cloud environments to train large-scale language models. GPT models automatically generate software code with user-defined prompts. In the future, resource-intensive IoT edge devices can be clustered to form edge devices to conduct local training and produce competent language models. Further, code generation can be activated on edge devices with all-around improvements in the edge space. Thus, cloud and edge AI phenomena are tuned towards the generative AI era.

Furthermore, generative AI also assists in software testing. Thus, software accuracy and dependability are being ensured. Test case generation and validation of software systems using test data, result in a high-quality software product. Moreover, generative AI can articulate different ways of software verification. That is, multi-dimensional checking can lead to the realization of multi-faceted software. GenAI-inspired automated debugging helps to accomplish software that fully adheres to the expressed initial requirements. In short, every aspect of the software engineering process is accelerated and even automated through the extraordinary power of generative AI solutions. GenAI impacts the entire software development lifecycle (software design, development, testing, deployment, operations, management, observability, and insights generation towards improvement). With a sustained focus on generative AI, we will see more advancements in how generative AI brings premium capabilities to the increasingly penetrative, pervasive, and persuasive domain of software engineering. Dedicated and determined work is initiated and implemented in the multimodal generative AI field. Other focus domains include graph AI, event-driven generative AI, agentic AI, and so on. So, it is not an exaggeration to state that the field of software engineering is at the cusp of a more significant paradigm shift.

Besides LLM-powered code creation, AI has become an increasingly essential tool in automated software testing. There are AIOps platforms and toolkits for collecting and crunching all kinds of operational data of **information and communication technologies** (**ICT**) systems and business workloads to emit essential insights in time. Furthermore, software security is ensured through real-time and AI-backed security data analytics. Similarly, software systems' other non-functional requirements/quality attributes (scalability, reliability, availability, and so on) are elegantly fulfilled by leveraging competent AI models. Thus, the hugely complicated software engineering is being augmented, accelerated, and automated through the intelligent leverage of noteworthy improvisations being unearthed and rolled out in the AI landscape. In this book, we will illustrate how AI comes in handy in drastically transforming every step of software engineering and how it changes how software is being developed, examined, debugged, delivered, deployed, run, observed, managed, and improved. With the widespread adoption and adaptation of cloud-native principles, software construction is bound to change drastically. That is, software products, solutions, and services are to be composed of purpose-specific and agnostic microservices. As cloud-native architecture patterns are fast maturing and stabilizing, the software industry is gleefully heading toward the cloud-native software engineering paradigm. There are two distinctive stages in which AI is to make several noteworthy breakthroughs:

- **Creative stage**: Here, software development experts interact with AI systems, submitting their knowledge of business domains and practices to AI systems. Project requirements, architecture, design, and acceptance criteria can be met through several iterations. That is, use case and test case documents will be produced to be formally accepted by project sponsors.
- **Delivery stage**: During this stage, competent AI tools are used to generate, test, and deploy the code. Software engineers are used to polish the generated code. There are AI-driven software testing tools. This stage will result in **Minimum Viable Products (MVP)**, deployment scripts, and technical and user guide documents. Further on, AI can assist in identifying bugs and suggesting solutions. Ultimately, with AI support and suggestions, producing high-quality software products, solutions, and services is relatively easy and swift.

In short, language models have revolutionized the way software is engineered, verified, and allowed to be used.

Multimodal generative AI for software engineering

We discussed unimodal generative AI previously. Now, the trend is to leverage the astonishing power of multimodal generative AI in which text, images, and audio fuse to produce advanced intelligence systems that can handle and produce multimodal data combined and comprehensively. Initially, AI systems could handle textual, visual, and audio data separately. Now, some technologies and tools fuse all the different data formats to give users enriching experiences. The real-world is stuffed with various IoT sensors, actuators and devices. The data emitted is multi-structured from IoT environments. Thus, it is mandatory to have next-generation intelligent systems capable of receiving, processing and making sense of multimodal data. Hence, the idea of multimodal generative AI is capturing the imagination of many these days. Further on, in the highly digitised world, digital data and content come with multiple data modalities. Thus, whether it is a real-world environment or a digital environment, the necessity for multimodal generative AI systems is always there without any iota of doubt. Fusing multimodal data and analysing the fused to emit synchronised output is the need of the hour. Here are the prominent roles of multimodal generative AI systems:

- **Text-to-image generation**: **Deep neural networks** (**DNN**), such as **convolutional neural networks** (**CNN**) and **recurrent neural networks** (**RNN**), exist. These neural network architectures can translate textual descriptions into visual representations. Firstly, text gets encoded into a semantic space, and a decoder creates a corresponding image from there. This closes the gap between text and vision.

- **Image-to-text generation**: By combining feature extraction and NLP capabilities, multimodal generative AI can generate image textual descriptions, image captioning, and content generation.
- **Audio-to-image generation**: Textual data becomes visual content and vice versa. Multimodal generative AI can also generate images from audio inputs. This is done through the fusion of audio processing and image synthesis techniques. Using GANs, multimodal generative AI transitions soundscapes into visual representations.

Applications and implications of multimodal generative AI

Many applications are carefully conceived and concretized through various innovations realized in the multimodal generative AI space. Besides paramount assistive technology, content creation and media synthesis are well-known contributions. The business and use cases for this technology are limitless.

As indicated above, multimodal generative AI can simultaneously generate text, images, videos, and audio. Therefore, multimedia content creation is being streamlined and speed up with the help of multimodal GenAI. With systems capable of analyzing text and image data, there is an opportunity for better understanding, and the subsequent responses will be more relevant for chatbot users. Visual assistants will be more cognitive and competent. Learners' experiences will be more personalized and tailored to their preferences. The healthcare sector will see a massive boost with service providers, consumers, and specialists empowered by multimodal generative AI. A few blogs, articles, white papers, and research papers illustrate the power of multimodal generative AI in accelerating the software engineering steps.

Multimodal generative AI generates visual elements like wireframes, **user interface** (**UI**) components, or flowcharts directly from software feature details. Then, it translates visual mock-ups or diagrams into corresponding code snippets. This automated translation contributes to accelerated software coding. Code errors will be minimal. Multimodal generative AI can suggest relevant code segments and snippets using code context and visual elements. The software design will be drastically simplified. Based on the code structure, the software documentation preparation activity gets automated. Distributed software teams can coherently collaborate and coordinate to finish the software building assignment neatly and quickly without any risks. Software prototypes and MVPs can be quickly realized. There are several challenging aspects in producing sophisticated and scalable software products. AI technologies and tools have shown acumen in addressing the limitations so that AI and its advanced incarnations ultimately will be a game-changing phenomenon for the critical field of agile software engineering. AI has become the core and central aspect of software engineering these days. Besides the much-insisted optimization, automation of every activity and orchestration of all the automated things are eloquently achieved through AI. Primarily, generative AI adorns itself with reverberating capabilities to shine in the software field.

Agentic AI for software engineering

AI agents are getting much attention as they have the power to work together to solve complex tasks. They assist with multi-step reasoning. Agents are inherently powered to do planning, decision-making, and automation. Experts say that 2024 was the prime year for generative AI, and this year (2025) and subsequent years, the idea of agentic AI will become pervasive across vertical industries. Complicated tasks are being automated through a dynamic collection of AI agents. Large, small, and vision language models are increasingly widely adopted and adapted to domain-specific and agnostic tasks. AI agents decisively empowered by such language models are being designated as the way forward to fulfill the ideals of agentic AI. In this section, we will focus on how the end-to-end lifecycle management of software engineering is being taken care of by the distinct advancements achieved in the agentic AI space.

Core characteristics of agentic AI

Agentic AI can optimize complex workflows and adapt to technology and business changes. This much-trumpeted feature of adaptability goes a long way in boosting business productivity. The much-insisted business transformation is to see the reality with the fast-evolving agentic AI paradigm. Its features are:

- **Autonomy:** AI agents have the capability to initiate and implement tasks with minimal intervention from human users. Once the goals and objectives are set, AI agents take care of everything with all the precision and perfection.
- **Reasoning**: AI agents exhibit greater reasoning power by leveraging advanced and accurate LLMs, multimodal LLMs, **retrieval-augmented generation** (**RAG**) frameworks, vector databases, knowledge graphs, and other automated tools. Decisions can be made based on contextual information and other trade-offs.
- **Reinforced learning**: Using the proven trial and error method, AI agents dynamically and insightfully interact with their environments, learning and evolving by receiving feedback.
- **Workflow optimization**: Efficient execution of multi-step processes.

As the world insists on intelligent automation mechanisms, agentic AI is being adopted vehemently and vigorously. In other words, business transformation approaches and architectures will be more tuned to be agentic-centric, and AI agents return the foundational elements of agentic AI architecture. Multifaceted agents team up together to accomplish bigger and better assignments. Internally and externally, AI agents gain all the necessary competencies to be at the centre of attention and attraction. AI agents and human interactions become more natural and nuanced through additional tools.

Elucidating different agent categories

AI agents will be good at aggregating and delivering information from diverse sources. There are many types of AI agents emerging and evolving fast. Typically, the well-known agents include routers, orchestration, and workflows. End-to-end workflows are fully executed by different agents working together purposefully by identifying the right APIs, functions, tools, and so on. That is, flawless user request fulfilment is facilitated through well-written agents. The ancient concept of agent-oriented programming will be revisited and revitalised with the fast-stabilising and maturing concept of agentic AI. An expert has come up with an explanation for the following AI agents that promise to be game-changing for the agentic AI paradigm:

- **Generative information retrieval agents**: These agents retrieve and disseminate the proper knowledge to users. These work well in less-regulated environments
- **Prescriptive knowledge agent**: AI started its career as predictive technology. AI can prescribe knowledge to users on different topics with its newly acquired generative power.
- **Dynamic workflow agents**: Agents can dynamically change workflows to reflect the changes in the underlying environment
- **User assistant agents**: These agents are designed, developed, and deployed to assist users in their everyday assignments and engagements.

The standout feature of agentic AI is the intelligent orchestration of diverse AI agents to perform complex tasks and multi-step reasoning requirements. Simple and small tasks can be automated, and many can be orchestrated to achieve complicated jobs. Multiple teams within an organisation can collaborate and share their unique capabilities to address significant challenges and concerns. Each team can operate independently, yet each team is aligned to accomplish any business strategy neatly.

The second aspect is that agents can integrate with external agents on a need-basis to fulfil varying needs. The essential agent characteristics of interoperability, portability, flexibility, and manageability help agents be adaptive, resilient, robust, and versatile in their operations, offerings, and outputs. Agents can instigate a suite of innovations and disruptions to envision intelligent enterprises.

Accentuating the architecture of agentic AI systems

The surging popularity of agentic AI originates from its decision-making capability. AI agents consider different facets, weigh possible outcomes, and respond to unforeseen problems. AI agents use language models, RAG, and other tools to gather problem-solving abilities. AI-powered agents are dynamic and suited to dynamic environments. Hence, agentic AI systems can be viable and valuable for the ensuing knowledge era. As per the prevailing situation, strategy adjustment is another noteworthy capability of AI agents. ML, deep learning, and RL algorithms and models substantially empower agents to be adroit in their actions and reactions. Learning from a large amount of cleaned data by identifying hidden patterns and articulating the correct outcomes are the top strengths of agents. The whole process is explained in an easy-to-understand manner, as follows:

1. **User provides instruction**: The user offers a prompt in natural language. The agentic AI system neatly understands and interprets the user's intent. If further clarification is needed, the system checks with the user before embarking on the next set of actions.
2. **Agentic AI system plans, allocates, and executes work**: The agentic AI system now converts the prompt into tasks and subtasks. There can be agents and subagents for completing the identified tasks and subtasks. These agents, equipped with domain knowledge, will leverage different functions and tools to coordinate and complete the assignments on time. Agents abstract the use of RAG for knowledge retrieval from internal and external sources. Vector databases and knowledge graphs are the prominent information sources. AI agents entirely abstract several connectivity and collaboration tasks.

Language models contribute as the reasoning engine. To refine output, the agent may check with the user to guarantee enhanced accuracy in their understanding and contribution. Increasingly, RL enables AI agents to be spot-on in their actions and articulation. Agent performance evaluation, optimisation, deployment, observability, and improvement are essential in setting up and sustaining breakthrough agentic AI. An AI agent typically consists of the following three main components:

- **Prompt**: The user query or goal that an agent must understand and accomplish within the specified constraints. A prompt is generalized as a blueprint for the agentic AI system to showcase its unique power. A prompt acts as a compass guiding all the participating agents to finish the assigned work with all sagacity and sincerity. As told above, a prompt gets subdivided into a collection of tasks that can be done by many agents individually or collectively.
- **Memory**: This serves as a dynamic repository for keeping up-to-date knowledge and experiences. AI agents use it to gain a more profound and decisive understanding of the context. With clear-cut context information, agents make insightful decisions. The prompt plus context derived is the input to LLMs to produce the correct responses.
- **Tools**: Several tools are critically enabling agents to do multiple things that were found difficult by conventional AI systems. The prominent tools include functions, APIs, web searching, calculators, calendars, and so on. Additional services are being systematically added to agents to do bigger things.

In short, it all starts with a user's input in their natural language. The user understands what needs to be done, interprets and reasons for the decisions made, generates and executes workflows, and produces the output. RL involves learning and course correction; hence, workflow steps can be optimized.

A **single-agent system** comprises an AI agent, which can be powered up through several tools. Specific problems are being tackled through single-agent systems that can operate autonomously. Agents decide and execute a step-by-step plan by leveraging the reasoning power of LLMs and utilizing the tools' unique capabilities. The agent creates a winning strategy to complete the user's goals (simple or complex) and plans their execution insightfully. The core and central aspect of agentic behaviour is leveraging internal and external tools by considering the overall objectives and constraints. Prompt engineering is also an essential ingredient for the agents' success. Creating a competent prompt enhances the accuracy of the output.

Single-agent systems are comparatively easy to design, build, and manage. They have lower communication and collaboration complexities. The challenge of fulfilling consistency is hugely reduced in single-agent systems. Nevertheless, adaptivity, flexibility, scalability, and extensibility are challenging in single-agent systems. The following figure represents the macro-level architecture of single-agent systems:

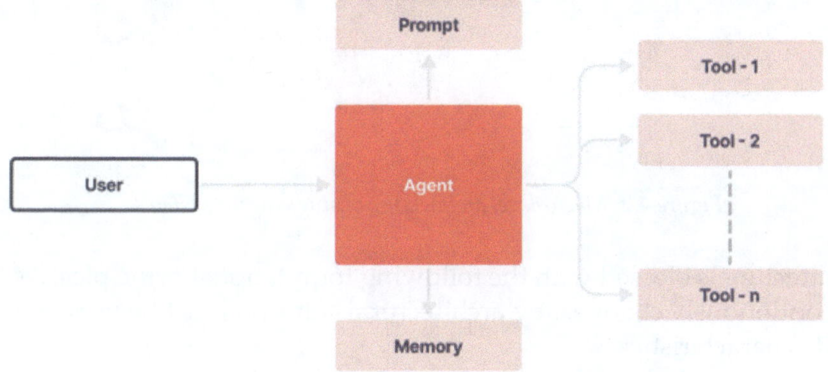

***Figure 4.1**: Macro-level architecture of single-agent systems*

With the more expansive and broader adoption of single-agent systems, the arrival of **multi-agent systems** (**MAS**) is gaining traction. Such advanced systems are enabled through multiple independent agents. A language model for reasoning power supports each agent. In conjunction with many LLMs, tools, and knowledge repositories, multiple agents voluntarily collaborate to address complex problems. Multiple agents' coordinating and collaborating nature comes in handy in fulfilling more significant requirements. Agents may be horizontal or vertical. MAS is decisive and dextrous. Additional agents can be incorporated as needed. MAS can handle newer problem domains elegantly. MAS is inherently fault-tolerant and scalable to solve newer challenges efficiently.

Refer to the following figure:

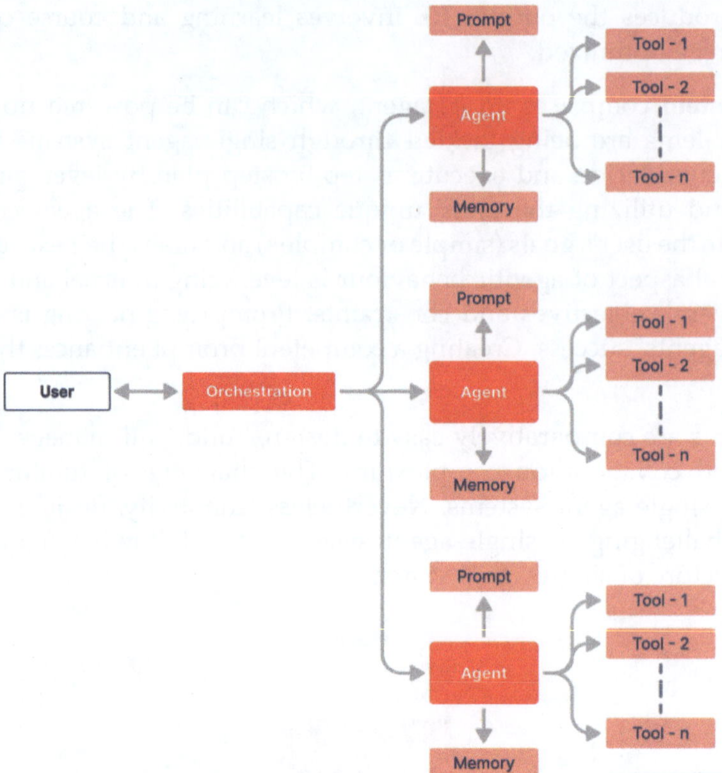

***Figure 4.2:** Macro-level architecture of single-agent systems*

Agentic AI architecture is blessed with the following foundational principles. As business and IT landscapes continuously change, any architectural solution must be versatile and resilient. Let us discuss its characteristics:

- **Modularity**: This typically represents subdividing complex structures into easily manageable modules. A complex function is segmented into its different tasks. Such a separation of concerns goes a long way in significantly reducing development, management, and improvement complexities. Multiple modules can be aggregated to perform specific tasks with clarity. The modularity principle has been proven and promising approach in software engineering. Every software application is being prepared and presented as a modular one. Modularity is formally defined as loosely coupled and highly cohesive. Refactoring is relatively easy with modular applications. In the recent past, MSA has been fully primed for producing and using modular microservices. The modularity enables the seamless and spontaneous composition of process-aware, event-driven, cloud-hosted, enterprise-scale, production-grade, and microservices-centric applications. With AI agents maturing and stabilising fast, pundits recommend agentic AI systems that are modular from the ground up.
- **Scalability**: AI agents must be scalable to match businesses' growing expectations.

As the underlying cloud-native infrastructure modules are elastic, the software applications and services running on them can exhibit scalability. Scalable applications can handle spikes in user loads. Agents can also scale out by solving problems across business domains. On the technical side, scalability guarantees software systems' continuous availability. The requirements, such as business continuity, get fulfilled through adaptive agentic systems.

- **Interoperability**: Agents interact with one another to produce valuable results. Using standardised communication protocols and data formats, agents can talk with one another to share their unique functionalities. Businesses can attain greater efficiency with interoperable agents. Microservices are interoperable by abstracting the implementation from interfaces. APIs facilitate applications and agents' finding, communicating, and collaborating.
- **Path-breaking with RL**: Continuous or lifelong learning is vital for agentic AI systems to be correct and relevant to their users. Through learning, AI agents gain additional knowledge. Agents utilise the distinct power of reinforcement learning to be adroit in their deliveries. RL systems naturally evolve in power by interacting with their environments and carefully learning from feedback. RL-driven agents optimise their decisions and responses over time.

With a dazzling array of enabling technologies and tools, AI pioneers have recently expounded on several real-world use cases. Agentic AI is being proclaimed as the next-generation AI technology. Worldwide organisations and institutions are exploring and exploiting the agentic AI paradigm to provide premium and path-breaking services to their clients and consumers.

AI leaders say business behemoths and start-ups can optimise AI workflows by aligning agents with their specific functional areas. Many of the repetitive and routine tasks can be automated within workflows. AI agents promise intelligent workflow or process automation. There are **Robotic Process Automation** (**RPA**) platforms and systems today. However, the future will belong to agentic AI-powered process automation. The trustworthiness and transparency needs, which are sorely missing in traditional AI, will be restored by agentic AI. Thus, there is a critical movement from AI models to AI agents. Like MSA, agentic architecture is gaining colossal market and mind shares. Agent communication and orchestration are to guarantee automated decision-making and action. Agentic AI systems gain the necessary knowledge in an automated manner to accomplish business processes with minimal human instruction.

Agentic AI paradigm for software engineering

We discussed how agentic AI has gained the credibility to represent the next-generation AI. With the related technologies and tools maturing fast, the world is keenly embarking on the agentic AI era. Let us learn how agentic AI impacts and influences software engineering:

- **Software quality management**: Software quality is indispensable for users when investing in software solutions. Businesses can also confidently run high-quality software systems in production environments. Thus, software research and engineering teams work together to unearth and use breakthrough methods to ensure the highest quality. As seen previously, the arrival of AI is seen as a positive signal for the field of software engineering. The paradigm of agentic AI is especially suited to bring dramatic improvements in building high-quality software products and services. There are several practices and techniques for improving software quality. Software engineering teams meticulously establish coding standards and focus on code reviews. Further on, teams do software testing and debugging to have error-free software source code. Moreover, teams swiftly respond to software incidents and vulnerabilities with alacrity. As software systems become critical for business transformation, leveraging advanced and artistic AI models and agents to bring forth adaptivity in cognitively constructing high-quality software is gaining momentum. By incorporating the features and facilities offered by AI agents, software teams can sharply enhance software engineering efficiency. Learning from already established codebases, deeply and decisively understanding software source code, capable of generating new source code, ensuring strict compliance to coding standards, modelling and detecting incoming threats, scanning hidden vulnerabilities, and so on, are being methodically automated through AI agents.

- **Code acceleration**: With several dramatic improvisations in the generative AI domain, text-to-code models and agents substantially empower software engineers. These agents can generate source code from simple text descriptions in any preferred programming language. Such a facility speeds up the transition from concept to code. By creating boilerplate code structures in an automated fashion, test-to-code AI agents greatly help software developers.
- **Automated code reviews and quality checks**: AI agents perform automated code reviews to pinpoint weaknesses and holes to exploit. Agentic AI can automatically analyse code changes, flag potential deviations and issues, and verify whether code segments or snippets have gone against predefined standards. This technologically enabled automation streamlines and speeds up code reviews. The long-standing goal of high-quality source code gets fulfilled swiftly through the smart leverage of agentic power.
- **Incident response automation**: Intelligent incident management is critical for systematically reducing software-related impacts on business operations. Agentic AI can improve the incident response process by automatically triggering predefined protocols when an incident occurs. AI can also generate comprehensive incident reports that help track all the incident and response details.
- **Continuous integration and testing automation**: Automated software testing keeps software reliable and risk-free. Any software changes are minutely monitored so as not to introduce bugs. Agentic AI can automate software testing and continuous integration, a prominent aspect of DevOps. If any new or updated code is committed, an AI agent preemptively turns into combat action to test the code. Other pertinent actions on the submitted source code can be accelerated and automated. Thereby, software teams can focus on other critical areas.

Thus, the agentic AI paradigm can be a silver bullet for the struggling field of software engineering. Agentic AI emboldens software engineering to match the growth rate of hardware engineering. Having understood the strategic sound contribution of AI agents, software experts are exploring the various ways of beneficially integrating AI agents into the software development process. Trendsetting AI models, language models, tools, RAG libraries, prompt engineering, context information retrieval, vector databases, and knowledge graphs collectively dramatically power up software engineering.

Conclusion

AI is advancing fast and enticing every functional domain to leverage its advancements artistically. The positive and potential improvements being achieved in the AI space energize every industry vertical to systematically explore how AI impacts and influences each of them. AI is steadily moving from predictive to generative. The next version of agentic AI is dawning, and there are many talks and write-ups on the transformative power of AI agents. Software engineering is one of the prime domains that would benefit massively if the extraordinary power of AI were used methodically.

As discussed in this chapter, software engineering is becoming complicated due to the insistence on incorporating advanced features and functionalities into software solutions to meet growing expectations. Due to the multiplicity and heterogeneity of software engineering technologies and tools, the software development, deployment, and management complexities are consistently rising. Moreover, organizations and institutions want software-driven business automation solutions quickly. Thus, there are endeavors to devise ways to accelerate software production. There is a suite of exemplary and agile programming techniques, faster software design mechanisms, plenty of low or no-code platforms, AI-enabled GitHub Copilots, and DevOps, **site reliability engineering** (**SRE**), platform engineering, and **value stream management** (**VSM**) toolkits. With the massive adoption of generative and agentic AI principles and practices, the long-pending goal of the accelerated and accurate software-building mission is to see the grandiose reality. In this chapter, we explained how the smart leverage of ground-breaking AI techniques can be a game-changing phenomenon for the illustrious software engineering field.

Multiple choice questions

1. **Which of the following technologies is emerging to support internal developer platforms (IDPs) in next-generation software engineering?**

   a. Platform engineering
   b. Manual programming
   c. Standalone systems
   d. Paper-based documentation

2. **Which of the following is a major contribution of AI in software development?**

   a. Manual coding only
   b. Code generation and completion

c. Reducing internet speed

d. Eliminating programming languages

3. **How does AI help in debugging and error detection?**

   a. By deleting entire code automatically

   b. By ignoring errors in the code

   c. By analysing code and suggesting fixes

   d. By converting code into hardware

4. **What is the role of AI in predictive analytics in software engineering?**

   a. Writing hardware drivers

   b. Predicting project timelines and risks

   c. Replacing developers completely

   d. Increasing project cost

5. **Which of the following best describes a core characteristic of agentic AI?**

   a. Only performing single-step tasks

   b. Manual intervention for every decision

   c. Ability to plan, reason, and make decisions autonomously

   d. Limited to data storage only.

6. **Why are AI agents considered powerful in software engineering?**

   a. They only execute predefined static instructions

   b. They cannot collaborate with other agents

   c. They can work together to solve complex, multi-step tasks

   d. They replace all human developers completely

Answers

1	a
2	b
3	c
4	b
5	c
6	c

Chapter 5

Study on AI Tools That Can Generate Software Source Code

Introduction

An AI code generator is a computer program incorporating AI models. Thus, computer programs help engineers write code more swiftly and precisely. AI-enabled code generators automatically create code snippets, elements, and complete applications. This chapter will discuss the critical code-generation tools (OpenAI Codex, CodeT5, GitHub Copilot, etc.) and their prominent features. ChatGPT-4 and its multimodal capabilities can generate text representations from image content.

In addition to increasing productivity, AI code generators are changing the way developers approach problem-solving. These tools help the change from manual coding to AI-assisted programming, where engineers focus on design logic and creativity. On the other hand, AI handles repetitive tasks. They also encourage collaborative development by offering real-time debugging support, intelligent recommendations, and automatic documentation. The integration of computer vision, **natural language processing** (**NLP**), and reinforcement learning into code production is predicted to completely transform software engineering in the future, making it more accessible, efficient, and user-friendly than it has ever been before.

Structure

In this chapter, we will cover the following topics:

- Overview of AI in code generation
- AI tools assisting developers
- AI in automating repetitive code tasks
- Accuracy and limitations of AI-generated code
- Future trends in AI-generated code
- Generative AI in coding

- Ethical and security implications of AI-generated code

Objectives

This study focuses on AI tools that have the capability to automatically generate software source code, significantly transforming the way software is developed. With advancements in **machine learning** (**ML**) and NLP, tools such as GitHub Copilot, OpenAI Codex, and others are able to understand user inputs in natural language and convert them into working code snippets or even complete programs.

These tools can assist developers by reducing coding time, minimizing human error, and accelerating the software development lifecycle. The study explores how such tools are being adopted in various sectors, their limitations, and the importance of human oversight to ensure correctness, security, and ethical use, particularly in the Indian software development context, where demand for rapid and scalable solutions is growing.

Overview of AI in code generation

AI-enabled code generation tools are becoming powerful day by day. It is one of the important uses in the field of software development. AI tools and models can generate code with the help of ML and NLP for the purpose of generating complete or partial code for incomplete snippets.

OpenAI codes and GitHub Copilot are examples that help programmers finish code. Code generated through AI is not just increasing productivity, but also making the code almost bug-free.

Additionally, these AI-based code generators are very helpful for both experienced and inexperienced developers. While learners can understand coding logic easily, experts can save time by automating repetitive code. Developers still need to have a strong understanding of basic programming concepts in order to evaluate, verify, and optimize the generated code. In this way, AI is a useful assistant rather than a replacement for human intelligence.

Popular AI code generation tools

The majority of code generation tools help software developers to write code quickly and with accuracy. Various code generation tools are becoming popular. These tools support almost all types of programming languages and can work for all types of development environments.

From speed-up to coding type to deploying the software has become easy through these tools, helping in improving the productivity and efficiency of IT companies. These tools are also very helpful for students to learn programming.

Many AI tools for automated code generation are discussed in *Chapter 2, Empowering Software*

Engineering with Artificial Intelligence, including Devika AI, GitHub Copilot, OpenAI Codex, Polycoder, DeepCode, and Cogram.

These AI technologies are gaining enormous popularity since they simplify coding for beginners and boost productivity for experienced workers. They offer real-time guidance, error reduction, faster prototyping, and an all-around more effective approach. Due to their increasing use in academic institutions, tech startups, and large IT corporations, these technologies are increasingly essential for modern software engineering techniques. As AI develops, these technologies will have an even bigger impact on how Indian developers construct applications, making coding more imaginative, user-friendly, and productive. In this chapter, these tools will be discussed in more detail.

Table 5.1 shows AI tools for code generation:

Tool	Description
GitHub Copilot	GitHub Copilot is a smart coding assistant that continuously learns from millions of code sources and facilitates the writing of faster and cleaner code. Copilot uses context to predict the next line.
AmazonCodeWhisperer	It supports IDEs, VS Code, and JetBrains. Java, Python, and JS are the main languages. It allows programmers to create secure and effective code by scanning the code for security problems and issuing warnings in addition to autocompletion.
Gemini	Gemini is not just for generating code but also for debugging and explaining the code in detail. More than 20 programming languages can be handled by Gemini, including C++, Java, Python, Go, etc.
CodeGeeX	It is an AI-enabled code generating engine that easily interfaces with VS Code and is a very adaptable tool for developers in a variety of fields because it supports several programming languages.
Replit Ghostwriter	It enables developers to write, test, and deploy code straight from their browser without the need to install any software.
PolyCoder	It supports C programming, and it is famous for its lightweight code and is available as open-source. It is a helpful tool for system-level programming activities because it is particularly favoured for producing lightweight and clear code structures.

Table 5.1*: AI tools*

AI that can create code

Code generator through AI makes the development process easier, faster, and more accurate. A number of well-known AI code generation tools have drawn a lot of interest due to their capacity to support and expedite software development. One of the most popular tools that offers real-time code suggestions right in the developer's IDE is GitHub Copilot, which is powered by OpenAI Codex. Additional tools that provide context-aware recommendations, bug fixes, and intelligent code completion include Amazon CodeWhisperer, Tabnine, and Replit Ghostwriter.

Benefits of AI code generation

AI code generation tools can boost developer productivity and efficiency, which may result in quicker and perhaps more accurate coding. They can speed up coding and support faster speed up development. Code generated through AI tools is more accurate in comparison to manual coding and hence reduces bugs. It also helps in efficient development and enhances productivity.

Programmers can complete tasks faster with the help of AI-enabled code generation tools available today. These tools significantly increase developers' productivity and improve efficiency. These technologies speed up the development cycle by automating various things, including code recommendations and automated debugging. Since code generated by AI technology is generally more accurate than code written by hand, it helps in error reduction as well. All things considered, the enhanced productivity, efficiency, and ease of creation of AI technologies help both experienced and inexperienced developers. The following figure illustrates the benefits of AI in code generation:

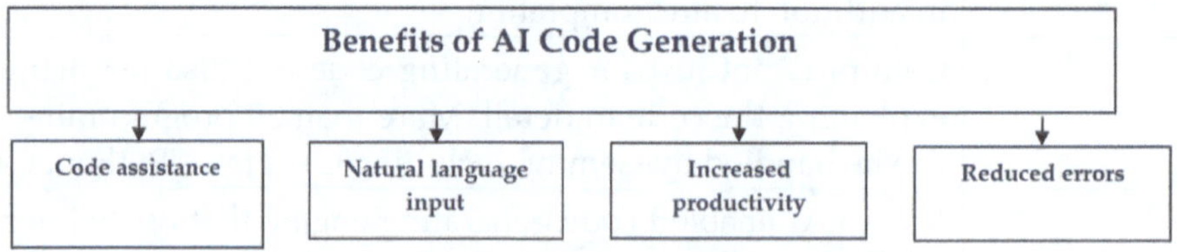

Figure 5.1: Benefits of AI code generation

There following list outlines several benefits of using AI for code generation:

- **Code assistance**: Based on context, AI can construct whole functions, write fragments of code, or recommend completions. AI code creation facilitates the rapid development of features or applications.

  AI-enabled code assistance assists developers by analyzing the project's context and producing full functions, composing code segments, or recommending precise completions. This facilitates the rapid and more accurate development of features or applications. AI-powered recommendations can minimize the likelihood of logical errors during implementation and save time.

  Additionally, this kind of clever support enables beginners to learn coding efficiently and helps experts do challenging projects with ease. It enhances code standards, makes projects more consistent, and makes the development process go more smoothly. This type of assistance is particularly helpful for Indian software teams in hectic settings where timely delivery and quality are equally crucial.

Key points of code assistance include:

- o Helps generate full functions based on project context.
- o Writes partial code snippets to save time.
- o Suggests accurate code completions instantly.
- o Reduces chances of logical errors during development.
- o Supports beginners in learning coding more easily.
- o Improves code quality and team consistency.

- **Natural language input**: Natural language input is frequently supported by AI code generation systems, enabling developers to express their goals in plain English. The development process is then streamlined, and coding becomes more approachable as the AI converts this description in natural language into code, because of this feature, developers can avoid becoming mired down in syntactic nuances and instead concentrate on design and logic.

  AI code generation systems often support natural language input, allowing developers to articulate their objectives in simple English. The AI then translates this natural language description into code, streamlining the development process and making coding more approachable. This feature allows developers to focus on design and logic rather than getting bogged down in syntactic intricacies.

  Additionally, because AI technologies support natural language, both experienced and inexperienced Indian programmers find them to be very helpful. Instead of needing to commit complex syntax or library functions to memory, developers only need to describe what they want to build, and the AI will provide relevant code quickly. It is because it saves time and boosts confidence that teams can focus more on creativity and problem-solving than on tedious coding tasks.

  Key points of natural language input include:

  - o Developers can explain tasks in simple English.
  - o AI converts natural language descriptions into working code.
  - o Reduces dependency on remembering complex syntax.
  - o Helps focus on design and logic instead of coding details.
  - o Useful for both beginner and experienced Indian developers.
  - o Saves time and improves confidence during development.

- **Increased productivity**: AI can speed up development by generating code rapidly and automating repetitive coding activities, and suggesting completions, thereby increasing productivity. AI-generated code can also help quickly build prototypes or proofs of concept.

By producing code rapidly, automating tedious operations, and making intelligent completion suggestions, AI significantly increases developer productivity. This helps teams stay consistent throughout their projects while also saving time. AI-generated code is frequently detailed enough to quickly create prototypes or proofs-of-concept, freeing up engineers to concentrate more on honing concepts rather than creating everything from scratch. In general, it contributes to a development workflow that is quicker, more effective, and simpler.

Key points of increased productivity include:

- Rapid code generation speeds up development.
- Automates repetitive coding tasks effectively.
- Provides smart completion suggestions to reduce effort.
- Helps in the quick creation of prototypes and POC models.
- Allows developers to focus more on creativity and logic.
- Overall workflow becomes faster and more efficient.

- **Reduced errors**: Through syntax checking, AI-driven systems identify and suggest fixes for syntactic problems, improving coding accuracy. AI-driven code completions reduce typos and errors by suggesting appropriate syntax and structures. Additionally, by considering the coding environment, AI reduces the likelihood of errors and provides recommendations that are more accurate.

  By identifying possible errors before the developer runs the program, AI-powered tools also significantly contribute to preserving code quality. These systems examine the surrounding code, comprehend the intended logic, and offer astute recommendations that reduce typical mistakes. In addition to saving crucial debugging time, this aids novices in learning proper coding techniques right away. In general, AI turns into a trustworthy coding companion that continuously helps programmers write safer, cleaner, and more effective code.

  Key points of reduced errors include:

  - Detects syntax errors and provides corrections.
  - Suggests accurate syntax and structure to avoid mistakes.
  - Understands coding context to reduce logical errors.
  - Helps maintain clean, high-quality code.
  - Saves debugging time by catching issues early.
  - Helps beginners follow correct coding practices.

AI tools assisting developers

AI tools help developers assist software developers in various ways. Intelligent automation, coding suggestions, code generation, and code optimization are the main benefits of using AI tools.

These tools can understand natural language, so it has become even easier to develop the code. So, developers can begin with natural language input, where they describe their goals in English language and AI converts these descriptions into functional code. Further, contextual code assistance helps in completing the functions and recommends relevant completions of code, which is also handled by AI.

AI tools assist developers by offering debugging insights and real-time speed improvements. These tools examine the code even before it is run to find logical errors, inefficiencies, or security threats. Developers can avoid wasting time on manual testing and fixes as a result. AI-enabled suggestions and optimization guidance improve the overall quality of the product, making the development process faster, smarter, and more reliable for both inexperienced and experienced programmers.

AI in automating repetitive code tasks

In software development, repetitive coding is crucial and takes enough time. AI plays an important role in automating these operations. AI-enabled powered tools can handle tasks like writing boilerplate code, establishing class structures, and configuration file setup effectively.

AI analyzes codebase trends and brings intelligent recommendations or completes the code automatically. Such tools help in increasing the productivity and consistency in software development and maintenance. As a result, software development and maintenance have become faster and more dependent on AI.

Instead of wasting time on monotonous tasks, AI-driven automation allows developers to concentrate on the most rational and creative areas of the project. Teams can focus on system design, optimization, and innovation when AI handles regular coding tasks. This lowers the likelihood of human error and tiredness while also improving the overall quality of the software. Such automation has proven essential to fulfilling deadlines and producing high-quality software solutions quickly in many Indian IT firms.

The following figure illustrates how AI can automate repetitive code tasks:

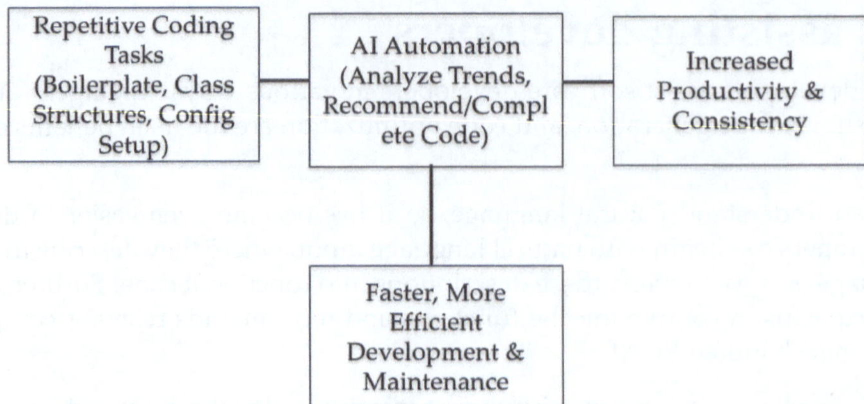

***Figure 5.2:** From repetitive work to efficient development*

Accuracy and limitations of AI-generated code

AI-generated code has more accuracy in comparison to manual coding, but developers need to be very careful about the code generated through AI tools. These tools can effectively generate accurate code in very little time, but developers need to review the code carefully. These tools can effectively produce syntactically accurate code and provide useful recommendations, but they cannot always comprehend the entire project context or particular business logic, which could result in functional errors.

Furthermore, the generated code may occasionally have inefficiencies or security flaws that need to be manually reviewed. It is crucial to view AI-generated code as a helpful tool rather than a comprehensive solution in the Indian software development context, where projects frequently entail domain-specific needs. To guarantee that the finished product satisfies quality standards and project objectives, human oversight, testing, and validation are still crucial.

Future trends in AI-based code generation

With trends suggesting a shift towards more intelligent, context-aware, and collaborative development environments, AI-based code creation is set for substantial growth and innovation in the future. Future developments should make it possible for AI tools to comprehend intricate project needs more fully, work in unison with development workflows, and facilitate multilingual coding on a variety of platforms.

It is anticipated that features like code optimization, real-time team communication, automated issue fixes, and customized coding recommendations based on developer habits would gain prominence. These trends have the potential to significantly alter the way code is created and maintained in the Indian software sector, where there is a constant need for quicker and more effective development. Developers will gain from more intelligent support as AI is incorporated more thoroughly into IDEs and cloud-based platforms, freeing them up to concentrate more on creativity and problem-solving.

Generative AI in coding

The process of using ML and AI to generate code on a user's request using any tool is very popular and time-saving. Code can be generated based on best practices and a natural language description of the desired code. In coding, this means the AI can generate code, complete functions for the purpose of creating code comments, finish code snippets, rework existing code, or create new software.

Gemini Code Assist is one of the example tools that can be used by developers to generate new code or to update existing code for the purpose of software maintenance. Generative AI is a subset of AI and is designed to generate content based on existing patterns of data. The main focus of Gen. AI is to create content, including text, audio, and video. It can be applied across various domains and has the potential to revolutionize creativity.

Generative artificial intelligence (**GenAI**) and **large language models** (**LLMs**) are transforming both personal and professional lives by providing digital assistance. Helping in managing content, communication, and productivity from digital assistants that handle emails to virtual chatbots and can interact with the company data across industries, languages, and specialties.

These technologies are ushering in a new era of convenience, productivity, and connectedness, from supercharged digital assistants that handle our emails to virtually omniscient chatbots that can interact with company data across industries, languages, and specialties. It helps in the automation of a huge variety of manual tasks, leading to the saving of time and effort. Consequently, it improves efficiency by generating code, analyzing data, automating the content creation, and so on.

Gen AI not just helps professional experience but also improves personal experiences by showing personalized recommendations for songs, movies, news, products to buy, investments to be made, and so on. All that can produce new content, including text, photos, music, and videos, is known as GenAI. It learns patterns from data that already exists and produces new outputs in response to that learning.

GenAI is a class of ML models that can create new data that resembles the training data. In coding, AI can generate code, functions can fix bugs, and optimize. On the other hand, gen AI is able to generate a complete end-to-end experience by generating entirely new output instead of predicting the provided data based on self-generated content.

Ethical and security implications of AI-generated code

Although AI-generated code is quick and easy, developers need to be aware of the significant ethical and security issues it raises. Relying only on AI-generated code carries a high risk because it may have hidden faults, security holes, or logical problems. Automated technologies may unintentionally add vulnerabilities that hackers could exploit if the code is not carefully reviewed.

Ethical concerns include copyright violations, plagiarism, and the AI's opaque code writing process. Sometimes, AI approaches might generate code that imitates existing proprietary software without the developer's awareness. Human supervision is therefore essential at all levels. Developers must review, test, and validate AI-generated material to ensure it is safe, distinct, and complies with the law.

To guarantee responsible use of AI technologies, best practices such as thorough code reviews, security scanning, documentation checks, and adherence to ethical standards should always be followed. This ensures that throughout the software development lifecycle, AI will remain a helpful tool rather than a risk.

There are many ethical and security implications of AI-generated code, as shown in the figure:

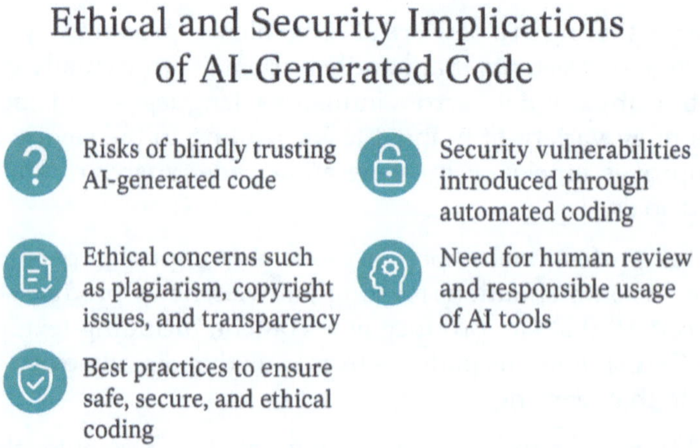

Figure 5.3: *Ethical and security implications of AI-generated code*

Conclusion

This chapter explored critical code-generation tools (OpenAI Codex, CodeT5, GitHub Copilot, etc.) and their prominent features and capabilities. It also examined ChatGPT-4, and its multi-modal capabilities can generate text representations from image content.

The chapter covered various popular AI code generation tools, including GitHub Copilot, Amazon CodeWhisperer, CodeGeeX, and many more. Further, the chapter explains the benefits of AI code generation, such as code assistance, natural language input, and many more.

The next chapter will discuss the AI-powered tools to enhance the stages of software development. To make sure that AI technologies are used safely, best practices like thorough code reviews, security scanning, documentation checks, and following ethical standards should always be used.

Questions

1. What is the role of AI in code generation?
2. How does AI improve coding efficiency?
3. In what ways do AI tools assist developers?
4. How do AI tools impact software development speed?
5. What are the limitations of AI-generated code?

Answers

1. AI in code generation automates the development of code by producing whole functions, code fragments, or structural templates from natural language descriptions or existent code context. It understands programming patterns and automatically applies best practices using learned models. By automating tedious coding tasks and reducing human labour, AI allows developers to focus more on design and problem-solving. Additionally, it ensures more consistency and faster development of coding assignments.
2. AI boosts coding efficiency by generating code quickly, automating time-consuming tasks, and providing intelligent, context-aware suggestions. It lowers logical and syntactic errors through the use of real-time inspections and suggestions. AI also expedites prototyping, enabling engineers to get from concept to implementation faster. By reducing physical work, it allows teams to focus more on innovation and high-level design.
3. By producing code, making suggestions for enhancements, identifying mistakes, and automating tedious chores, AI technologies assist developers and free them up to concentrate on logic and design.
4. AI tools assist engineers by generating code snippets, suggesting improvements, and quickly spotting potential errors. By automating repetitive tasks like configuring settings and writing boilerplate code, they significantly reduce the amount of time needed for development. These tools also look at code patterns to suggest optimal solutions and best practices. As a result, developers may focus more on logic, creativity, and producing the best possible programs.

5. The disadvantages of AI-generated programming include the potential for logical errors and security vulnerabilities that may not be immediately apparent. AI occasionally produces erroneous or unproductive responses, especially in complicated or unique contexts outside of its training data. An excessive dependence on AI may hinder a developer's capacity to address significant issues. Therefore, to ensure code quality, accuracy, and compliance with project criteria, human review is required.

Multiple choice questions

1. **Which of the following is a limitation of AI-generated code?**
   a. It always produces error-free and optimal solutions.
   b. It may contain logical errors and security vulnerabilities.
   c. It eliminates the need for human review.
   d. It can fully replace experienced developers.
2. **What is a primary function of generative AI in coding?**
   a. Debugging only
   b. Creating user interfaces automatically
   c. Generating code snippets and complete functions
   d. Compiling source code into executables
3. **Which input method is often used by generative AI to produce code?**
   a. Voice commands only
   b. Binary code input
   c. Natural language descriptions
   d. Manual code rewriting
4. **Which of the following is an example of a popular AI code generation tool?**
   a. OpenAI Codex
   b. Adobe Photoshop
   c. Microsoft Excel
   d. AutoCAD
5. **GitHub Copilot is primarily designed to:**
   a. Manage cloud storage
   b. Suggest and generate code in real-time
   c. Create graphic designs
   d. Compile hardware schematics

Answers

1	b
2	c

3	c
4	a

5	b

CHAPTER 6

AI-powered Tools to Enhance the Stages of Software Development

Introduction

AI-powered tools are integral to software development, providing significant advantages at each stage of the **software development lifecycle** (**SDLC**). From planning and design to coding, testing, deployment, and maintenance, **artificial intelligence** (**AI**) can enhance efficiency, improve quality, and enable automation in almost every SDLC aspect. These tools leverage AI and **machine learning** (**ML**) techniques to automate tasks, enhance decision-making, and improve the quality and speed of software development.

SDLC is a structured process that software engineers and developers use to design, develop, test, deploy, and maintain software applications. It defines the phases of creating software and provides a systematic approach to delivering high-quality software products.

Generative AI, a subset of AI, is revolutionizing how software is developed and maintained by automating creative and repetitive tasks throughout the SDLC. It can generate design diagrams, write optimized code, create test cases, predict bugs, and even produce deployment scripts. By learning from vast datasets and existing codebases, generative AI tools like GitHub Copilot and ChatGPT assist developers in producing faster, more reliable, and efficient solutions. This integration not only reduces human error and development time but also enhances innovation, allowing teams to focus on higher-level problem-solving and strategic decision-making.

Structure

In this chapter, we will cover the following topics:

- Usage of AI tools in software development
- Industry standards and compliance in SDLC

Objectives

This chapter aims to explore the integration of AI-powered tools within the SDLC and demonstrate how they enhance efficiency, accuracy, and automation across all phases. It aims to provide a comprehensive understanding of how AI-driven technologies optimize requirement analysis, system design, coding, testing, deployment, and maintenance by reducing human effort, minimizing errors, and accelerating decision-making.

This chapter highlights the transformative role of AI in modern software development by analyzing the impact of AI-powered tools such as **natural language processing** (**NLP**) for requirement gathering, ML for predictive analysis, AI-assisted code generation, and automated testing frameworks. Furthermore, it equips readers with insights into the latest AI advancements and their practical applications in SDLC, enabling organizations to streamline development processes, enhance software quality, and maintain a competitive edge in the evolving technological landscape.

Usage of AI tools in software development

AI tools are increasingly playing a key role in streamlining various stages of software development. From planning and design to coding, testing, deployment, and maintenance, AI can enhance efficiency, improve quality, and enable automation in almost every aspect of SDLC. The different phases of the SDLC are:

1. Planning and requirement gathering
2. Design and architecture
3. Coding/development
4. Testing
5. Deployment
6. Maintenance and monitoring
7. Documentation and knowledge sharing

These phases are illustrated in the following figure:

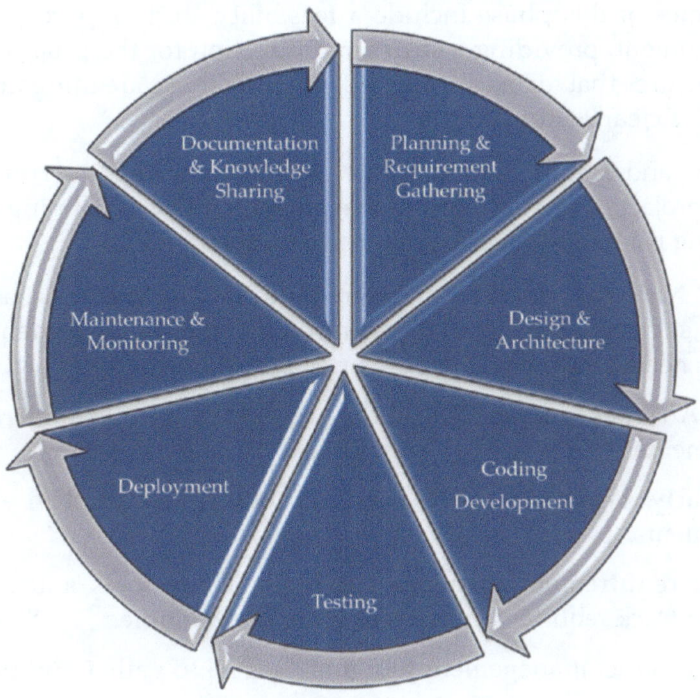

Figure 6.1: Different phases of SDLC

Let us now go over the respective phases of SDLC.

Planning and requirement gathering

Planning and requirement analysis are crucial early phases of SDLC, as they set the foundation for the entire project.

The planning phase is the foundation of the SDLC, where project goals, feasibility, and resource requirements are identified. This phase ensures that the project is viable and aligns with business objectives. A well-structured plan is crucial for reducing project risks, optimizing resources, and setting clear expectations. Proper planning helps stakeholders establish a shared vision, preventing scope creep and ensuring a streamlined development process.

The activities involved are:

- Understanding user needs and business objectives.
- Conducting interviews, surveys, and workshops with stakeholders.
- Documenting functional and non-functional requirements.
- Defining project timelines, budgets, and resource allocation.

The primary outcomes of this phase include a feasibility study report, project charter, and risk assessment document, providing a structured direction for the project's development. A well-defined plan ensures that teams are aligned, potential risks are mitigated, and the project moves forward with a clear roadmap.

AI tools for planning and requirement analysis assist in gathering, interpreting, and refining user requirements, project estimation, risk management, and even defining software features. Refer to the following list to build a comprehensive understanding:

- **NLP tools**: NLP can be used to automatically analyze text-based requirements documents, such as user stories or feature descriptions, and identify key elements such as user needs, business rules, or constraints. For example:
  - **spaCy**: An open-source NLP library to extract entities and relationships from requirements.
  - **Grammarly**: While primarily a writing tool, it can assist in ensuring clarity in requirements.
- **AI-powered requirement management tools**: These tools automatically generate, validate, and track requirements in real-time. For example:
  - **Aha!**: A product management tool that uses AI to gather and prioritize customer feedback.
  - **Jira with AI plugins**: Jira integrates AI tools to help define and track user stories, epics, and overall project progress.
- **Project estimation tools**: AI-based estimation tools predict the time, cost, and resources required to complete a project. For example:
  - **Function point analysis tools:** AI models that use historical data to estimate function points and overall project effort.

Generative AI is rapidly transforming the SDLC by automating tasks, improving efficiency, and enhancing creativity at every stage. In requirement analysis, generative AI can analyze natural language documents, emails, and user stories to automatically extract functional and non-functional requirements. The details are as follows:

- It can identify inconsistencies or missing details.
- It can generate requirement templates or visual representations of user needs.
- **Example**: Using GPT-like models, stakeholders can input high-level project ideas, and the AI can produce a structured requirement document.

Design and architecture

Design and architecture are crucial stages in the SDLC. They involve creating a blueprint for how the software will work, ensuring scalability, reliability, and maintainability. Create the architecture and design of the software.

The objective of the design phase is to create a comprehensive system blueprint based on the requirements gathered in the previous phase. This phase focuses on defining the system architecture, technical stack, data structures, and user interface design to ensure a well-structured, efficient, and scalable solution. A well-designed system facilitates smooth implementation, reduces complexities, and meets all technical and functional requirements. This phase also incorporates security, maintainability, and scalability considerations to ensure the longevity of the software solution.

The activities involved are:

- Defining project timelines, budgets, and resource allocation.
- High-level design (System architecture).
- Low-level design (Detailed component design).
- Database design and selection.
- UI/UX design.

The outcome of this phase includes detailed design documents, system architecture diagrams, database structures, and prototypes, which act as a blueprint for the coding phase. A well-structured design ensures the system's efficiency, reliability, and ease of maintenance. By having a solid design foundation, developers can efficiently implement the system, reducing the chances of errors and the need for significant modifications later in the development process.

AI tools in design and architecture can assist developers and architects in automating tasks, making better design decisions, and predicting future challenges. These tools help generate software architecture, create UI/UX designs, analyze performance, and optimize code for scalability. Refer to the following list to build a comprehensive understanding:

- **Automated code generation**: AI can assist developers by automatically generating code based on high-level design or specifications. For example:
    - o **GitHub Copilot**: Powered by OpenAI's Codex, this tool helps developers write code faster by suggesting code snippets.
    - o **Tabnine**: An AI-powered code completion tool that offers suggestions based on the context of the code being written.
- **AI for UI/UX design**: AI tools in this area help automate design processes, generate prototypes, and enhance user experience through pattern recognition. For example:
    - o **Uizard**: An AI tool that converts hand-drawn sketches into fully functional user interface prototypes.
    - o **Figma + AI plugins**: Figma has AI-powered plugins for design assistance, auto-layout, and more.

- **Adobe Sensei**: Adobe's AI and ML platform that assists in optimizing designs and improving user experience.

During the design phase of software development, generative AI plays a significant role in improving creativity, accuracy, and efficiency. The details are as follows:

- It can automatically generate UML diagrams, flowcharts, wireframes, and architecture sketches from simple text descriptions.
- This helps teams quickly visualize system structures and workflows without manual drawing.
- AI can suggest modular and scalable design patterns or system architectures based on best practices and past project data.
- It also creates UI/UX prototypes, offering layout ideas that follow usability and aesthetic design principles.
- Designers and developers can refine these AI-generated designs to meet specific project needs.
- This process saves time and reduces manual effort while maintaining design accuracy.
- Generative AI ensures consistency and standardization across complex systems.

As a result, teams can focus more on innovation, functionality, and user experience rather than repetitive design documentation.

Coding/Development

The implementation phase is the core of the SDLC, where developers convert the approved system design into actual source code. The main objective of this phase is to build a functional and robust software system while adhering to coding standards, security guidelines, and best practices. This phase ensures that the software meets functional, performance, and security requirements. Proper version control, modular development, and adherence to coding principles contribute to a maintainable and scalable software product.

The activities involved are:

- Setting up the development environment and tools.
- Writing code according to the design specifications.
- Adhering to coding standards and best practices.
- Version control using tools like Git.

The primary outcomes of this phase include a fully developed software system, unit test reports, and updated technical documentation to facilitate future maintenance and enhancements.

A properly implemented system ensures that the software operates correctly according to the design specifications. The quality of the implementation directly affects the software's security, performance, and maintainability. A well-written and structured codebase results in fewer defects and easier debugging and enhancement in the later stages.

AI tools for coding help developers write, refactor, and maintain code more efficiently, reducing errors and improving productivity. Let us go over them:

- **AI-assisted code completion**: These tools suggest code snippets and solutions in real-time, saving time on boilerplate coding. For example:
  - **GitHub Copilot**: Uses ML to help developers by suggesting lines of code and entire functions.
  - **Kite**: An AI-powered coding assistant for Python, JavaScript, and other languages.
  - **Codota**: AI-based code completion and suggestions for Java and Kotlin.
- **Code refactoring and optimization**: AI tools can refactor code automatically to improve performance or readability. For example:
  - **Refactoring.guru**: Provides tips and patterns for improving existing code.
  - **SonarQube:** Though primarily a code quality tool, SonarQube can analyze code for potential improvements with AI-enhanced suggestions.

Generative AI greatly supports developers in writing code more efficiently and accurately by automating several aspects of the coding process, as outlined in the following list:

- **Code generation**: AI tools can automatically produce *boilerplate or repetitive code* from simple, high-level instructions given by developers. This helps eliminate the need to write lengthy, repetitive functions manually and ensures consistency in coding style and structure.
- **Code completion and suggestions**: Tools such as GitHub Copilot and Tabnine use AI models trained on vast codebases to provide *context-aware code snippets* and intelligent suggestions. These tools can predict what a developer is likely to write next, making the coding process faster and more intuitive.
- **Refactoring and optimization**: Generative AI can analyze existing code and suggest ways to *improve performance, readability, and efficiency*. It can identify redundant code, optimize algorithms, and even detect potential logical errors before execution.

By automating these tasks, generative AI *reduces development time, minimizes coding errors,* and allows developers to focus on solving complex problems rather than repetitive syntax. Overall, it improves productivity, ensures higher code quality, and accelerates software delivery, especially in large-scale and collaborative development environments.

Testing

The testing phase is crucial for ensuring that the developed software is functional, secure, and free of defects. The objective of this phase is to systematically identify and eliminate bugs, security vulnerabilities, and performance issues before the software is deployed. Testing validates that the software meets all functional and non-functional requirements and ensures a seamless user experience. It also minimizes risks associated with software failures, ensuring that the final product performs as expected under various conditions.

The activities involved are as follows:

- Writing test cases and performing unit testing, integration testing, system testing, and acceptance testing.
- Identifying and fixing bugs.
- Verifying the system against requirements (functional, non-functional, and security testing).

The outcomes of this phase include a detailed test report, defect resolution documentation, and validation reports confirming the software's readiness for deployment. The testing phase ensures the software is reliable, secure, and meets quality standards before reaching end-users. A well-tested software system reduces downtime, improves user confidence, and enhances overall system stability. Ensuring the product is free of critical defects before deployment leads to a smoother transition and fewer post-deployment issues.

AI tools for testing help automate test generation, test execution, bug detection, and regression testing, speeding up the process and increasing accuracy, as outlined in the following list:

- **AI-powered test automation**: AI tools can automatically generate and run test cases, including unit tests, integration tests, and UI tests. For example:
    - o **Testim**: An AI-powered test automation tool that helps in creating and maintaining automated tests.
    - o **Mabl**: Uses ML to identify and run tests, and adapt to changing UIs and workflows.
    - o **Applitools**: AI-powered visual testing tool that can detect visual bugs across multiple platforms and devices.
- **Predictive bug detection**: AI can analyze code and predict where bugs are likely to occur or identify existing bugs based on past data. For example:
    - o **Sentry**: An error-tracking tool that uses ML to detect and categorize bugs in real-time.
    - o **DeepCode**: AI-powered code review tool that can identify potential security vulnerabilities and bugs.
- **AI for load testing**: AI can simulate real user traffic patterns for load testing and predict system performance under heavy load. For example:

- **BlazeMeter**: Uses ML to analyze and simulate real-world usage scenarios for load testing.
- **Flood.io**: Leverages AI to provide smarter load testing and real-time insights into performance bottlenecks.

Generative AI is transforming the software testing process by automating the creation of test cases, scripts, and scenarios, making testing faster, more accurate, and more efficient. The details are as follows:

- **Unit test generation**: AI can automatically *generate test cases* by analyzing the code's logic, structure, and functionality. This ensures that every function or module is tested thoroughly without requiring manual effort. It helps developers validate that each part of the program works as expected.
- **Bug prediction**: Generative AI can *predict potential defects or vulnerabilities* in the code even before it is executed. By studying coding patterns and historical bug data, it highlights risky areas where issues are likely to occur, allowing developers to fix them early in the process.
- **Scenario simulation**: AI tools can *simulate different testing scenarios*, including edge cases and complex user behaviors, to ensure that the software performs well under various conditions. This helps identify rare bugs that traditional testing methods might miss.

By automating these processes, generative AI enables *higher test coverage, quicker bug detection, and improved software reliability*. It reduces the manual workload for testers, speeds up the testing cycle, and ensures that software products are more stable and secure before release.

Deployment

The deployment phase is responsible for releasing the software to the production environment and making it available to end-users. The goal of this phase is to ensure a seamless transition from development to live operations with minimal disruptions. This phase involves installing the software on production servers, finalizing system configurations, and conducting final checks to ensure a smooth launch. A successful deployment ensures that the software operates as intended in a real-world setting and that users can start utilizing its functionalities effectively.

The activities involved are as follows:

- Setting up production servers and environments.
- Performing final **user acceptance testing** (UAT).
- Deploying the software using **continuous integration/continuous deployment** (CI/CD) pipelines.
- Updating system configurations and monitoring tools.

The key outcomes of this phase include a fully operational software system, deployment reports, and comprehensive user guides to assist in smooth adoption by end-users. A successful deployment ensures system stability, user acceptance, and readiness for operational use. Proper deployment planning prevents downtime, enhances security, and ensures that the software integrates well into the existing infrastructure. Additionally, user training and support help in maximizing software adoption and effectiveness in real-world use cases.

AI tools for deployment help automate and optimize the deployment process, ensuring smooth CI/CD. Refer to the following list to build a comprehensive understanding:

- **AI for CI/CD**: AI tools help automate the entire build, test, and deployment pipeline, optimizing each stage. For example:
    - **CircleCI**: An AI-powered CI/CD platform that automates deployments and integrates with testing tools.
    - **Travis CI**: Another CI/CD tool that can integrate AI-based testing and deployment.
- **Automated rollback and monitoring**: AI systems can monitor live deployments and roll back if an issue is detected. For example:
    - **ArgoCD**: A Kubernetes-native tool that automates deployment with AI-based rollbacks and error detection.
    - **Rollout.io**: Uses AI to monitor application performance and rollback if an anomaly is detected.

Generative AI plays a crucial role in improving and automating software deployment pipelines, making the process faster, more reliable, and error-free. The details are as follows:

- **Configuration generation**: AI can automatically generate optimized deployment scripts and configurations for various environments such as development, testing, staging, and production. This eliminates the need for repetitive manual setup and ensures that each environment is properly configured according to best practices. As a result, deployment becomes more consistent, reducing human errors and setup time.
- **Predictive deployment analysis**: Using data from past deployments and system performance, generative AI can predict potential risks, failures, or compatibility issues before deployment actually occurs. It analyzes system dependencies, version mismatches, or performance bottlenecks and alerts developers in advance. This proactive approach helps in minimizing downtime and improving deployment success rates.
- **Automated CI/CD integration**: Generative AI can seamlessly integrate with CI/CD pipelines, automating tasks like code testing, building, and deployment. It ensures that updates move smoothly from development to production without manual intervention.

Overall, by combining automation and intelligence, generative AI enhances efficiency, reliability, and scalability in deployment pipelines, allowing teams to release software faster with fewer errors and better performance.

Maintenance and monitoring

The maintenance and support phase ensures the software's long-term sustainability by addressing any issues that arise after deployment. The objective of this phase is to provide continuous improvements, fix software defects, enhance performance, and ensure security updates. This phase also focuses on adapting the software to evolving business needs and technological advancements. Maintenance is essential to extend the software's lifespan, improve user satisfaction, and ensure compliance with industry standards and security protocols.

The activities involved are as follows:

- Bug fixes and patching.
- Enhancements based on user feedback and market requirements.
- Regular updates for security, performance, and functionality.
- Providing technical support and documentation.

The outcomes include software updates, maintenance logs, technical support reports, and enhancements to improve UX and system performance. Effective maintenance ensures that the software remains robust, secure, and relevant over time. Regular updates and optimizations improve system efficiency and reliability, ensuring that the software continues to meet business needs and technological advancements effectively.

AI tools for maintenance and monitoring enable predictive maintenance, performance optimization, anomaly detection, and overall system monitoring. Let us go over them:

- **AI-based monitoring and anomaly detection**: AI tools analyze logs, metrics, and system behavior to detect anomalies and predict failures before they occur. For example:
    - **New Relic**: An AI-powered monitoring tool that helps detect and resolve performance bottlenecks in real-time.
    - **Datadog**: Uses ML to provide insights into application performance, automatically detecting anomalies.
- **Automated issue resolution**: Some AI systems can automatically resolve issues identified during maintenance or operational monitoring. For example:
    - **IBM Watson AIOps**: AI-driven system that predicts and resolves IT incidents to minimize downtime.
    - **BigPanda**: Uses ML to correlate and resolve incidents in IT operations.

- **Predictive maintenance tools**: AI tools predict system failures or security vulnerabilities before they happen, reducing downtime and maintenance costs. For example:
    - o **Uptake**: AI for predictive maintenance in industrial software applications.
    - o **Honeywell Forge**: Uses AI and IoT to monitor industrial systems and predict maintenance needs.

During the *maintenance and monitoring phase*, generative AI plays an essential role in ensuring that software systems remain stable, efficient, and up to date. The details are as follows:

- **Generating documentation**: After every update, patch, or change, generative AI can automatically *create detailed documentation* that explains what has been modified and why. This saves developers valuable time and ensures that all updates are clearly recorded for future reference, improving transparency and team collaboration.
- **Predictive maintenance**: By analyzing historical logs, error reports, and performance data, AI can forecast potential system failures or breakdowns before they happen. This allows teams to take preventive actions, reducing system downtime and improving reliability. Predictive maintenance helps organizations plan repairs or upgrades in advance, saving both time and cost.
- **Automated issue resolution**: Generative AI can identify recurring bugs or performance issues and suggest possible fixes based on previous resolutions or best practices. In some cases, it can even automatically apply small patches or configuration adjustments.

Overall, generative AI makes maintenance and monitoring more proactive, data-driven, and efficient, helping teams detect problems early, respond faster, and keep the software performing smoothly throughout its lifecycle.

Documentation and knowledge sharing

Documentation and knowledge sharing play a crucial role in SDLC by ensuring that all processes, system functionalities, and operational guidelines are well-documented for future reference. This phase involves creating comprehensive technical documents, user manuals, and system guides to support developers, testers, and end-users. Proper documentation enhances maintainability, reduces onboarding time for new team members, and helps in troubleshooting issues efficiently.

The activities involved are:

- Document system architecture, processes, and functionalities in detail.
- Develop user guides, technical manuals, and FAQs covering all system aspects.
- Conduct structured training sessions, workshops, and knowledge transfer meetings.
- Establish and continuously update internal knowledge bases and repositories.

- Implement version control for documentation to track changes and improvements.
- Collect feedback from users and stakeholders to enhance documentation clarity and usability.
- Ensure compliance with industry standards and best practices in documentation.

The outcome of this phase includes a structured and accessible knowledge base, complete documentation covering all system functionalities, and well-prepared training materials for both technical and non-technical users. Organizations can achieve long-term sustainability, efficient system maintenance, and streamlined knowledge transfer across teams by focusing on proper documentation and knowledge sharing. This phase ultimately supports the continuity and scalability of the software system, ensuring smooth transitions in case of personnel changes or future system enhancements.

AI tools for documentation help automate the generation of documentation, making it easier to maintain up-to-date records of code and system design. Refer to the following list to build a comprehensive understanding:

- **AI documentation assistants**: AI tools help in generating technical documentation, **application programming interface (API)** references, or code comments automatically. For example:
  - o **Scribe**: Uses AI to automatically generate documentation for code and APIs.
  - o **DocuSign and AI integration**: Used for automating legal and contract documentation associated with software development.
- **Knowledge base systems**: AI can be used to maintain and organize knowledge bases for development teams, helping with internal documentation and collaboration. For example:
  - o **Guru**: An AI-powered knowledge management tool that automatically organizes and retrieves knowledge within teams.
  - o **Confluence and AI**: Uses AI to suggest content and structure knowledge management in teams.

Refer to the following table:

SDLC phase	AI-powered tools	Benefits
Planning and requirement analysis	1. IBM Watson 2. ChatGPT API 3. Akkio 4. ReWceptiviti 5. Lucidchart AI	• Automates requirement gathering and analysis. • Enhances risk assessment and feasibility analysis. • Extracts insights from stakeholder feedback. • Identifies potential project challenges early.
Design	1. Adobe Sensei 2. Sketch2Code 3. Archistar 4. Figma AI 5. Microsoft Visio AI	• Automates UI/UX design improvements. • Transforms sketches into working code. • Optimizes system architecture for efficiency. • Enhances design accuracy using AI-driven analytics.
Development (Coding)	1. GitHub Copilot 2. Tabnine 3. DeepCode 4. CodeT5 5. JetBrains AI Assistant	• AI-assisted code generation reduces development time. • Improves code quality and efficiency. • Detects and fixes syntax and logical errors. • Provides real-time coding suggestions.
Testing	1. Applitools 2. Testim 3. Selenium with AI 4. Mabl 5. Functionize	• Automates test case generation and execution. • Enhances visual testing and UI validation. • Reduces manual effort in software testing. • Improves test accuracy and defect detection.
Deployment	1. Google Cloud AI 2. AWS DevOps Guru 3. Azure AI DevOps 4. Harness AI 5. Kubernetes AI	• Automates deployment and infrastructure management. • Detects deployment failures before they occur. • Optimizes resource allocation and scaling. • Enhances CI/CD pipeline efficiency.

Maintenance and monitoring	1. Datadog AI 2. New Relic AI 3. AIOps by Splunk 4. IBM Cloud Pak for AIOps 5. Dynatrace AI	• Detects and resolves software performance issues. • Predicts system failures before they impact users. • Automates incident response and log analysis. • Enhances system monitoring and anomaly detection.
Documentation and knowledge sharing	1. Confluence AI 2. Notion AI 3. Microsoft Copilot 4. Google Bard 5. Guru AI	• Automates documentation summarization. • Enhances knowledge retrieval using AI-driven search. • Assists in generating technical documentation. • Improves collaboration and information sharing.

***Table 6.1**: AI-powered tools in SDLC phases and their benefits*

The following figure visually explains how generative AI contributes to every stage of the development lifecycle from requirement analysis to deployment:

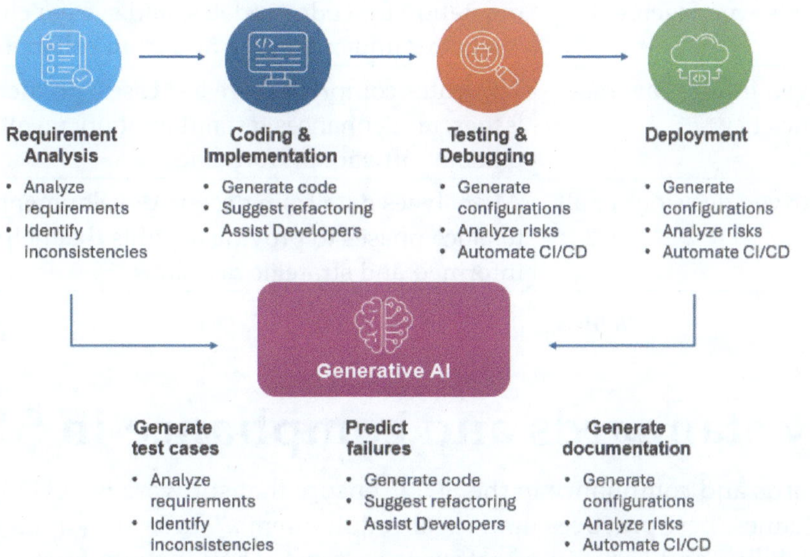

***Figure 6.2**: Generative AI in software development*

The figure demonstrates that during requirement analysis, AI helps in analyzing and validating requirements. In the coding and implementation phase, it assists developers by generating code and suggesting refactoring. During testing and debugging, AI automates configuration generation, predicts risks, and enhances CI/CD processes. For deployment, it ensures smooth and reliable delivery by analyzing potential risks and automating repetitive steps. Additionally, the image shows how AI continuously generates test cases, predicts failures, and creates documentation, thus making the overall development process more intelligent, automated, and efficient.

Generative AI also offers significant advantages across all stages of the SDLC. It not only speeds up development but also improves the quality and reliability of software. Automating documentation and testing ensures better knowledge management and thorough verification. Additionally, AI provides insights that enable **data-driven decisions**, making the development process more strategic and efficient. The following table summarizes the key benefits of using generative AI in SDLC:

S.No.	Benefit	Description
1	Faster development with reduced manual effort	Generative AI automates repetitive and time-consuming tasks such as code generation, testing, and documentation, enabling quicker software delivery.
2	Enhanced code quality and fewer errors	AI tools assist in writing cleaner, optimized, and error-free code by identifying bugs and suggesting improvements during development.
3	Better documentation and knowledge management	Automatically generates accurate and updated documentation for code, updates, and system changes, ensuring better understanding and team collaboration.
4	Improved testing coverage and efficiency	AI creates comprehensive test cases, predicts potential issues, and enhances test automation, resulting in more reliable software performance.
5	Data-driven decisions at all stages	AI analyzes data from design, development, and maintenance phases to provide insights that help teams make informed and strategic decisions.

Table 6.2: Benefits of generative AI in SDLC

Industry standards and compliance in SDLC

Industry standards and compliance in the SDLC ensure that software is developed following approved guidelines, best practices, and legal requirements. These standards help maintain the quality, reliability, and security of software systems. They include frameworks like ISO 9001 for quality management, ISO/IEC 27001 for information security, and CMMI for process maturity. Compliance with these standards also ensures that software products meet data protection and privacy laws such as GDPR and HIPAA, helping organizations build user trust and avoid legal risks.

Incorporating compliance throughout the SDLC from requirement gathering to deployment ensures that each phase follows secure and ethical practices. For example, during the design stage, developers can follow security architecture principles, while in testing, compliance tools can verify adherence to coding standards and detect vulnerabilities. This structured approach not only improves software quality but also makes maintenance and audits more manageable.

AI and generative AI are now transforming how compliance is managed in SDLC. AI-powered tools can automatically scan code for security issues, suggest improvements, and monitor adherence to standards in real-time. Generative AI can help generate documentation, compliance checklists, and even secure code templates that align with industry regulations. These technologies reduce human errors, save time, and make compliance more proactive rather than reactive, ensuring that software remains safe, efficient, and compliant throughout its lifecycle:

Area	Standard/Regulation	Purpose	AI and generative AI contribution
Quality management	ISO 9001	Ensures software quality and continuous improvement.	AI tracks performance metrics and suggests process optimizations.
Information security	ISO/IEC 27001	Protects data and manages security risks.	AI detects anomalies and predicts potential breaches.
Software process management	IEEE 12207/ CMMI	Standardizes software life cycle activities.	Generative AI automates documentation and compliance reporting.
Data privacy	GDPR, HIPAA	Protects personal and sensitive information.	AI flags privacy violations and generates compliance summaries.
Application security	OWASP Top 10	Prevents common software vulnerabilities.	AI tools auto-scan code and generate secure code snippets.

***Table 6.3**: Industry standards and how AI supports compliance*

Table 6.3 highlights key industry standards commonly applied in the SDLC and explains how AI and generative AI technologies assist in maintaining compliance and improving efficiency across each area. It shows the connection between traditional frameworks and modern AI-driven practices.

Conclusion

SDLC provides a structured approach to software creation, ensuring efficiency, quality, and scalability. Each phase, from planning to maintenance, plays a critical role in delivering a robust software product that meets business and user needs. The integration of AI tools across these phases has significantly improved productivity, accuracy, and decision-making. AI-driven solutions streamline requirement gathering, optimize design, enhance coding efficiency, automate testing, and ensure seamless deployment and maintenance. As AI continues to evolve, its role in software development will become even more prominent, helping organizations build innovative, high-quality software at an accelerated pace. Embracing AI-powered SDLC methodologies will be crucial for staying competitive in the ever-evolving technological landscape. AI has transformed software engineering, with generative AI playing a vital role in optimizing the SDLC.

Generative AI is transforming the SDLC by making it more automated, intelligent, and efficient. It reduces manual effort, enhances software quality, and accelerates delivery across all stages. As AI continues to evolve, its integration into SDLC will further optimize development processes and drive innovation in software engineering.

Industry standards and compliance ensure that software development remains secure, reliable, and aligned with legal and quality requirements. These standards build user trust and support sustainable, high-quality software delivery.

The next chapter discusses how AI tools automate resource allocation in IT infrastructure. It also explains how AI-driven solutions help reduce costs and boost efficiency. Furthermore, the chapter discusses AI's role in maintaining consistency.

Multiple choice questions

1. **What is the primary role of AI in the SDLC?**
    a. Increasing hardware cost
    b. Manual documentation
    c. Automating tasks and improving decision-making
    d. Network management

2. **How does AI reduce human effort during the planning phase of SDLC?**
    a. By writing source code
    b. By analyzing historical project data for estimation
    c. By executing test cases
    d. By managing databases

3. **Which AI technique is mainly used to assist in requirement gathering?**
   a. Computer vision
   b. Robotics
   c. NLP
   d. Cryptography

4. **AI-powered NLP tools help in requirement analysis by:**
   a. Generating hardware designs
   b. Extracting and classifying requirements from text
   c. Running performance tests
   d. Monitoring servers

5. **What is the primary function of AI-powered test automation tools like Testim and Mabl?**
   a. Manual bug fixing
   b. Test case generation and execution
   c. Code deployment
   d. Network security

6. **Which AI tool assists in real-time monitoring and automatic issue detection?**
   a. GitHub Copilot
   b. Dynatrace
   c. Selenium
   d. JIRA

7. **Which of the following is a key benefit of using generative AI in SDLC?**
   a. Increased manual effort
   b. Faster code and documentation generation
   c. Higher development cost
   d. Reduced test coverage

8. **AI-powered tools enhance different stages of SDLC primarily by:**
   a. Eliminating developers
   b. Automating tasks and improving accuracy
   c. Increasing project complexity
   d. Slowing development

9. **AI-powered design and architecture tools help in building scalable systems by:**
   a. Ignoring performance constraints
   b. Recommending optimal architectures and resource usage
   c. Reducing system security
   d. Increasing manual design work

10. **Which of the following tools helps developers by providing AI-driven code completion?**
   a. Jenkins
   b. GitHub Copilot
   c. Tableau
   d. Dynatrace

11. **How do AI-driven code completion tools impact developer productivity?**
   a. Increase syntax errors
   b. Slow down coding
   c. Reduce repetitive coding tasks
   d. Eliminate testing

12. **AI contributes to software maintenance by:**
   a. Performing hardware upgrades
   b. Predicting failures and detecting anomalies
   c. Writing user manuals only
   d. Stopping system monitoring

13. **Which AI tools are commonly used for maintenance and monitoring?**
   a. MS Word and Excel
   b. Dynatrace and New Relic
   c. Photoshop and Figma
   d. Eclipse and NetBeans

14. **How do AI-powered documentation tools improve collaboration?**
   a. By increasing manual documentation
   b. By generating outdated documents
   c. By automatically creating and updating documentation
   d. By limiting information sharing

15. **How does generative AI improve efficiency and accuracy in software development?**
    a. By increasing human errors
    b. By automating content generation and reducing ambiguity
    c. By eliminating SDLC phases
    d. By focusing only on testing

Answers

1	c
2	b
3	c
4	b
5	b
6	b
7	b
8	b
9	b
10	b
11	c
12	b
13	b
14	c
15	b

CHAPTER 7
AI for IT Infrastructure Resource Optimization

Introduction

This chapter will cover how the increasing complexity of **information technology** (**IT**) infrastructure requires innovative solutions to enhance efficiency, reduce costs, and ensure security. **Artificial intelligence** (**AI**) has emerged as a transformative technology, enabling organizations to optimize resources, automate processes, and strengthen cybersecurity measures. By integrating AI-driven tools, businesses can enhance operational efficiency, improve energy management, and ensure the reliability of their IT systems.

AI helps companies save money in many ways. It can predict when machines need fixing, which helps reduce sudden breakdowns by about 50%. It also manages cloud costs by using smart tools to control how much computer power is used, so companies do not pay for more than they need. Studies show that using AI tools for cloud cost management can save 20 to 30% on bills. Moreover, AI-based maintenance can cut repair costs by 10 to 40% and help machines last longer. Additionally, AI-driven energy efficiency solutions, such as smart load balancing and AI-optimized cooling systems, significantly reduce power consumption in data centers. Automation through AI minimizes human intervention, streamlining IT operations with self-healing systems and **Robotic Process Automation** (**RPA**).

AI helps improve cybersecurity. It finds and stops threats early. It follows industry rules and standards. It protects data using behavior analysis and encryption. AI also makes IT systems work better. It improves how networks run and manages data storage in a smarter way. It provides tools that adjust to users' needs. These tools help people with disabilities use technology more easily. All these features make IT systems stronger, safer, and more reliable.

This chapter examines how AI-driven solutions enhance IT resource management in key areas, including cost efficiency, energy conservation, automation, security, and performance. By adopting AI-powered strategies, businesses can achieve a competitive edge, enhance sustainability, and ensure the long-term reliability of their IT ecosystems.

Structure

In this chapter, we will cover the following topics:

- AI for IT infrastructure resource optimization
- Energy efficiency
- Automation and minimal human involvement
- Data security and privacy
- Performance and accessibility enhancement

Objectives

By the end of this chapter, you will understand how AI enhances IT infrastructure by improving efficiency, reducing costs, and strengthening security. The key objectives of this chapter include understanding AI-driven cost optimization through predictive maintenance and cloud cost management, exploring AI's role in improving energy efficiency using smart load balancing and renewable energy integration, and learning about AI-powered automation through **artificial intelligence for IT operations** (**AIOps**) and RPA. It will examine how AI strengthens data security using threat detection, behavioral analysis, and encryption, and help the reader discover how AI boosts IT performance through network optimization and user-centered accessibility tools, which adapt systems to meet the needs of users with different abilities.

By achieving these objectives, readers will gain a clear understanding of AI's transformative impact on IT infrastructure, including its role in promoting sustainability, automation, and operational excellence.

AI for IT infrastructure resource optimization

This chapter discusses how AI-powered tools help achieve cost optimization, energy efficiency, automation, data security, and performance in IT infrastructure. AI is transforming IT infrastructure management by enabling smarter automation, optimizing resources, and enhancing security.

The following figure illustrates the IT resources optimization process:

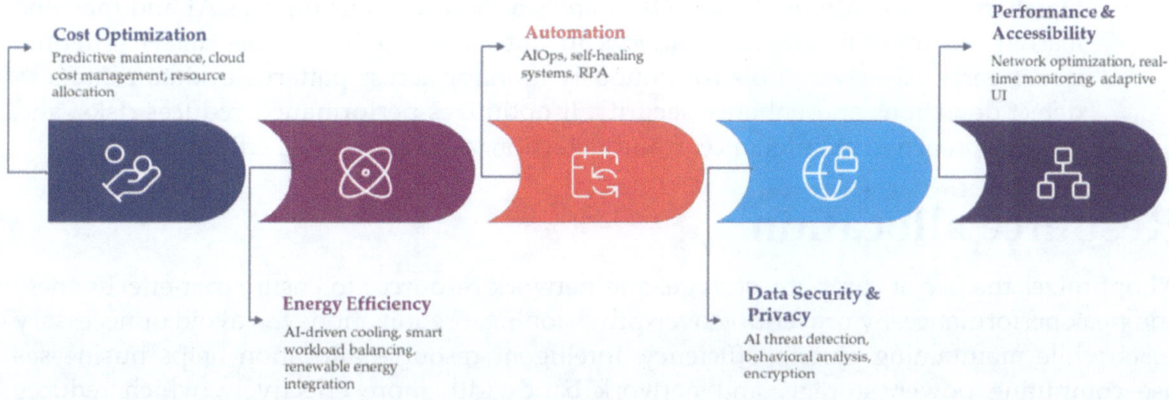

Figure 7.1: IT resources optimization process

Here is a breakdown of how AI-powered tools contribute to various key aspects.

Cost optimization

Cost optimization reduces expenses while improving efficiency, quality, and performance. It involves identifying wasteful spending and streamlining operations. Businesses also use automation and adopt cost-effective technologies. By analyzing data and applying lean methods, they eliminate inefficiencies. This helps prioritize essential investments and maximize value. Cost optimization is an ongoing process. It ensures financial sustainability, competitiveness, and growth. AI further enhances cost optimization. It improves resource allocation, enables predictive maintenance, and reduces both operational and capital expenditures.

Predictive maintenance

Predictive maintenance uses data analytics, sensors, and AI to anticipate equipment failures before they happen. AI predicts hardware issues and schedules maintenance ahead of time, reducing downtime and repair costs. Analyzing patterns and real-time data helps businesses lower expenses, extend asset life, and improve efficiency. It also enhances safety and ensures that equipment runs smoothly and reliably.

Some predictive maintenance tools are:

- **SAP predictive maintenance and service**: SAP predictive maintenance and service is a cloud-based solution that uses IoT, AI, and analytics to predict equipment failures and optimize maintenance schedules. It uses machine learning to estimate the remaining useful life of IT equipment, enabling proactive maintenance. This helps businesses cut downtime, reduce costs, and increase asset longevity. Leveraging real-time data enhances operational efficiency, improves service quality, and ensures proactive maintenance strategies.

- **Databank's anomaly detection**: Databank's anomaly detection uses AI and machine learning to identify unusual patterns in data, helping businesses detect potential issues early. AI-driven tools continuously monitor access patterns in data centers to detect deviations and enhance security. It optimizes performance, reduces risks, and ensures proactive maintenance, fraud detection, and operational efficiency.

Resource allocation

AI optimizes the use of compute, storage, and network resources to ensure cost-effectiveness and peak performance. By preventing over-provisioning, organizations can avoid unnecessary costs while maintaining system efficiency. Intelligent resource allocation helps businesses use computing power, storage, and network bandwidth more effectively, which reduces operational expenses. AI-driven automation further streamlines resource management, ensuring a balanced infrastructure without overspending.

Some resource allocation tools are:

- **Juniper Networks AI data center solution**: One example of an AI-driven tool is Juniper Networks' AI data center solution. This solution provides high-capacity, lossless networking designed for AI training. It optimizes data flow, ensuring smooth communication between AI workloads while preventing congestion and packet loss. With intelligent automation and scalable architecture, it boosts performance, efficiency, and reliability, allowing organizations to handle demanding AI applications with ease. This solution reduces latency and maximizes throughput, enabling faster model training and better operational efficiency in AI environments.

- **Arista AI networking solutions**: These are specifically designed to support AI workloads. They offer high-performance, low-latency networking, optimizing data flow and enhancing scalability. These solutions ensure efficient connectivity for advanced AI applications and training by intelligently managing network traffic. With their robust architecture, they enable seamless communication between AI systems, helping to reduce bottlenecks and improve overall system performance, making them ideal for data-heavy AI environments.

- **NVIDIA Blackwell Ultra AI chips**: These chips are designed to boost AI workload efficiency in data centers. They provide superior performance and optimized power usage. These chips enable faster processing, improving model training speed. They also support seamless scalability and enhance computational power for advanced AI applications.

- **Micron and Seagate AI storage solutions**: These are designed for high-performance AI workloads. They ensure fast data access, efficient storage management, and seamless scalability. These solutions improve AI processing by optimizing data throughput, reliability, and capacity. This makes them ideal for demanding AI-driven applications.

Cloud cost management

AI-powered tools like AWS Cost Explorer, Azure Cost Management, and Google Cloud Recommender help manage cloud spending. They analyze cloud usage and find areas of waste. These tools offer suggestions to lower costs and improve how resources are used. This helps businesses avoid overspending and make better use of their cloud services.

Some cloud cost management tools are:

- **AWS Cost Explorer**: It helps businesses understand their AWS usage and spending. It shows detailed cost trends over time. The tool allows users to set custom time ranges, view usage by service, and filter by account. It also provides cost forecasts to support better budgeting. With these insights, businesses can plan ahead and manage cloud resources more efficiently.

- **Azure Cost Management**: It helps businesses track cloud spending in real-time. It sends budget alerts and offers cost-saving suggestions. The tool identifies waste and improves how resources are used. This helps organizations control expenses and increase cost efficiency.

- **Google Cloud Recommender**: It is an AI-powered tool that reviews how cloud resources are used. It suggests actions like resizing virtual machines and removing unused resources. These recommendations help businesses lower cloud costs and use their resources more effectively.

- **CloudHealth by VMware**: A multi-cloud management platform that provides deep cost analytics, governance policies, and automated optimization insights. It helps organizations track cloud spending, enforce budget controls, and improve overall financial management of cloud resources.

- **Apptio Cloudability**: This tool delivers real-time cost monitoring, forecasting, and rightsizing recommendations across multiple cloud platforms. It helps businesses allocate resources efficiently, optimize spending, and ensure cost-effective cloud operations with detailed financial insights.

AI-powered cooling systems

AI-powered cooling systems optimize energy use by adjusting power based on real-time conditions. These systems help maintain the right temperature at all times. They improve energy efficiency and lower electricity bills. They also reduce environmental impact and cut operating costs. This ensures reliable performance in data centers and industrial settings.

The key components are as follows:

- **Sensors and IoT devices**: Monitor environmental conditions.

- **AI algorithms**: Detect cooling inefficiencies such as overcooling and sudden energy spikes. They adjust system settings to reduce waste. This helps save energy and maintain stable temperatures.
- **Automated cooling adjustments**: Dynamically control fans, **heating, ventilation, and air conditioning** (HVAC), and liquid cooling.

For example, in 2016, Google used DeepMind AI to improve data center cooling. The AI system reduced cooling costs by 40%. This showed how AI can significantly lower energy use in large facilities.

Energy efficiency

AI enhances energy efficiency by intelligently optimizing power consumption across IT infrastructures. Google's DeepMind AI adjusts cooling resources based on real-time data. This reduces energy waste and cuts operational costs. At the same time, it keeps the data center running efficiently. In one case, it helped Google lower cooling energy use by 40%, supporting sustainable and eco-friendly operations.

Smart load balancing

AI-driven smart load balancing intelligently distributes workloads evenly across multiple systems to ensure efficient performance. By preventing any single system from becoming overloaded or underused, it helps maintain stability and reliability in operations. This approach minimizes energy waste, reduces downtime, and enhances the overall efficiency of computing environments. In data centers and cloud platforms, such AI-based management ensures that power and resources are utilized more effectively and sustainably. As a result, organizations can achieve improved performance, lower operational costs, and reduced environmental impact. The key features of AI-driven smart load balancing are as follows:

- **Vertiv's AI load management**: It is designed to handle high-power AI workloads efficiently. It intelligently manages energy distribution across systems to ensure optimal performance and protect sensitive liquid cooling systems. By preventing overheating and balancing power usage, it helps maintain stable and reliable operation in data centers.

  This technology enhances cooling efficiency, reduces energy waste, and supports continuous performance even under heavy computational loads. Vertiv's solution is especially useful in AI-driven data centers and high-performance computing environments, where maintaining energy efficiency, reliability, and system safety is essential for achieving consistent and sustainable performance.
- **Enhance energy efficiency and reduce costs**: It optimizes power usage by analyzing data and predicting performance. Enhancing energy efficiency and reducing costs are key goals in modern AI-driven and industrial systems. By using intelligent data

analysis and performance prediction, power usage can be optimized to achieve maximum efficiency. Advanced AI algorithms continuously monitor system performance, workload patterns, and energy consumption in real-time. Based on this data, the system automatically adjusts power distribution to ensure that energy is used only where and when it is needed.

This smart optimization process helps prevent unnecessary energy waste, lowers electricity costs, and improves the overall sustainability of operations. It also reduces the strain on hardware, leading to longer equipment life and fewer maintenance requirements. In industrial environments and AI-based applications, such optimization ensures that machines and servers run at their best performance levels without consuming excessive energy.

By improving energy utilization, organizations can significantly cut operational expenses and reduce their carbon footprint. This not only benefits the company financially but also contributes to environmental conservation. Overall, optimizing power usage through data-driven analysis and predictive performance modeling enhances both efficiency and sustainability, making it an essential strategy for industries and data centers aiming for smarter, greener, and more cost-effective operations.

AI-optimized cooling systems

AI-based thermal management systems use intelligent prediction to identify temperature patterns and automatically adjust HVAC settings in real-time. By analyzing data from sensors and environmental conditions, the AI optimizes cooling and airflow to maintain ideal temperatures for equipment operation. This real-time adjustment helps reduce unnecessary energy consumption, prevent overheating, and extend the lifespan of hardware components. As a result, organizations can significantly lower their operational costs while improving system reliability and energy efficiency. In data centers and industrial environments, such AI-driven systems play a crucial role in maintaining stable performance and ensuring continuous operation under varying workloads. Moreover, they contribute to sustainability by minimizing energy waste and reducing the overall carbon footprint. These intelligent solutions not only improve performance but also support eco-friendly and cost-effective infrastructure management. The key features of AI-based thermal management systems are as follows:

- **Siemens AI cooling optimization**: It uses an advanced network of smart sensors to continuously monitor cooling systems in real-time. These sensors collect temperature and load data from various points within data centers or industrial facilities. Using AI-driven analysis, the system automatically adjusts cooling levels based on current conditions, ensuring that energy is used efficiently without overcooling or wasting resources. This intelligent control helps maintain consistent temperature levels, preventing equipment overheating while minimizing energy consumption.

  As a result, operational costs are significantly reduced, and overall system performance is improved. Siemens' AI-based cooling solution not only enhances energy efficiency but also promotes sustainable operations by cutting down on unnecessary power usage. Its ability to dynamically respond to changing workloads and environmental conditions ensures stable, reliable, and eco-friendly temperature management in modern industrial and data center environments, supporting both performance and cost optimization goals.

- **EkkoSense AI software**: It is an advanced solution designed to provide real-time monitoring and intelligent insights for data centers. It continuously analyzes temperature, power usage, and airflow across the facility to detect potential thermal and power-related risks before they can affect operations. By using AI-driven analytics, the system helps operators understand exactly where inefficiencies exist and recommends corrective actions to maintain optimal environmental conditions.

  The software dynamically optimizes cooling and energy distribution, ensuring that power is used only where it is needed. This reduces energy waste, lowers operational costs, and minimizes the strain on cooling systems and IT equipment. As a result, data centers can achieve higher efficiency and sustainability while maintaining consistent performance levels.

  EkkoSense also improves reliability by preventing overheating and ensuring stable thermal conditions, which are critical for the smooth functioning of IT infrastructure. By offering actionable insights and predictive maintenance capabilities, it helps operators make smarter, data-driven decisions. Overall, EkkoSense AI software supports energy-efficient, cost-effective, and reliable operations in data centers, helping organizations reduce their carbon footprint and enhance system performance without compromising safety or uptime.

Renewable energy integration

AI plays a vital role in modern energy management by enabling the seamless integration of renewable energy sources such as solar, wind, and hydro power. Through advanced data analytics, AI can accurately forecast power demand by analyzing real-time data, historical usage patterns, and environmental factors. This predictive capability allows energy systems to adjust generation and distribution efficiently, ensuring that the right amount of power is produced and utilized at the right time.

By intelligently balancing supply and demand, AI helps optimize the use of renewable energy resources, reducing the need for conventional fossil fuels. This not only minimizes energy waste but also significantly cuts down operational costs for industries and utilities. The system ensures consistent energy availability even when renewable sources fluctuate due to weather or time of day.

Incorporating AI into renewable energy management enhances sustainability and supports a greener energy future. It enables better decision-making, promotes energy efficiency, and reduces the overall carbon footprint. As a result, organizations can achieve both economic and environmental benefits by transitioning toward cleaner, smarter, and more resilient energy systems.

The key features of AI-driven renewable energy integration are as follows:

- **Cadence's reality DC insight platform**: It is an advanced AI-powered solution designed to enhance energy efficiency and performance in data centers. It uses AI to continuously monitor and optimize power usage, ensuring that every component operates at peak efficiency. The platform collects and analyzes data from various sensors, power meters, and cooling systems, offering real-time visibility into the overall energy performance of the facility.

  One of the platform's main strengths is its ability to track critical metrics such as **Power Usage Effectiveness** (**PUE**), cooling efficiency, and equipment load. By monitoring these parameters, the system helps identify inefficiencies or abnormal behavior that could lead to performance issues or energy waste. When irregularities or potential faults are detected, the AI system alerts operators, enabling them to take timely corrective actions before problems escalate into costly downtime.

  In addition to improving reliability, the platform helps organizations reduce energy consumption and operational costs. By optimizing cooling systems, balancing equipment loads, and enhancing power distribution, it supports a more sustainable and environmentally friendly approach to data center management.

  Overall, Cadence's Reality DC Insight platform ensures stable, efficient, and eco-conscious data center operations. It empowers IT and facility teams with actionable insights, making it easier to maintain reliability, lower costs, and achieve long-term sustainability goals through intelligent, data-driven decision-making.

- **NVIDIA and Schneider Electric digital twin**: It is an advanced AI-driven virtual modeling technology designed to enhance power efficiency and sustainability in data centers and industrial operations. A digital twin is a virtual replica of a physical system that continuously mirrors real-world performance through data collected from sensors and connected devices. By using AI and simulation techniques, this technology allows organizations to visualize, analyze, and optimize their energy usage in real-time.

  The digital twin simulates various operational scenarios to predict how systems will behave under different conditions. This helps engineers and operators identify inefficiencies, potential energy waste, and areas where performance can be improved without interrupting actual operations. Through these simulations, companies can test energy-saving strategies and implement the most effective ones in the real environment.

  By integrating NVIDIA's high-performance AI computing with Schneider Electric's expertise in energy management, the platform provides accurate insights into power distribution, cooling efficiency, and equipment performance. It reduces operational costs by minimizing energy wastage while maintaining reliable and stable system performance.

Overall, the NVIDIA and Schneider Electric digital twin supports smarter, greener, and more resilient infrastructure. It empowers organizations to achieve greater energy efficiency, optimize operations, and contribute to sustainability goals by combining real-time data, predictive analytics, and intelligent automation.

AI-powered UPS management

AI-powered **Uninterruptible Power Supply** (**UPS**) management systems are designed to optimize battery performance and improve overall power reliability in critical infrastructure. By using AI, these systems intelligently monitor power demand and battery status in real-time. This allows them to distribute energy efficiently and ensure that backup power is available exactly when needed.

The AI continuously analyzes usage patterns to prevent unnecessary energy waste and overcharging, which helps extend the battery's lifespan. As a result, maintenance requirements are reduced, and the system remains more cost-effective over time.

By enhancing battery efficiency and optimizing energy flow, AI-powered UPS management contributes to smoother operations during power interruptions. It not only improves reliability but also promotes sustainability by minimizing energy loss and reducing operational costs.

The following list outlines the key features and benefits that make AI-powered UPS management an essential part of modern infrastructure systems:

- **Eaton's Intelligent Power Manager (IPM)**: It is an advanced software solution that uses artificial intelligence to optimize the performance of UPS systems. It is designed to ensure efficient battery usage and maintain reliable power delivery across data centers and industrial environments. By combining real-time monitoring with AI-driven analytics, the software provides deep insights into power usage, system health, and energy distribution.

  The IPM software continuously collects data from connected power devices and analyzes it to predict potential issues before they occur. Through predictive analytics, it can anticipate power fluctuations or battery degradation, allowing operators to take timely preventive actions. The system also includes automated response features that help maintain uninterrupted operations during power disturbances or failures, reducing downtime and ensuring business continuity.

  Beyond reliability, Eaton's IPM enhances energy efficiency by intelligently managing power loads and optimizing battery performance. This leads to lower operational costs and reduced energy waste, supporting sustainability goals. In essence, the intelligent power manager enables smarter, safer, and more efficient energy management, making it an essential tool for organizations that depend on continuous power availability and optimal system performance.

- **Schneider Electric's EcoStruxure IT**: It is an advanced, AI-driven platform designed to optimize power management and ensure reliable performance in critical infrastructures. The system intelligently manages UPS systems by using real-time data and predictive analytics to enhance battery performance and prevent potential power disruptions. By continuously monitoring the health and performance of connected devices, EcoStruxure IT ensures stable and uninterrupted power delivery even in demanding environments.

  One of the platform's key strengths is its ability to enable remote monitoring and management. Operators can access detailed system information from anywhere, allowing for quick responses to potential issues and better operational control. The platform's AI capabilities also support predictive maintenance by identifying signs of wear or malfunction before they lead to failures, thereby minimizing downtime and maintenance costs.

  In addition to reliability, EcoStruxure IT promotes energy efficiency by optimizing power usage across all connected systems. This not only reduces operational expenses but also contributes to sustainability by minimizing energy waste. Overall, Schneider Electric's EcoStruxure IT provides a smart, secure, and efficient solution for managing critical power infrastructure, ensuring improved reliability, reduced costs, and a greener, more sustainable operation.

- **Vertiv's Liebert Trinergy Cube**: It Vertiv's Liebert Trinergy Cube is an advanced AI-powered UPS system designed to deliver efficient and reliable power management for data centers and enterprise environments. It uses AI to intelligently control and distribute power, ensuring that energy is used efficiently and evenly across systems. Maintaining balanced power loads helps prevent energy waste and supports optimal system performance under varying operational conditions.

  The Trinergy Cube continuously collects and analyzes real-time data from connected equipment. Its built-in analytics provide predictive maintenance capabilities, allowing the system to detect potential issues before they cause failures or downtime. This proactive approach helps maintain operational stability while reducing maintenance costs and improving system reliability.

  Another key advantage of Vertiv's Liebert Trinergy Cube is its focus on battery optimization. By monitoring battery health and usage patterns, it ensures proper energy allocation, extends battery lifespan, and reduces the likelihood of unexpected power losses.

Overall, the Liebert Trinergy Cube enhances power efficiency, reliability, and sustainability in critical infrastructure. With its AI-driven intelligence and adaptive performance, it enables modern data centers and enterprises to achieve consistent uptime, reduced energy consumption, and long-term operational efficiency.

Table 7.1 presents a comprehensive overview of various AI-powered technologies that are transforming modern energy management systems. Each of these solutions leverages AI to enhance efficiency, reliability, and sustainability in data centers, industrial environments, and energy infrastructures. From balancing workloads to optimizing cooling, integrating renewable energy, and managing UPS systems, these technologies play a crucial role in achieving smarter and greener operations. The comparison highlights their purpose, working mechanisms, benefits, and application areas, providing a clear understanding of how AI contributes to energy optimization and sustainability goals:

Technology	Purpose	How it works (AI functionality)	Key benefits	Application areas
Smart Load Balancing	To evenly distribute workloads and optimize energy usage across systems.	Uses AI algorithms to analyze real-time system loads and automatically balance workloads between servers or devices.	Prevents overloads and underuse, reduces energy waste, enhances performance, and improves sustainability.	Data centers, cloud platforms, and large-scale IT infrastructures.
AI-Optimized Cooling Systems	To maintain ideal thermal conditions and reduce cooling energy consumption.	Uses AI to predict thermal patterns, adjust HVAC settings in real-time, and optimize airflow.	Reduces energy use, prevents overheating, lowers operational costs, and increases equipment lifespan.	Data centers, industrial environments, and high-performance computing setups.
Renewable Energy Integration	To maximize the use of renewable power and minimize fossil fuel dependence.	Uses AI to forecast power demand, analyze consumption trends, and balance energy from renewable sources.	Enhances sustainability, lowers energy costs, and reduces carbon footprint.	Smart grids, renewable energy plants, and sustainable industrial systems.
AI-Powered UPS Management	To ensure reliable power backup and optimize battery performance.	Uses AI to monitor battery health, predict failures, and distribute energy intelligently during power fluctuations.	Improves reliability, extends battery life, reduces downtime, and minimizes energy waste.	Data centers, critical infrastructures, and industrial power systems.

Table 7.1: Overview of AI-powered energy optimization technologies

Automation and minimal human involvement

AI-powered automation plays a major role in simplifying and improving various business operations. By using advanced algorithms and data-driven systems, AI can manage repetitive and time-consuming tasks that earlier required constant human supervision. This allows organizations to work more efficiently while saving both time and effort. Automation ensures that processes run smoothly and consistently, leading to fewer mistakes and improved accuracy across different departments.

In the supply chain sector, for example, AI helps in predicting product demand, maintaining the right inventory levels, and managing transportation routes effectively. These systems can analyze large amounts of data in real-time to forecast future needs and optimize delivery schedules. As a result, goods move faster through the supply chain, customers receive their products on time, and companies can reduce waste and operational costs.

Overall, AI-based automation reduces the need for manual intervention and allows employees to concentrate on higher-level strategic tasks, such as planning and innovation. It also ensures that businesses remain competitive in a fast-changing market. With enhanced efficiency, cost-effectiveness, and reliability, AI-driven automation is transforming how organizations operate, making their processes smarter, faster, and more adaptable to future challenges.

AI-driven IT operations

It uses AI and ML to improve and automate various tasks within IT systems. Instead of relying only on human monitoring and manual troubleshooting, AIOps platforms analyze vast amounts of data from multiple sources to identify, predict, and solve issues automatically. This helps organizations manage complex IT infrastructures more efficiently and with greater accuracy.

Popular AIOps tools such as *Dynatrace*, *Moogsoft*, and *Splunk AI* are designed to continuously monitor system performance and detect irregularities in real-time. When a problem arises, these tools can immediately alert the IT team or even take automatic corrective actions to resolve the issue. This proactive approach reduces system downtime, sometimes by as much as 40%, and ensures that services remain stable and reliable for users.

Beyond problem-solving, AIOps also provides valuable insights into system performance and resource utilization. By learning from historical data, it can forecast potential failures and recommend preventive measures. As a result, IT teams can focus more on innovation and strategic planning rather than routine maintenance. Overall, AIOps enhances the speed, reliability, and efficiency of modern IT operations, making them more intelligent and adaptive to changing business needs.

Self-healing systems

Self-healing systems represent one of the most powerful applications of AI in IT infrastructure management. These systems are designed to automatically detect, diagnose, and fix issues without waiting for human intervention. Using AI and ML, they continuously monitor the performance of servers, applications, and networks to identify irregular patterns or potential faults before they escalate into serious problems. This proactive monitoring ensures that any disruption is handled quickly, often before users even notice that an issue occurred.

The concept of self-healing revolves around automation and intelligence working together. When AI identifies an anomaly, it analyzes the root cause and applies corrective actions immediately, such as restarting services, reallocating resources, or patching affected components. Unlike traditional systems that rely on manual troubleshooting, self-healing systems act independently and in real-time. This greatly reduces downtime, minimizes errors, and ensures smoother operations across all IT environments.

Moreover, self-healing systems improve overall reliability, resilience, and efficiency in organizations. They help IT teams focus on strategic initiatives instead of spending time fixing repetitive issues. Over time, these systems also learn from past incidents, improving their ability to predict and prevent future failures. As a result, businesses experience higher uptime, better performance, and reduced maintenance costs. In essence, AI-driven self-healing systems create a more stable, intelligent, and self-managing IT ecosystem that keeps operations running seamlessly with minimal human effort.

Chatbots and virtual assistants

AI-powered chatbots and virtual assistants are transforming the way organizations handle IT support and customer service. Tools such as *IBM Watson* and *Microsoft Copilot* use AI to understand user queries, provide instant responses, and perform tasks that would otherwise require human assistance. These smart assistants can diagnose common IT issues, offer real-time troubleshooting steps, and even execute automated fixes, making the entire support process faster and more efficient.

By managing routine queries and repetitive tasks, chatbots significantly *reduce the manual workload* on IT teams. This allows professionals to focus on more complex or strategic issues that require deeper analysis. The use of AI ensures quick response times and accurate solutions, improving overall user satisfaction and minimizing downtime in daily operations.

Furthermore, virtual assistants continuously learn from past interactions, enabling them to become smarter and more efficient over time. They can integrate with various IT management systems to provide personalized support, system alerts, and performance updates. As a result, organizations benefit from enhanced productivity, smoother workflows, and improved service quality. In short, AI-driven chatbots and virtual assistants not only streamline IT operations but also create a more responsive and user-friendly support environment.

AI-enabled RPA

AI-enabled RPA combines the power of AI with automation tools to simplify and speed up everyday business and IT operations. It is designed to handle repetitive, rule-based tasks that usually take a lot of time and effort when done manually. By automating these processes, AI-enabled RPA reduces human error, improves accuracy, and ensures tasks are completed much faster and more efficiently.

In IT service management, AI-enabled RPA can perform various operations such as ticket categorization, data entry, and report generation without human assistance. This not only saves time but also allows IT professionals to focus on more complex and strategic activities. For instance, in customer service departments, RPA bots can automatically respond to common queries, assign tickets to the right teams, and even generate replies. This can reduce the average handling time by up to 60%, significantly improving overall service quality and customer satisfaction.

Moreover, by streamlining workflows and ensuring consistency, AI-enabled RPA enhances both business productivity and technology management. It creates a more reliable, scalable, and efficient working environment, helping organizations deliver faster results with fewer resources. Ultimately, it enables businesses to operate smarter and more effectively in a highly digital world.

Data security and privacy

AI plays a vital role in strengthening data security and protecting user privacy. It continuously monitors networks and systems to identify unusual patterns or suspicious activities that might indicate a potential threat. By doing this in real-time, AI can detect and stop cyberattacks before they cause harm.

AI systems also help organizations find and fix vulnerabilities that could be exploited by hackers. Through machine learning, they analyze large volumes of data to predict possible security risks and recommend preventive actions.

Additionally, AI ensures compliance with data protection laws and industry regulations, reducing the chances of data breaches or misuse. By safeguarding sensitive information and maintaining user trust, AI not only improves cybersecurity but also supports a safer and more reliable digital environment for both organizations and their customers.

AI-powered threat detection

AI-powered threat detection systems play a crucial role in modern cybersecurity by monitoring and analyzing network activity in real-time. Tools like *Darktrace*, *CrowdStrike*, and *IBM Security QRadar* use AI and ML to detect potential cyber threats quickly and accurately.

For example, IBM Security QRadar gathers and analyzes massive amounts of security data from across an organization's network. It uses advanced analytics to identify unusual behavior, highlight high-risk incidents, and reduce false alarms that often waste time and resources.

By continuously learning from past data and global threat intelligence, QRadar can recognize new attack patterns and predict possible security breaches. This proactive approach allows security teams to respond faster and more efficiently, often stopping cyber threats before they cause major damage. In this way, AI enhances both the speed and reliability of threat detection in today's digital environment.

Behavioral analysis

Behavioral analysis uses AI to monitor and understand how users normally interact with systems and networks. By applying techniques like **User Behavior Analytics** (**UBA**) and *anomaly detection*, AI establishes a baseline of regular user activity. When any action deviates from this normal pattern, such as unusual login times or unexpected data transfers, the system flags it for further investigation.

These AI-driven methods help organizations quickly identify insider threats, data breaches, or unauthorized access attempts that might otherwise go unnoticed. For instance, *Capital One* implemented AI-based UBA to track employee access behaviors and detect irregular data movements. This proactive monitoring helped the company prevent potential data leaks and strengthen its overall cybersecurity measures.

By continuously learning from user behavior, AI-powered behavioral analysis provides early warning signs of security risks, enhancing both data protection and trust within digital environments.

Automated compliance monitoring

AI-powered automated compliance monitoring helps organizations follow legal and regulatory standards with greater accuracy and efficiency. It continuously scans and analyzes data across systems to detect any activities that may violate compliance rules or security policies. By doing this in real-time, AI ensures that potential issues are identified and addressed before they lead to serious consequences.

This technology supports adherence to important regulations such as GDPR and HIPAA, which govern data privacy and security. Through automation, it reduces the need for manual audits, lowers the chances of human error, and saves valuable time for compliance teams.

By proactively monitoring operations and enforcing policies, AI-driven compliance systems help businesses minimize risks, avoid penalties, and maintain trust with customers. Overall, automated compliance monitoring strengthens both data protection and organizational accountability in an increasingly regulated digital world.

AI-powered encryption

AI-powered encryption is an advanced method of protecting sensitive information by using artificial intelligence to automate and strengthen the encryption process. Traditional encryption techniques rely on predefined algorithms, but AI takes this a step further by continuously learning and adapting to new types of cyber threats. This ensures that data remains secure, even as attackers develop more sophisticated methods to breach systems.

By automating encryption, AI helps organizations safeguard their data without the need for constant manual intervention. It can detect potential vulnerabilities, automatically apply stronger encryption methods, and manage encryption keys more securely. This not only enhances data protection but also ensures compliance with global security standards and privacy regulations.

A great example of this technology in action is **Darktrace**, whose AI systems autonomously detect and prevent **ransomware attacks** in real-time. By combining encryption with intelligent threat detection, AI ensures that unauthorized users cannot access or alter sensitive data. Ultimately, AI-powered encryption creates a smarter, more adaptive layer of defense that helps businesses maintain trust, privacy, and security in an ever-evolving digital landscape.

AI plays a transformative role in enhancing cybersecurity across various domains. It not only helps organizations detect and respond to threats in real-time but also ensures data privacy, compliance, and overall system resilience. The following table summarizes key AI-driven cybersecurity applications and their functions as discussed:

AI application	Description	Example/Key benefit
AI-powered threat detection	Uses AI and machine learning to monitor network activity, detect unusual patterns, and identify potential cyber threats in real-time.	Tools like IBM Security QRadar, Darktrace, and CrowdStrike help detect and respond to attacks before they cause serious damage.
Behavioral analysis	Analyzes user activity through UBA and anomaly detection to identify insider threats or unauthorized access.	Capital One uses AI-driven UBA to monitor employee behavior and prevent data leaks.
Automated compliance monitoring	Continuously checks for policy violations and ensures adherence to regulations like GDPR and HIPAA using automated AI systems.	Reduces audit workload, minimizes human error, and ensures ongoing regulatory compliance.
AI-powered encryption	Automates encryption processes to protect sensitive data and adapts to new cyber threats to strengthen security.	Darktrace AI autonomously prevents ransomware attacks and enhances data privacy.

***Table 7.2:** Key AI applications in cybersecurity*

Performance and accessibility enhancement

AI plays a vital role in improving both the performance and accessibility of IT systems. By continuously monitoring hardware, software, and network operations, AI can quickly detect and resolve potential issues before they affect users. This proactive monitoring helps maintain system stability and ensures that applications and services run smoothly without unexpected interruptions.

AI-driven tools use real-time data analysis to identify performance bottlenecks, optimize resource allocation, and predict possible failures. As a result, downtime is significantly reduced, allowing organizations to operate more efficiently and reliably. This not only saves time and costs but also enhances user trust in digital platforms.

In addition to performance optimization, AI enhances *accessibility* by ensuring that users experience consistent and seamless interactions across multiple devices and networks. Whether it is a mobile app, website, or enterprise system, AI adjusts settings automatically to provide the best possible experience for all users.

Overall, AI's ability to combine intelligent monitoring with real-time problem-solving leads to higher operational efficiency, improved system reliability, and a more engaging user experience. This makes AI an essential technology for maintaining smooth, accessible, and high-performing IT environments.

AI-powered network optimization

AI dynamically adjusts bandwidth to ensure efficient data flow by using techniques such as reinforcement learning or adaptive **quality of service** (**QoS**) models. These AI models analyze network traffic in real-time and make adjustments based on traffic patterns, prioritizing critical data and reducing latency. By continuously optimizing network performance, this approach improves connectivity, enhances overall system efficiency, and ensures a seamless user experience across various digital platforms. Let us go over the following:

Arista AI networking solutions are designed to optimize network performance for AI workloads by leveraging techniques like parallelism and GPU data sharding. These solutions manage data flow efficiently, ensuring low-latency communication between AI processors and storage systems. By distributing data across multiple GPUs and parallel processing units, they enhance connectivity, reduce bottlenecks, and ensure seamless scalability for high-performance computing environments, such as AI model training and large-scale data processing.

Intelligent storage management

AI has revolutionized how organizations handle data through *intelligent storage management*. Instead of relying on manual data organization, AI automates the entire process from storing and categorizing data to retrieving it when needed. By analyzing usage patterns and access frequency, AI determines where and how data should be stored for the best performance and efficiency.

One of the key benefits of AI-driven storage management is its ability to *optimize data retrieval and tiering*. Frequently used data is stored in faster, high-performance storage systems, while less critical data is automatically moved to cost-effective storage tiers. This ensures that resources are utilized efficiently without compromising speed or reliability.

Moreover, intelligent storage management supports *scalability* by adapting to growing data volumes in real-time. As business needs evolve, AI dynamically allocates storage resources to maintain performance and prevent bottlenecks. This automation not only reduces operational costs but also minimizes human errors and improves overall data accessibility.

In essence, AI-powered storage systems make data management smarter, faster, and more flexible, providing modern IT infrastructures with the reliability and efficiency they need to support digital growth.

AI-driven accessibility tools

AI-driven accessibility tools are designed to make technology more inclusive and user-friendly for everyone, including individuals with disabilities. These tools use advanced technologies such as speech-to-text and NLP to enable voice recognition and hands-free navigation. This allows users to interact with devices and applications easily, even without using traditional input methods like keyboards or touchscreens.

Additionally, computer vision and adaptive AI algorithms help interfaces automatically adjust to a user's specific needs in real-time. For example, screen brightness, font size, or layout can be modified based on user preferences or behavior.

Over time, these AI models continuously learn from user interactions, improving accuracy and personalization. By enhancing digital accessibility, AI empowers individuals with greater independence and convenience, ensuring equal access to information and technology across different platforms and devices.

Real-time monitoring and performance tuning

AI continuously monitors workloads to detect inefficiencies and optimize performance. It dynamically adjusts resources in real-time, ensuring smooth operations and minimal downtime. This proactive approach enhances system efficiency, reduces latency, and improves overall productivity in IT environments. Refer to the following table:

Aspect	How AI helps	Key benefits
Cost optimization	Predictive maintenance, cloud cost management, and resource allocation.	Reduced operational costs and optimal resource use.
Energy efficiency	AI-driven cooling, smart workload balancing, and renewable energy integration.	Lower power consumption, reduced carbon footprint.
Automation	AIOps, self-healing systems, RPA.	Fewer manual errors, improved efficiency.
Data security and privacy	AI threat detection, behavioral analysis, and encryption.	Prevents cyber threats, ensures compliance.
Performance and accessibility	Network optimization, real-time monitoring, adaptive UI.	Faster processing, better user experience.

***Table 7.3:** AI-powered IT resources optimization benefits*

Conclusion

In this chapter, we discussed how AI is transforming IT infrastructure by enhancing efficiency, reducing costs, and strengthening security. Through AI-driven automation, predictive analytics, and intelligent resource management, businesses can optimize operations, improve energy efficiency, and bolster cybersecurity. AI also plays a critical role in workload distribution, performance monitoring, and improving digital accessibility through technologies like speech recognition and adaptive interfaces. As IT environments evolve, integrating AI will be key to maintaining competitive advantage, sustainability, and reliability. Embracing AI-driven infrastructure will lead to significant gains in operational effectiveness and long-term scalability.

In the next chapter, we are going to learn about AI and workload plus infrastructure optimization.

Multiple choice questions

1. **What is one of the primary ways AI helps with cost optimization?**
    a. Increasing manual troubleshooting
    b. Predictive maintenance to reduce downtime
    c. Ignoring cloud costs
    d. Disabling security features

2. **How does AI improve energy efficiency in data centers?**
   a. By increasing power consumption
   b. Through AI-driven cooling and smart load balancing
   c. By shutting down systems randomly
   d. Reducing the need for IT staff

3. **What is AIOps primarily used for?**
   a. Managing social media accounts
   b. Automating IT operations and issue resolution
   c. Replacing all human employees
   d. Disrupting IT workflows

4. **Which AI-powered solution helps prevent insider threats in IT security?**
   a. Behavioral analysis
   b. Disabling security logs
   c. Increasing manual monitoring
   d. Ignoring network anomalies

5. **What does AI-driven accessibility focus on?**
   a. Limiting network bandwidth
   b. Improving user experience for individuals with disabilities
   c. Reducing IT infrastructure performance
   d. Removing automated support systems

6. **How do AI-powered cooling systems optimize energy use?**
   a. By predicting heat patterns and adjusting HVAC settings
   b. By shutting down cooling systems permanently
   c. By running cooling systems at full power constantly
   d. By ignoring temperature variations

7. **Which of the following is an AI-driven tool used for threat detection?**
   a. Darktrace
   b. Excel
   c. Photoshop
   d. Notepad

8. **How does AI enhance cloud cost management?**
    a. By analyzing cloud usage and suggesting cost-saving strategies
    b. By increasing unnecessary storage allocation
    c. By recommending over-provisioning of resources
    d. By ignoring cloud resource allocation

9. **What is one key benefit of AI in IT infrastructure?**
    a. Increased power consumption
    b. Reduced operational costs and improved efficiency
    c. More manual intervention
    d. Reduced data security

10. **What role does AI play in IT performance monitoring?**
    a. Adjusts workloads dynamically to ensure efficiency
    b. Ignores real-time data
    c. Disables system logs
    d. Requires constant manual monitoring

11. **What is the purpose of AI-driven encryption in IT security?**
    a. To automatically protect sensitive data from cyber threats
    b. To make data less accessible for authorized users
    c. To slow down data processing speeds
    d. To eliminate the need for passwords

12. **How does AI assist in workload management?**
    a. By distributing workloads dynamically to balance resource usage .
    b. By assigning all workloads to a single server
    c. By ignoring real-time resource allocation needs
    d. By shutting down servers randomly

13. **Which of the following AI technologies enhances storage management?**
    a. Intelligent tiering and data retrieval automation
    b. Manual file transfers between systems
    c. Increasing redundant data storage without organization
    d. Disabling automated data sorting

14. **How does AI contribute to automation in IT operations?**
    a. By reducing manual intervention and improving efficiency
    b. By making IT processes more complex and difficult to manage
    c. By requiring constant human oversight
    d. By eliminating the need for IT personnel entirely

15. **What is a major advantage of AI-powered network optimization?**
    a. Improved bandwidth allocation and reduced latency
    b. Increased network congestion
    c. Reduced connectivity for remote users
    d. Decreased system reliability

Answers

1	b
2	b
3	b
4	a
5	b
6	a
7	a
8	a
9	b
10	a
11	a
12	a
13	a
14	a
15	a

Join our Discord space

Join our Discord workspace for latest updates, offers, tech happenings around the world, new releases, and sessions with the authors:

https://discord.bpbonline.com

CHAPTER 8
AI and Workload Infrastructure Optimization

Introduction

In today's digital world, companies are under pressure to work faster, smarter, and more efficiently. Managing large workloads and complex IT systems can be challenging and time-consuming. That is where **artificial intelligence** (**AI**) plays a key role. AI helps organizations by automating repetitive tasks, improving decision-making, and making better use of time and resources. From answering customer questions using chatbots to automatically adjusting server loads or creating smart employee schedules, AI can handle many responsibilities that were once manual.

This not only reduces the burden on employees but also boosts overall productivity and accuracy. AI is also changing how infrastructure is managed; it can predict problems before they happen, save energy, improve security, and help businesses plan for the future.

This chapter explores how AI is being used to optimize both workload and infrastructure in various industries. Real-life examples and case studies are included to show how businesses are already benefiting from AI-powered tools and systems. By understanding these applications, readers can see how AI is shaping a more efficient and intelligent future for work.

Structure

In this chapter, we will cover the following topics:

- AI's role in managing workload
- Workload distribution and optimization
- AI and infrastructure optimization
- AI challenges in infrastructure optimization
- Future trends of AI in optimization

Objectives

This chapter aims to provide a comprehensive understanding of how AI is revolutionizing workload and infrastructure optimization across various industries. One of the main objectives is to explain how AI can automate repetitive and time-consuming tasks such as data entry, scheduling, and customer service, thereby freeing up employees to focus on higher-value work. It also highlights how AI supports smarter decision-making through predictive analytics and real-time data analysis, allowing organizations to make more informed and faster business decisions. Additionally, the chapter discusses how AI helps optimize the use of both digital and human resources through techniques such as dynamic allocation, intelligent shift planning, and real-time monitoring, ultimately improving productivity and efficiency.

Another key focus of this chapter is to showcase real-world examples and case studies from companies like Netflix, Amazon, UPS, and Google, which demonstrate the practical impact of AI in managing workloads and infrastructure. The chapter also aims to help readers understand how AI enhances infrastructure operations through automated scaling, energy efficiency, predictive maintenance, and improved network performance. At the same time, it addresses the major challenges of AI adoption, including job displacement, data quality issues, integration with legacy systems, and security concerns. Finally, the chapter explores future trends such as autonomous systems, edge AI, **explainable AI** (**XAI**), AIOps, and sustainable computing. By the end of the chapter, readers will have a solid foundation in the applications, benefits, limitations, and emerging directions of AI in workload and infrastructure optimization.

AI's role in managing workload

AI is revolutionizing how organizations manage workforce efficiency, productivity, and operational balance. By integrating intelligent systems into daily workflows, businesses can reduce human error, minimize burnout, and enhance overall performance. The following are key ways AI contributes to efficient workload management:

- **Automation of repetitive tasks**: AI-driven tools, such as **Robotic Process Automation** (**RPA**) and machine learning algorithms, can handle repetitive, time-consuming tasks, freeing employees to focus on strategic and creative work. Tasks such as data entry, customer support via chatbots, and scheduling can now be efficiently managed by AI. AI not only speeds up these processes but also reduces the likelihood of human error, ensuring greater accuracy and consistency in operations. By automating routine and repetitive processes, AI enables organizations to reduce operational costs and increase employee productivity.

    - **Case study: AI-powered customer support**: Companies like Amazon and Google utilize AI-driven chatbots to handle customer inquiries, significantly reducing human workload while improving response times and efficiency. These AI chatbots are capable of learning from past interactions, allowing them to continuously improve their ability to resolve customer queries without human intervention.

This level of automation not only enhances customer satisfaction but also reduces the pressure on human support teams, allowing them to focus on more complex customer issues.

AI is playing a transformative role in optimizing workload management and IT infrastructure. As shown in *Figure 8.1*, AI contributes significantly to several critical areas, including automation of repetitive tasks, dynamic resource allocation, enhanced decision-making, and energy efficiency. These capabilities help in streamlining operations, reducing costs, and improving overall system performance. The visual representation highlights how AI-powered systems are integrated across various components to enable intelligent workload distribution and infrastructure optimization:

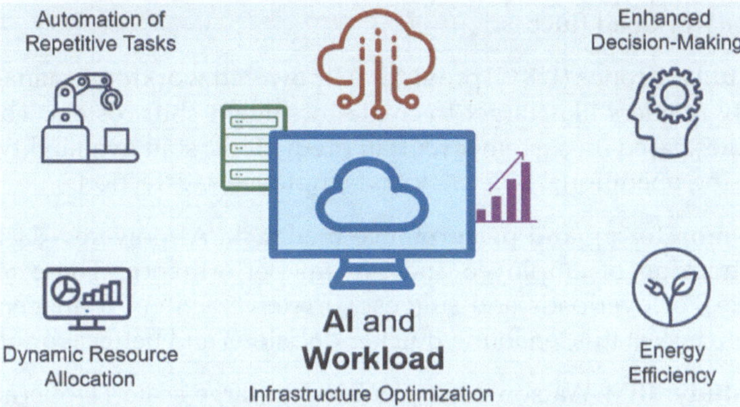

***Figure 8.1**: AI and workload infrastructure optimization*

- **Enhanced decision-making**: AI enhances decision-making by analyzing vast amounts of data quickly and accurately. Predictive analytics, pattern recognition, and recommendation systems help managers make informed choices, reducing the cognitive workload on employees. With the power of machine learning and AI-driven data analytics, businesses can make data-driven decisions with greater confidence, reducing risks and increasing overall operational efficiency.
  - **Example:** Predictive analytics in healthcare—Hospitals use AI to analyze patient data and predict disease outbreaks, reducing the workload on doctors and optimizing patient care strategies. AI-based predictive analytics tools help identify patterns in vast datasets, allowing healthcare professionals to allocate resources more effectively, streamline diagnostics, and provide more personalized treatment plans to patients.
- **Dynamic resource allocation:** AI dynamically allocates digital and human resources based on current workloads. It monitors system performance, user demand, and task urgency to adjust CPU usage, memory, bandwidth, or staff efforts in real-time. This

ensures optimal resource use, minimizes downtime, and maintains service quality without manual intervention.

- **Case study**: Netflix uses AI-driven systems to automatically scale its cloud infrastructure during sudden viewership spikes (e.g., a new season release). AI algorithms analyze server demand patterns and allocate resources accordingly, ensuring uninterrupted streaming without wasting capacity during low-demand times.

- **Intelligent scheduling and shift management**: AI optimizes employee shift schedules by balancing business needs with individual preferences, legal requirements, and workload predictions. It minimizes manual scheduling errors, ensures fair workloads, and prevents employee fatigue. AI also adjusts schedules dynamically in response to absences or workload fluctuations.
  - **Case study**: Kronos (UKG) provides AI-powered workforce management software used by retailers like Target to create intelligent shift rosters. The system adapts schedules based on customer footfall predictions, staff availability, and labor laws, increasing operational efficiency and employee satisfaction.
- **Real-time monitoring and performance feedback**: AI-powered dashboards provide real-time tracking of employee and system performance. These tools flag delays, inefficiencies, or overloads and suggest corrective actions. Managers receive instant insights into task status, enabling quicker decisions and better workload control.
  - **Case study:** IBM Watson AIOps is used in large-scale IT operations to monitor system logs and metrics. It detects anomalies in real-time, notifies teams, and even initiates self-healing actions. This reduces incident response time and prevents larger system failures.
- **AI-based task prioritization and routing**: AI analyzes tasks, their dependencies, deadlines, and available resources to prioritize and assign them intelligently. It ensures that urgent or high-value work is completed first and by the most suitable personnel or system, improving turnaround time and workload clarity.
  - **Case study**: Zendesk uses AI to route customer service tickets to the most appropriate support agent. The AI analyzes ticket urgency, keywords, language, and past agent performance to ensure faster and more accurate responses, optimizing agent workload and improving customer satisfaction.
- **Predictive workload management**: AI leverages historical and real-time data to forecast future workload patterns. This includes anticipating peak periods, resource bottlenecks, and project delays. Predictive models help organizations prepare for demand surges, schedule maintenance, and deploy the right personnel or infrastructure ahead of time. This reduces system overload, improves planning accuracy, and increases overall productivity.

- **Case study**: **United Parcel Service** (**UPS**) uses AI to predict package volumes during holiday seasons. Their AI models analyze shipping history, weather, and customer trends to proactively adjust logistics operations and workforce planning, significantly reducing late deliveries and overwork during peak periods.

Workload distribution and optimization

AI-powered systems analyze workload patterns and optimize task distribution. Smart scheduling software, AI-driven project management tools, and workload-balancing algorithms ensure that resources are utilized efficiently, preventing burnout and increasing productivity. AI-based workload distribution allows organizations to allocate resources where they are needed most, reducing inefficiencies and improving overall performance.

Case study

AI-powered workload optimization—TechNova Inc., a mid-sized software development company, faced recurring challenges with uneven workload distribution among its project teams. Some teams were overburdened with tasks and missed deadlines, while others had idle time, leading to inefficiencies, employee burnout, and missed project goals.

The challenges are as follows:

- Uneven task allocation.
- Missed deadlines and low productivity.
- Employee dissatisfaction due to overwork or underutilization.

The solution is as follows:

- TechNova implemented an *AI-driven project management tool* integrated with:
  - Smart scheduling algorithms.
  - Predictive analytics.
  - Machine learning-based workload balancing.
- The system analyzed:
  - Individual employee skills and past performance.
  - Real-time availability.
  - Task complexity and urgency.
  - Historical project timelines and workload trends.
- The implementation is as follows:
  - **Task forecasting**: AI predicted future workload spikes based on project cycles.

  - **Skill-based allocation**: Tasks were automatically assigned to team members best suited for them.
  - **Dynamic rescheduling**: If a task took longer than expected, the system adjusted deadlines and reassigned resources in real-time.
  - **Burnout prevention alerts**: The system flagged when an employee was at risk of burnout due to a high workload and suggested redistribution.

The results are as follows:

- 30% increase in on-time project deliveries.
- 20% improvement in employee satisfaction scores.
- 25% reduction in idle resources.
- More consistent workload distribution across departments.

Personalized work experiences

AI can adapt work processes to individual employee strengths and weaknesses, improving efficiency. Intelligent assistants suggest the best workflow, automate mundane tasks, and even provide real-time feedback to employees to enhance performance. By tailoring work experiences to individual capabilities, AI enables employees to maximize their productivity and job satisfaction.

Case study

Personalized workflows—FinEdge Solutions, a global financial consulting firm, employs over 2,000 professionals handling complex client portfolios and data analysis. The firm struggled with high turnover among analysts, citing repetitive tasks, low engagement, and generic workflows that did not align with individual working styles or strengths.

The challenges are as follows:

- Employees felt undervalued and overburdened with routine tasks.
- Analysts with different strengths were given similar workflows.
- No real-time performance feedback or personalized support system.

The solution is as follows:

- FinEdge integrated an *AI-driven employee experience platform* that used machine learning and intelligent assistants to:
  - Analyze individual work habits, strengths, and preferred work styles.
  - Automate repetitive tasks like report generation, client follow-ups, and data entry.
  - Offer personalized workflow suggestions and time management strategies.

    o Deliver real-time feedback and microlearning tips tailored to each employee's improvement areas.

The implementation highlights are as follows:

- **Behavioral AI models**: Tracked user behavior (e.g., time spent on tasks, peak productivity hours).
- **Intelligent virtual assistant**: Suggested optimal work schedules and flagged priority tasks.
- **Customized dashboards**: Employees received daily insights and nudges (e.g., *You are most productive between 10 and 12 AM, schedule your deep work then*).
- **Performance feedback engine**: Provided instant feedback on task quality and completion efficiency with coaching tips.

The results are as follows:

- 40% reduction in time spent on repetitive tasks.
- 25% improvement in task completion efficiency.
- Significant rise in employee engagement scores.
- Lower attrition rate among junior analysts (down by 18%).
- Improved productivity consistency across teams.

Here is a comprehensive table that outlines the key roles of AI in managing workload across various domains. The topics covered demonstrate how AI enhances operational efficiency, improves decision-making, optimizes resource allocation, and tailors work experiences to individual needs. Each entry includes a brief explanation. These roles go beyond traditional automation, showing how AI contributes strategically to workforce management and system performance. The table also highlights AI's impact on predictive analytics, real-time monitoring, and intelligent task management. Together, these insights provide a clear understanding of how AI transforms modern workload handling:

S.No.	AI application area	Description	Real-world example
1.	Automation of repetitive tasks	Handles routine jobs like data entry, emails, and chat support.	Amazon uses AI chatbots for customer service.
2.	Enhanced decision-making	Uses data analysis and pattern recognition to guide better decisions.	Hospitals use AI to predict disease outbreaks.
3.	Dynamic resource allocation	Adjusts computing or staff resources in real-time based on workload.	Netflix scales servers using AI during spikes.

4.	Intelligent scheduling	Creates employee rosters based on demand, preferences, and legal compliance.	Target uses Kronos for AI-based scheduling.
5.	Real-time monitoring and feedback	Tracks task and system performance to suggest improvements.	IBM Watson AIOps for IT operations monitoring.
6.	AI-based task prioritization	Sorts tasks based on urgency and assigns them to suitable personnel.	Zendesk routes support tickets using AI.
7.	Predictive workload management	Forecasts workload trends to prevent overload and bottlenecks.	UPS predicts package volumes using AI.
8.	Personalized work experiences	Adapts workflows to employee strengths for better engagement.	FinEdge customizes tasks based on analyst habits.

Table 8.1: *AI-related workload management*

AI and infrastructure optimization

To achieve infrastructure optimization, AI enables intelligent monitoring, automation, and decision-making across various operational domains. The following are key areas where AI significantly contributes to optimizing infrastructure:

- **Dynamic resource allocation**: AI helps allocate computing resources dynamically based on real-time demand. Cloud platforms use AI-driven scaling mechanisms to optimize server loads and minimize resource wastage. AI-powered resource allocation ensures that businesses can scale up or down based on operational needs without incurring unnecessary expenses.
    - **Example**: **AI in cloud computing**: Companies like Microsoft and AWS use AI to manage cloud resources, automatically scaling applications up or down based on demand. AI-driven cloud computing allows organizations to optimize their infrastructure costs while ensuring high availability and performance.
- **Predictive maintenance**: AI-powered predictive analytics detect potential infrastructure failures before they occur. This reduces downtime, enhances system reliability, and lowers maintenance costs by addressing issues proactively. AI-driven predictive maintenance uses sensor data and historical performance records to identify potential equipment failures before they happen.
    - **Case study**:
        - **AI in manufacturing**: Factories use AI-driven predictive maintenance to monitor machine conditions, preventing unexpected failures and reducing

repair costs. This proactive approach minimizes production downtime and enhances overall operational efficiency.

- **Network traffic management**: AI algorithms optimize network performance by analyzing traffic patterns, detecting anomalies, and managing bandwidth allocation. This ensures seamless data flow and reduces latency issues in digital workplaces. By leveraging AI-driven network optimization, businesses can prevent bottlenecks and improve network security.
- **Energy efficiency and cost reduction**: AI-driven infrastructure management helps optimize energy usage in data centers. Smart cooling systems, workload balancing, and automated power adjustments reduce energy consumption, leading to cost savings and sustainability benefits. By optimizing power consumption, businesses can reduce their environmental impact while lowering operational costs.
- **AI-driven capacity planning**: AI enables accurate infrastructure capacity planning by analyzing historical usage data, seasonal trends, and projected business demands. It helps organizations scale up or down based on forecasted needs, reducing unnecessary investments and avoiding performance bottlenecks.
    - **Case study:**
        - **Facebook (Meta)** uses AI to predict data center capacity requirements. Their AI tools analyze user growth, engagement patterns, and compute loads to plan future hardware deployments, ensuring seamless service and cost-effective expansion.
- **AI in cloud resource optimization**: AI continuously monitors cloud workloads and dynamically adjusts resource allocations to maintain performance while minimizing idle time and cost. It automates scaling decisions, rightsizing virtual machines, and selecting optimal pricing tiers.
    - **Case study**:
        - **Airbnb** implemented AI-driven optimization to manage its AWS cloud infrastructure. The AI system identifies underused instances and automatically resizes or shuts them down, reducing cloud spend without impacting performance.
- **Intelligent data center management**: AI manages cooling, power distribution, and server workloads in data centers to ensure efficient operations. It identifies inefficiencies, predicts potential failures, and automates environmental controls to reduce energy use and extend equipment life.
    - **Case study**:
        - **Google** applied DeepMind AI in its data centers, which led to a 40% reduction in cooling energy by adjusting airflow and temperature based on real-time sensor data and machine learning predictions.

            - **Airbnb** implemented AI-driven optimization to manage its AWS cloud infrastructure. The AI system identifies underused instances and automatically resizes or shuts them down, reducing cloud spend without impacting performance.

- **Anomaly detection and security monitoring**: AI systems monitor network and infrastructure activity to detect unusual behaviors or threats. By identifying anomalies in traffic, performance metrics, or system logs, AI enables faster response to faults and security breaches.
    - **Case study**:
        - **Darktrace**, an AI cybersecurity firm, uses machine learning to monitor enterprise networks in real-time. One of their clients detected a ransomware attack within minutes using AI anomaly detection, preventing major data loss.
- **AI-based IT asset lifecycle management**: AI assists in managing the entire lifecycle of IT assets, from acquisition to decommissioning. It forecasts upgrade schedules, predicts hardware failures, and recommends optimal procurement strategies, improving ROI and reducing downtime.
    - **Case study**:
        - **Dell Technologies** uses AI in its ProSupport suite to monitor hardware health and suggest proactive maintenance or replacement. This reduces unplanned downtime and improves customer satisfaction.
- **AI-enhanced disaster recovery planning**: AI simulates various failure scenarios to optimize disaster recovery plans. It helps determine the best backup intervals, identifies critical systems for recovery prioritization, and tests readiness, ensuring resilience against outages or cyber incidents.
    - **Case study**:
        - **IBM Resiliency Services** uses AI to develop adaptive disaster recovery plans for enterprise clients. For example, a global bank used IBM's AI to simulate disaster events and adjust its recovery protocols, reducing recovery time by over 40%.

The following table summarizes ten key areas where AI plays a crucial role in infrastructure optimization. Each topic is explained in a simplified manner to highlight how AI enhances performance, reduces costs, and ensures system reliability across different IT environments. These roles go beyond automation, encompassing intelligent monitoring, predictive analytics, and proactive planning. Real-world case studies are also included to demonstrate how leading organizations are successfully applying AI to optimize their infrastructure. This provides a practical perspective on AI's transformative impact on modern infrastructure management:

S.No.	Optimization area	Function	Example/use case
1	Automated resource allocation	Scales server capacity based on demand.	AWS & Microsoft Azure auto-scale cloud resources.
2	Predictive maintenance	Detects potential equipment failures in advance.	AI is used in manufacturing to reduce breakdowns.
3	Network traffic management	Manages bandwidth and detects traffic anomalies.	AI for stable and secure data flow.
4	Energy efficiency	Optimizes energy usage through AI-controlled cooling and power adjustments.	Google's DeepMind cuts data center energy use.
5	Capacity planning	Forecasts future infrastructure needs.	Facebook uses AI to plan data center expansions.
6	Cloud resource optimization	Manages and resizes cloud instances automatically.	Airbnb saves costs through AI-managed AWS usage.
7	Intelligent data center management	Controls cooling, power, and server load efficiently.	AI reduces overheating and boosts reliability.
8	Security and anomaly detection	Spot threats and system failures through pattern analysis.	Darktrace prevents cyberattacks in real-time.
9	IT asset lifecycle management	Manages hardware lifecycle and schedules upgrades.	Dell's ProSupport suite monitors device health.
10	Disaster recovery planning	Simulates outages and plans recovery strategies.	IBM helps banks with AI-powered recovery models.

***Table 8.2**: AI and infrastructure optimization*

AI challenges in infrastructure optimization

AI is helping many industries improve how they manage and run their infrastructure. It can save time, reduce costs, and make systems work more smoothly. However, using AI also brings some challenges. These problems need to be solved to use AI in the right and effective way. Some challenges are related to people losing jobs or needing new skills, and others are about fairness, accuracy, and cost. Companies also face trouble when trying to mix AI with their old systems or when they do not have good data. Solving these issues is important to get the full benefits of AI.

The key challenges include:

- **Job displacement and workforce adaptation**: Automation raises concerns about job security as machines replace human roles. Organizations must focus on upskilling and reskilling employees to work alongside AI rather than be replaced by it. Companies must invest in workforce training programs to ensure that employees can transition into new roles that complement AI-driven automation.

- **Bias and ethical considerations**: AI systems rely on data, which may contain biases, leading to unfair workload distribution and infrastructure decisions. Transparency and ethical AI practices are crucial to ensure unbiased decision-making. AI developers must implement bias-mitigation strategies to promote fairness and equality in AI-driven systems.
- **Reliability and accountability**: AI tools are not infallible. Errors in AI-driven decision-making can lead to mismanagement of workload and infrastructure inefficiencies. Organizations must maintain human oversight to ensure accountability. Establishing clear guidelines for AI governance and human-AI collaboration can help mitigate these risks.
- **Data quality and availability**: AI needs clean, complete, and up-to-date data to work well. If the data is missing, wrong, or messy, AI will make poor decisions. Many companies struggle to collect and manage good data. Without good data, AI cannot optimize workload or infrastructure properly.
- **Integration with legacy systems**: Old systems are often not built to work with modern AI tools. Connecting AI to these systems is hard, slow, and costly. It may cause errors or downtime. Many companies must upgrade their systems first, which takes time and money, before using AI effectively.
- **High initial investment and maintenance cost**: Using AI can save money in the long run, but starting with it is expensive. Companies must spend on hardware, software, and skilled people. AI also needs regular updates and care. These costs make it hard for small businesses to use AI for optimization.
- **Security and privacy risks**: AI uses a lot of data, including private and important information. If not protected well, hackers can steal or misuse this data. This can lead to big problems for the company. So, strong security is needed, which adds more work and cost.

While AI offers significant benefits in workload and infrastructure optimization, its implementation is not without challenges. *Figure 8.2* illustrates some of the key obstacles organizations face when adopting AI technologies, including issues related to data quality, system integration, cost, and ethical concerns. Understanding these limitations is essential for developing effective and responsible AI strategies.

Figure 8.2: Challenges of AI in workload and infrastructure optimization

Future trends of AI in optimization

As AI technologies continue to evolve, their role in infrastructure and workload optimization is expected to grow significantly. Several emerging trends are shaping the future landscape, pushing organizations toward smarter, more efficient, and sustainable operations.

The following are some of the key future directions in which AI is expected to make a profound impact:

- **Autonomous infrastructure management**:
  - **Self-monitoring systems**: Future AI systems will automatically track their own performance and health. They will detect problems early without needing manual checks, making infrastructure more reliable and easier to manage.
  - **Self-healing capabilities**: AI will fix common system problems on its own, like restarting failed services or switching to backup systems. This reduces the need for human involvement in routine issue resolution.
  - **Reduced downtime**: With AI detecting and fixing issues quickly, systems will stay available more often. This leads to fewer service interruptions and less pressure on IT support teams.
- **AI at the edge**:
  - **Real-time decision making**: Edge AI processes data locally, allowing instant decisions without sending it to the cloud. This is crucial for fast-response systems like healthcare monitors or industrial machines.
  - **Reduced latency and bandwidth usage**: By processing data nearby, edge AI cuts delays and lowers internet use. This improves speed and saves costs, especially for remote or bandwidth-limited areas.

  - **Critical applications**: Edge AI will support important areas like self-driving cars, factory automation, and medical devices, where quick and reliable decision-making is essential.

- **Rise of artificial intelligence for IT operations (AIOps):**
  - **Big data and machine learning integration**: AI will analyze huge volumes of IT data to detect patterns, problems, and improvements. It helps IT teams understand system behavior more accurately and quickly.
  - **Predictive analytics**: AIOps platforms will predict potential issues before they happen. This allows teams to fix things early and prevent system failures or slowdowns.
  - **Automated incident resolution**: AI will solve common IT problems automatically, like restarting services or clearing logs. This reduces manual work and improves the speed of support.
- **Focus on sustainability and energy efficiency**:
  - **Green IT operations**: AI will help data centers use less energy by distributing tasks more efficiently. This supports environmentally friendly and cost-effective computing.
  - **Workload scheduling**: AI can shift heavy computing tasks to times when energy use is cheaper or more efficient. This helps save electricity and reduce environmental impact.
  - **Carbon footprint reduction**: Smart AI choices in infrastructure planning and workload management will reduce carbon emissions, supporting global sustainability goals.
- **XAI**:
  - **Transparency in decision-making**: Explainable AI will show why certain decisions or actions were made, helping teams understand the reasoning behind optimizations and changes.
  - **Trust and accountability**: When AI decisions are clear and easy to understand, people are more likely to trust them. This builds confidence in automated systems.
  - **Regulatory compliance**: XAI helps companies follow laws and regulations by keeping clear records of AI actions, supporting audits, and data use rules.
- **Deeper integration with cloud-native technologies:**
  - **AI in Kubernetes and containers**: AI will manage where to place containers, when to scale them, and how to recover from failures in modern cloud-based systems like Kubernetes.

- **Improved resource utilization**: AI will assign the right number of resources for tasks at the right time, reducing waste and improving system efficiency.
- **Resilience in hybrid/cloud environments**: AI will balance workloads between on-premise and cloud systems, improving performance and reducing costs in mixed environments.

AI is becoming more advanced as technology grows. In the future, it will offer even better ways to manage work and systems. These improvements will help businesses work smarter and save energy. AI will also be easier to understand and use.

The following table shows the main trends we are likely to see soon:

S.No.	Future trend	Description
1	Autonomous infrastructure	AI will self-monitor and fix systems without human intervention.
2	Edge AI	Data processed locally for fast and real-time decisions.
3	AIOps	Combines AI with IT operations to predict and resolve system issues.
4	XAI	AI decisions will become more transparent and easier to understand.
5	Sustainability and green computing	AI will reduce energy usage and carbon footprint in infrastructure management.
6	Cloud-native AI integration	AI will better manage containerized apps and hybrid cloud environments.

***Table 8.3**: Future trends in AI for optimization*

Conclusion

In this chapter, we covered how AI is transforming the way we handle work and manage infrastructure. It automates routine tasks, improves decision-making, predicts future workloads, and helps businesses respond faster to changes. With AI, companies can save time, reduce costs, and offer better services. However, using AI also brings challenges like job displacement, data security, and the need for high-quality data. To get the best results, organizations must carefully plan how they use AI and prepare their systems and teams for change. Looking ahead, trends like self-healing systems, edge AI, and sustainable computing will continue to grow. In short, AI is not just a helpful tool; it is becoming a key part of building smarter, faster, and more reliable workplaces.

In the next chapter, we are going to learn about the challenges of using AI in software development. These include problems like a lack of good data, difficulty in understanding AI decisions, and concerns about fairness and trust. Knowing these challenges helps us use AI more carefully and effectively.

Questions

1. What is the role of AI in automating repetitive tasks?
2. How does AI contribute to predictive maintenance?
3. Explain how AI helps in dynamic resource allocation.
4. Mention two benefits of using AI in infrastructure optimization.
5. What is XAI, and why is it important?
6. Describe how AI improves workload distribution and provide an example.
7. Explain the role of AI in intelligent shift scheduling and its impact on employees.
8. Discuss the challenges organizations face while implementing AI in workload optimization.
9. How does AI contribute to energy efficiency and cost reduction in data centers?
10. Elaborate on future trends in AI for workload and infrastructure optimization, such as AIOps and edge AI.

Multiple choice questions

1. **Which of the following is a benefit of AI in workload management?**
   a. Increased manual labor
   b. Higher human error
   c. Automation of repetitive tasks
   d. Reduced productivity
2. **What technology is often used for automating repetitive business processes?**
   a. Blockchain
   b. Augmented reality
   c. RPA
   d. Edge computing
3. **How does AI improve decision-making?**
   a. By hiring employee
   b. By flipping coins
   c. By analyzing large datasets
   d. By guessing
4. **Which company uses AI to scale its cloud infrastructure during traffic spikes?**
   a. Microsoft
   b. Netflix
   c. Oracle
   d. Facebook

5. **What does predictive maintenance aim to reduce?**
    a. Software updates
    b. System upgrades
    c. Equipment failure and downtime
    d. Staff meetings

6. **Which AI system is used by IBM for IT operations monitoring?**
    a. IBM Watson AIOps
    b. IBM Cloud Watch
    c. IBM Navigator
    d. IBM SecureOps

7. **What is the main purpose of intelligent shift scheduling?**
    a. To assign tasks randomly
    b. To increase workload
    c. To ensure fair and efficient work distribution
    d. To fire employees

8. **Which company uses AI to personalize work experiences for analysts?**
    a. Infosys
    b. FinEdge Solutions
    c. Adobe
    d. Accenture

9. **What role does AI play in energy efficiency?**
    a. Increasing electricity bills
    b. Enhancing cooling systems in data centers
    c. Turning off devices randomly
    d. Ignoring power use

10. **Which of the following is a future trend in AI?**
    a. Manual scheduling
    b. XAI
    c. Fixed infrastructure
    d. Human-only decisions

11. **AI helps optimize network performance by:**
    a. Adding more routers
    b. Analyzing traffic patterns
    c. Blocking IPs
    d. Restarting computers.

12. **Which AI tool is used for real-time ticket routing in customer service?**
    a. WhatsApp
    b. Salesforce
    c. Zendesk
    d. Skype

13. **What does AI do in disaster recovery planning?**
    a. Ignores incidents
    b. Simulates failure scenarios

c. Deletes old files
d. Sends random alerts

14. What challenge is caused by low-quality data in AI systems?

a. Better results
b. Faster training
c. Poor decision-making
d. Reduced costs

15. AI used at the edge helps in:

a. Cloud delays
b. Real-time decision-making
c. Slower bandwidth
d. Physical storage

Answers

1	c
2	c
3	c
4	b
5	c
6	a
7	c
8	b
9	b
10	b
11	b
12	c
13	b
14	c
15	b

CHAPTER 9
Challenges of Using AI in Software Development

Introduction

In contemporary software engineering, **artificial intelligence** (**AI**) has emerged as one of the most revolutionary trends. The way developers create, test, and release software is evolving thanks to tools like intelligent project management assistants, automated code generation, and problem detection systems. AI has permeated almost every phase of the **software development lifecycle** (**SDLC**), from ChatGPT-based coding helpers and GitHub Copilot to predictive analytics in project planning.

AI is a prime technology getting much attention these days. Software engineers are overwhelmingly exploring, experimenting, and expounding the unique contributions of AI in their everyday assignments. However, a few critical challenges must be surmounted to make AI the new normal for the software community. This chapter explains the brewing challenges and how they can be overcome.

The adoption of AI in software development is not without its roadblocks. However, with structured approaches to data quality, team training, system design, and ethical AI practices, these challenges can be transformed into opportunities for innovation. The chapter ends with recommendations and a framework for AI-readiness in software teams.

The use and acceptance of AI in software development with a structured approach will help in maintaining the quality of software in terms of optimized code and bug free software, but there are some challenges to the use of AI in software development.

Structure

In this chapter, we will cover the following topics:

- Challenges in adaptation of AI in software development
- AI and ethics
- Challenges in testing and validation

Objectives

AI is the ability of a computer system to learn and solve problems, and comprehend natural language that normally requires human intelligence. AI makes use of different models and algorithms that allow computer systems to process data, recognize patterns, and automate tasks for different purposes. The other book chapters discuss the opportunities and various benefits of AI in software engineering, and we shall also talk about the challenges in its adoption.

This chapter will discuss the challenges in the adaptation of AI in software development. The chapter will discuss major challenges, such as issues with data quality and ethical concerns. The chapter will also discuss the integration of AI with the existing system in terms of existing code, APIs used, interfaces in use, and even infrastructure restrictions. The AI adaptation challenges could be overcome by treating them as opportunities in different ways.

Challenges in adaptation of AI in software development

As we all know, we have various tools with capabilities to support artificial intelligence. We will examine the challenges encountered in integrating AI into software development. The adoption of AI tools to support software development.

On the other hand, there are specific challenges in implementing AI in software development. We will look in detail of all such difficulties. These challenges we can overcome to convert them to opportunities for innovation, team training, development, and designing AI ethics.

The chapter will discuss the challenges of AI adoption. No matter how much excitement and potential AI brings, there will always be challenges to overcome.

One of the key challenges is the lack of a clear AI strategy. There is often a disconnect between the team and the business owners. This can be overcome by defining a clear AI strategy and ensuring the use cases chosen align with the strategy and deliver business value to legacy systems. The same is illustrated in the following figure:

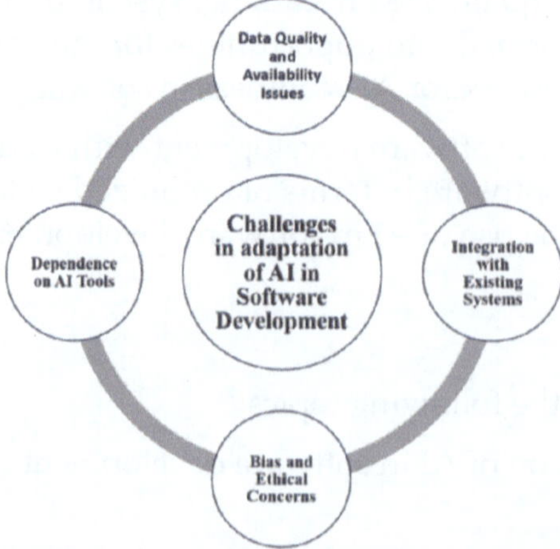

***Figure 9.1**: Challenges in adaptation of AI in software development*

Technical challenges

The major challenges in AI adaptation are:

- Data quality and availability issues
- Integration with existing systems
- Bias and ethical concerns
- Dependence on AI tools

Data quality and availability issues

For software engineering to successfully use AI, data availability and quality are essential. Inaccurate models, skewed outcomes, and eventually ineffectual AI solutions might stem from inadequate data. Assuring data timeliness, accuracy, completeness, and consistency is a major difficulty. Other problems include data silos and integrating AI with current systems.

Garbage in, garbage out (GIGO) is a simple but effective concept that highlights the importance of input in data quality. AI systems require large volumes of clean, relevant, and unbiased data. Poor data quality leads to inaccurate predictions or unreliable software behaviour.

For example, if user purchase history data is inconsistent or lacking across platforms, an Indian e-commerce company attempting to employ AI for consumer recommendation systems may encounter issues.

Data quality and data availability are the main challenges in the adaptation of AI. The poor data can mislead models and, hence, can result in incompetent software. Labelled dataset, synthetic data generation, and data cleaning can be very helpful to overcome this issue. Labelled dataset, synthetic data generation, and data cleaning may solve this problem. Monitoring of data will also help in improving data quality.

Several tactics can be used to overcome data quality and availability issues:

- **Incomplete data**: If the customer's purchase history is not properly recorded, AI may fail to understand buying patterns.

  Example: A user buying from both the website and the mobile app may have split transaction records if the systems are not linked. The AI will then see incomplete behaviour.
- **Inconsistent data across**: Many companies operate across multiple platforms (website, Android app, iOS app, offline store). If these platforms do not sync properly, data becomes inconsistent.

  Example: A customer adds items to the cart in the app but purchases them in-store. The AI sees **abandoned cart** data online, assuming the customer did not buy, which leads to wrong recommendations later.

  The following figure illustrates various data challenges:

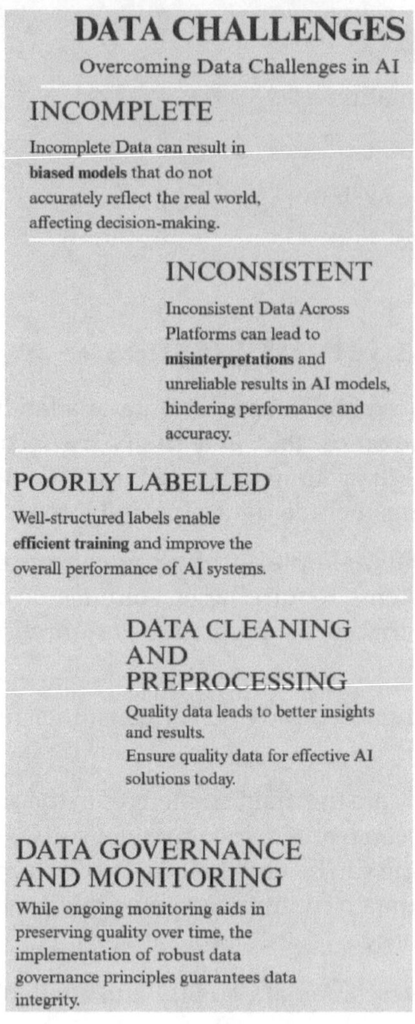

Figure 9.2: *Data challenges in AI*

- **Labelled datasets**: AI models are guaranteed to learn from accurate and representative data when high-quality, properly labelled datasets are curated.
- **Synthetic data generation**: To complement inadequate datasets, realistic artificial data can be produced by utilizing methods like data augmentation, simulation, or generative models.
- **Data cleaning and preprocessing**: The data's dependability and usability are increased by eliminating duplicates, managing missing values, standardizing formats, and fixing mistakes.
- **Data governance and monitoring**: While ongoing monitoring aids in preserving quality over time, the implementation of robust data governance principles guarantees data integrity.

Integration with existing systems

AI integration is difficult or even not possible with the old architectures. There are various complexities in fitting the AI components due to existing codebases, APIs, and workflows.

Most organizations already use legacy software and tools. Integrating AI solutions with these systems can be complex and costly.

For example, an Indian government agency may find it difficult to employ AI to digitize land records since outdated paper records are not standardized, which makes AI integration sluggish and prone to mistakes.

Complexities occur on several levels:

- **Existing codebases**: Without endangering system stability, legacy code may be difficult to change, poorly documented, and resistant to modification. It frequently takes a lot of reworking or reconstruction to incorporate AI functionality.
- **APIs and interfaces**: AI modules may find it challenging to interact and exchange data with one another in older systems due to a lack of clear or contemporary APIs.
- **Workflows and business logic**: Since AI processes are data-driven and iterative, established workflows might not be compatible with them, which could result in operational bottlenecks.
- **Infrastructure restrictions**: AI models may not operate well due to inadequate storage, antiquated servers, and low processing power.

Bias and ethical concerns

Software engineering (**SE**) functions like code development, issue identification, testing, project management, and hiring are increasingly utilizing AI. AI increases productivity, but it also presents ethical issues and bias that need to be addressed. Although AI has great potential in software engineering, concerns like justice, accountability, privacy, and prejudice must be carefully considered. In order for AI to truly assist engineers, the best strategy is to employ human oversight, a variety of data, safe procedures, and appropriate rules.

AI models trained on biased datasets can give unfair or discriminatory results. Ethical concerns arise when there is a lack of transparency or accountability.

For example, if the training data is not diverse, an AI-based job recruitment tool can inadvertently favor applicants from particular universities or backgrounds.

AI unintentionally inheriting biases from training data can cause a system to give misleading results. This section explains how bias manifests itself, the effects it has on software, and the necessity of ethical standards, openness, and a broad sample of data.

Data representation and algorithmic bias also help in making data ethical. The topic further discusses the adoption of ethical values and guidelines and the audit of the dame, as outlined in the following table:

Concern	Impact on SE	Possible solution
Bias in training data	Unfair or one-sided code recommendations	Use diverse datasets, biaschecks.
Lack of transparency	Hard to trust AI suggestions	More explainable AI,proper documentation.
Privacy risks	Data leak, misuse of IP	Secure storage,anonymization.
Accountability issues	Confusion over responsibility	Clear rules and ownership frameworks.
Job displacement	Fewer beginner-level opportunities	Upskilling, human–AIeamwork.

***Table 9.1**: Bias and ethical concerns in AI for SE*

Refer to the following list to build a comprehensive understanding:

- **Data representation bias**: The model is unable to make correct generalizations when particular people, categories, or situations are underrepresented.
- **Algorithmic bias**: If the parameters or design of the algorithm inadvertently favor particular results, bias may result even from objective data.
- **Adopt ethical guidelines**: Create structures that give justice, openness, and responsibility top priority when developing AI.
- **Employ diverse data sampling**: To reduce inadvertent bias, train models using representative and balanced datasets.
- **Frequent auditing**: Throughout the lifecycle of AI systems, keep an eye out for bias and conduct regular audits.

Dependence on AI tools

The fundamental programming and problem-solving abilities of developers might be undermined by an over-reliance on AI-driven development environments (such as code generation tools or intelligent debuggers). The necessity of striking a balance between automation and human skill is emphasized throughout the chapter.

Excessive reliance on AI may reduce critical thinking and problem-solving skills among software engineers. If the AI tools fail, productivity drops significantly.

For example, developers who use AI coding assistants, such as Copilot, risk becoming reliant on them and finding it difficult to generate code that is optimized without tool support.

There are many AI tools on which there is dependency which leads to kill the skill, so skill atrophy is the major challenge. As dependency on AI tools is increasing, it is also decreasing creativity and innovation. However, a balanced dependence on AI tools, ethical use, cautious integration, and high-quality data are all necessary for the effective deployment of AI in software development. While AI should be viewed as a supporting tool, human skills must continue to play a fundamental role. The details are as follows:

- **Skill atrophy**: Without completely comprehending the underlying logic, developers may rely more on AI recommendations rather than crafting streamlined, efficient code from scratch. Developers' own technical abilities may progressively deteriorate if they rely too much on AI-generated recommendations. They might eventually stop giving algorithms, optimization, and best coding techniques careful thought. This may make them less confident in their ability to solve challenging issues on their own. Developers must constantly practice manual code, critically evaluate AI-generated outputs, and keep up with fundamental programming principles in order to prevent such a drop in skill.
- **Decreased creativity**: Developers' capacity to innovate and think creatively may be weakened by automated solutions that restrict their exposure to different strategies.
- **Shallow debugging skills**: Developers may lose the capacity to systematically trace problems if AI technologies take over the majority of debugging activities. This is crucial in intricate, high-stakes situations.
- **Knowledge gaps**: Newer programmers may overlook fundamental ideas due to an ongoing reliance on automation, which could lead to a lack of long-term knowledge.

The following figure explores the various challenges of AI in s/w development, including data quality and availability issues, integration with existing systems, and dependency on various AI tools:

Figure 9.3: AI adaptation in software development

The other challenges are as follows:

- Skill gaps and training needs
- Performance and reliability challenges

Let us discuss them.

- **Skill gaps and training**: Formal training in ML and AI model deployment is typically lacking among software engineers. This disparity emphasizes how urgently upskilling and cross-disciplinary training are needed. In order to train engineers to effectively design, build, and maintain AI-powered systems, the chapter examines how industry and educational institutions might work together to develop the requisite AI capabilities.
- **Performance and reliability**: When used in dynamic, real-world settings, AI components, especially machine learning models, can exhibit unpredictable behaviour. The significance of thorough testing, ongoing model drift monitoring, guaranteeing explainability to ensure transparency, and putting procedures in place to preserve stability and dependability across system changes are all covered in this section.

AI and ethics

Although AI has the potential to revolutionize software development, overcoming these complex obstacles calls for a methodical, interdisciplinary, and moral approach. To fully reap the benefits of this potent technology, addressing these problems calls for strong engineering processes, ongoing learning, and a dedication to responsible AI principles.

AI is giving us a lot of new applications and providing benefits in every aspect of our lives. As AI moves out of the research labs into the real-world, more and more people are becoming aware of some ethical concerns. Data privacy, also known as information privacy, is the accessibility of an individual's data. Data plays a very important role in every domain of AI. In recent times, the amount of data that is generated by the use of gadgets and applications is huge, and organizations use data protection policies in order to safeguard it.

The personal data of the customers' applications needs a lot of data, which is collected from the user, like details about browsing history, geographic location, contact list, preferences, etc. This data is collected legally to keep a track of activities, including shopping cart preferences, places you visit, and content you see. Such information helps many websites to provide customized recommendations and notifications.

The ethical way to collect such data is for websites or mobile applications to ask for several permissions to access your systems. Most of the time, the data collected by various applications is ethical in nature, as the users agree to it by clicking on allow when the application asks for various permissions. To avoid any misuse of data, it is advisable not to give these permissions to all applications and websites. Rather, it is to be selected very carefully.

Challenges in testing and validation

Compared to standard software testing, AI testing and validation are more complicated. It is difficult to determine what is *correct* because AI models frequently provide multiple responses based on the situation, whereas traditional software provides fixed findings.

It is because of their unexpected behavior, which is mostly dependent on the quality and diversity of the training data, that AI systems are challenging to test and validate. Traditional testing methods are sometimes insufficient since AI models may react differently to new scenarios, edge cases, or unanticipated data patterns. To ensure accuracy, fairness, security, and reliability, extensive testing datasets, specific evaluation techniques, and continuous monitoring are required. Additionally, when an AI model functions as a black box, it becomes more difficult to verify its decision-making process and identify biases or mistakes. Organizations must use robust validation methods to ensure that AI systems function dependably and safely in real-world situations.

The following are the major challenges in testing and validation:

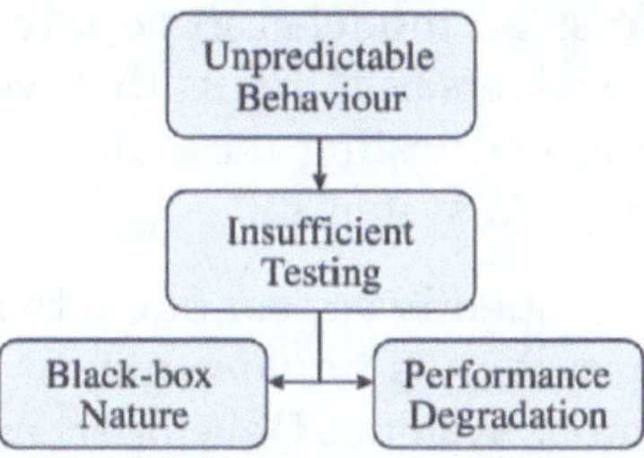

***Figure 9.4**: Challenges in testing and validation*

Testing and validating AI systems presents unique challenges that differ greatly from traditional software testing. The following points highlight the primary challenges to effectively testing and maintaining AI systems:

- **Non-deterministic outputs**: Unlike traditional software, AI models do not always produce predictable outcomes. Rather, their results are frequently context-dependent or probabilistic, making it challenging to determine what is actually *correct*. Furthermore, it is nearly impossible to test every potential combination of inputs, which makes validation even more difficult.

  In addition to these challenges, AI systems often need constant monitoring and retraining to remain effective because real-world data is constantly changing. If the model is not updated often, its accuracy may decline, producing forecasts that are unreliable in real-world situations. Organizations must also invest time and resources in creating trustworthy validation pipelines and simulation environments in order to thoroughly assess model behavior before deployment.

It is because of this, maintaining high-quality AI performance is an ongoing effort that requires careful attention, domain knowledge, and responsible monitoring, especially in application domains that are expanding quickly.

- **Defining correctness and performance metrics**: While evaluation measures (such as accuracy, precision, recall, F1-score, AUC, etc.) are important, they must be carefully selected in accordance with the objectives of the application. Performance on one metric may suffer if performance on another is optimized. It is crucial to compare performance to baseline models or human performance.

  In addition to these considerations, it is critical to ensure that the metrics used appropriately reflect real-world expectations. Sometimes a model performs incredibly well on paper but is inefficient when applied in real-world scenarios. Engineers must validate the model in a variety of contexts, including real-time and stressful scenarios, in order to understand its genuine behavior. By regularly assessing and improving these indicators, it is possible to maintain model reliability and guarantee that the system complies with both technical goals and user expectations.

- **Edge cases and outliers**: AI models can perform poorly or even fail completely when they face rare or adversarial inputs that were not properly included in the training data. Detecting and testing these unusual cases is a major challenge in ensuring the reliability of AI systems.

  These edge situations frequently appear out of the blue in real-world applications, particularly when the system is implemented in dynamic settings like banking, healthcare, or autonomous systems. Developers must constantly collect fresh data, update the model, and do stress testing because even one untested scenario can result in inaccurate or dangerous outcomes. Managing such uncommon occurrences becomes even more crucial in the Indian setting, where varied user behavior, linguistic variances, and unpredictable inputs are typical, to guarantee that AI systems stay trustworthy, equitable, and resilient in a variety of circumstances.

- **Continuous evaluation**: As real-world data distribution changes over time, AI models may perform worse in production (concept drift or data drift).

  Adds a substantial operational overhead by requiring ongoing monitoring, retraining, and re-validation. In real-world applications, continuous evaluation becomes essential since AI systems cannot be developed once and then forgotten. As user behavior, market trends, or environmental factors change, the model must be regularly assessed to ensure it continues to yield accurate and meaningful results. Organizations often require specialist teams and the appropriate infrastructure to monitor performance, identify issues early, and modify the model as necessary. This ongoing loop keeps the AI system up to date, reliable, and consistent with real-world expectations.

Conclusion

Software engineering is assimilating several breakthrough technologies to keep up with the progress of hardware engineering. AI is a main technology getting much attention these days. Software engineers are overwhelmingly exploring. There are many opportunities and uses of AI for software development. Along with the multiple benefits of AI in this field, there are various challenges also. This chapter discussed the challenges of using AI in software development. In this chapter, we covered various topics, including data quality, data availability issues, integration with existing systems, and dependence on AI tools. The chapter also talked about various ethical concerns. AI can expedite support requests, issue patches, and feature improvements.

In the next chapter, you will discover the impact of AI in transforming software design, development, debugging, documentation, deployment, delivery, and decommissioning.

Questions

1. How do data quality and availability issues affect AI development?
2. What challenges arise when integrating AI with existing systems?
3. What risks come from overdependence on AI tools in software development?
4. How can performance challenges affect AI-based software systems?
5. Why is reliability a concern when deploying AI tools in production?
6. Why is ethics important in AI development?

Answers

1. Incomplete or low-quality data might result in less reliable systems and erroneous model predictions. Consistent, pertinent, and representative datasets are essential for training AI models. Development might be delayed, and data collection or augmentation expenses may be raised by limited data availability. The effectiveness and reliability of AI-driven solutions are directly impacted by this.

   Bias can be introduced by low-quality data, producing unfair or incorrect results. Additionally, it lessens the model's capacity to generalize to actual situations. It is more difficult to develop specialized AI applications when domain-specific data is scarce. Successful AI development thus depends on ensuring appropriate data pretreatment, cleaning, and validation.

2. Integration often requires adapting legacy systems that were not designed for AI workflows. Compatibility issues, data format differences, and performance bottlenecks

can occur. Organizations may need additional infrastructure or middleware to connect AI models with current processes. This increases implementation complexity and project timelines.

The cost of adoption is further increased by the possibility that staff members need training in order to operate AI-enabled technologies efficiently. Sharing sensitive data among new AI components also presents security and privacy problems. The seamless integration of AI with developing systems requires constant upkeep and updates. Adoption may be further slowed by stakeholder resistance to change. In order to minimize risks, integration necessitates thorough planning, testing, and staggered implementation.

3. When developers rely too much on these technologies, they may begin to rely on AI-generated recommendations for even basic tasks, which might gradually diminish their creativity and analytical thinking abilities. Developers may find it difficult to debug complicated problems or come up with creative solutions on their own when they cease paying close attention to the logic of their code. Furthermore, the quality, security, and functionality of the product may be jeopardized if an AI tool generates biased, out-of-date, or technically incorrect recommendations and the developer accepts them without question. Therefore, in order to assure dependable and well-written software, engineers must maintain a balanced approach—using AI technologies as useful helpers while still applying their own expertise, judgment, and problem-solving skills.

4. Furthermore, the computational demand of AI models may rise sharply as organizations scale their applications, necessitating more infrastructure and upkeep. Budget and technological resources may be strained as a result, particularly in startup or academic settings. Adopting effective model-compression strategies, optimizing code, and selecting suitable deployment environments are crucial to overcoming such obstacles. Businesses can benefit from AI without sacrificing cost or performance with careful planning and optimization.

5. When AI models are exposed to fresh or changing data, they may exhibit unpredictable behavior. Functionality may be affected by software updates, model drift, or external API modifications. System reliability is jeopardized in the absence of adequate testing and backup plans. Stable and consistent performance is ensured by ongoing monitoring. Additionally, in order to maintain their AI systems' alignment with current requirements, organizations must devote effort to routine validation and fine-tuning. Developers can also spot early indicators of performance decrease with the aid of appropriate documentation and recurring audits. Teams may guarantee that the AI performs consistently even when the operational environment or data patterns change by taking a proactive stance.

6. By ensuring that technology develops in a way that benefits everyone, not just a chosen few, ethical AI practices also support long-term sustainability. It is simpler to construct

AI systems that are safe, inclusive, and in line with societal demands when developers and organizations adhere to ethical principles. In addition to boosting public trust, this promotes the broader use of AI in delicate fields like healthcare, finance, and education. In the end, ethics serve as a foundation that steers technical development in the proper direction, guaranteeing that AI stays a tool for empowerment rather than a source of danger.

Multiple choice questions

1. **Which of the following is a common challenge when integrating AI into software development?**
   a. Unlimited availability of high-quality training data
   b. Difficulty in ensuring the explainability of AI models
   c. Complete predictability of AI outcomes
   d. Guaranteed fairness in AI decision-making
2. **What does model drift refer to in AI-based software systems?**
   a. The AI model is becoming faster over time
   b. The AI model adapts automatically without retraining
   c. The AI model's performance is degrading due to changes in data patterns
   d. The AI model is producing random results
3. **One of the key challenges in deploying AI software in production environments is:**
   a. AI never needing updates after initial deployment
   b. Maintaining robustness across software updates
   c. AI always produces the same result for every input
   d. AI models requiring no monitoring
4. **Which of the following is a challenge related to AI ethics in software development?**
   a. Code compilation errors
   b. Bias in training data leading to unfair decisions
   c. Slow internet speed during model training
   d. Low resolution of training images
5. **Why is high-quality training data crucial for AI development?**
   a. It reduces the cost of cloud storage
   b. It ensures the AI model learns accurate and relevant patterns
   c. It guarantees AI will not require testing
   d. It eliminates the need for developers

6. **Which of the following is a key reason ethics is important in AI?**
   a. To increase the speed of AI algorithms
   b. To ensure fairness, transparency, and accountability
   c. To reduce the cost of data storage
   d. To improve internet connectivity

Answers

1	b
2	c
3	b
4	b
5	b
6	b

Join our Discord space

Join our Discord workspace for latest updates, offers, tech happenings around the world, new releases, and sessions with the authors:

https://discord.bpbonline.com

Chapter 10
Next-generation Developer Experience Enabled by AI

Introduction

Artificial intelligence (**AI**) is transforming the IT landscape across all domains, from automating routine maintenance tasks to driving strategic decision-making in operations. One of the key areas seeing substantial impact is the developer experience—the overall experience of software developers as they build, test, deploy, and manage applications. With the growing adoption of AI in **IT infrastructure and operations** (**IT I&O**), developers are beginning to interact with smarter tools, more automated environments, and self-healing systems.

This chapter explores how AI is revolutionizing the developer experience within modern IT ecosystems, improving productivity, reducing cognitive load, and enabling more agile and resilient software development practices.

Structure

The chapter covers the following topics:

- AI-powered development environments
- Intelligent CI/CD pipelines
- Smart infrastructure provisioning and management
- Enhanced observability and incident response
- Adaptive security and compliance
- Personalized developer workflows
- Collaborative AI and team productivity
- Enhanced coding efficiency with AI tools
- AI-driven code suggestions and autocompletion

- Improved collaboration and communication
- AI-enhanced debugging and troubleshooting
- AI-driven continuous learning for developers
- Evolving role of developers in the age of AI
- Challenges and considerations

Objectives

The primary objective of this chapter is to explore how AI is transforming the developer experience within the domain of IT I&O. As AI technologies become more integrated into development environments, this chapter aims to highlight the tools, techniques, and systems that are enhancing developer productivity, reducing manual effort, and supporting smarter decision-making throughout the software development lifecycle. It focuses on how AI empowers developers by automating repetitive coding tasks, offering intelligent code suggestions, simplifying infrastructure management, and accelerating debugging and deployment processes. This chapter also examines how AI contributes to a more personalized and streamlined workflow, allowing developers to focus on higher-value activities such as system design, innovation, and user experience.

Beyond technical advancements, the chapter also addresses the broader impact of AI on collaboration, learning, and job responsibilities. It aims to provide a balanced perspective on the opportunities and challenges AI introduces for developers, including the need for new skills, concerns around dependency, and the importance of transparency and ethical considerations in AI-driven tools. By the end of this chapter, readers will understand how AI is reshaping the developer's role—not by replacing human input, but by augmenting capabilities and fostering more efficient, adaptive, and intelligent development environments. This understanding will help both practitioners and learners to prepare for the evolving demands of software engineering in AI-driven IT operations.

As AI continues to reshape the software development lifecycle, it brings significant improvements in how developers build, deploy, and manage applications. AI tools are now integrated into many parts of the development process, making it faster, smarter, and more efficient. In this chapter, let us discuss the key areas of how AI is transforming modern development and operations practices, and build understanding.

AI-powered development environments

Modern **integrated development environments (IDEs)** now integrate AI-powered assistants that offer real-time code suggestions, error detection, and performance recommendations. These tools, such as GitHub Copilot or Amazon CodeWhisperer, rely on machine learning models trained on massive code repositories.

Impact on developers:

- Reduces time spent on boilerplate code.
- Assists with writing complex functions and debugging.
- Provides intelligent autocomplete features and documentation generation.
- Enhances code consistency and reduces syntax or logic errors.

When combined with AI-enabled infrastructure, these environments can also simulate runtime behavior, predict errors based on infrastructure dependencies, and suggest optimal deployment configurations.

As AI becomes more integrated into software development workflows, a variety of intelligent features are now available to support developers in writing, testing, deploying, and securing applications. These features not only increase efficiency but also help reduce human error and improve overall code quality. The following table highlights some key AI capabilities and how they benefit developers:

AI feature	Function	Benefit to developers
Code autocompletion	Predicts and completes code snippets.	Saves time and reduces typing errors.
AI-powered debugging	Analyzes errors and suggests fixes.	Speeds up bug resolution.
Smart testing	Selects and runs relevant test cases automatically.	Improves test efficiency and coverage.
Infrastructure automation	Provisions and scales infrastructure using AI.	Reduces manual DevOps work.
Predictive CI/CD	Flags potential build failures or performance issues.	Enables faster and more reliable deployments.
Personalized suggestions	Recommends files, tools, or shortcuts based on behavior.	Increases comfort and efficiency.
AI-driven security scanning	Identifies vulnerabilities during coding or deployment.	Ensures secure code earlier in the development process.

Table 10.1: AI features that enhance developer productivity

Intelligent CI/CD pipelines

AI is transforming **continuous integration and continuous deployment** (**CI/CD**) pipelines by making software delivery faster, more reliable, and error-free. Traditional CI/CD processes often face issues such as build failures, inefficient testing, and unexpected deployment errors. With AI integration, these challenges are being addressed through predictive and data-driven automation.

AI-powered pipelines can predict build failures before they occur by analyzing code patterns, commit histories, and test results. This proactive approach helps developers identify potential issues early, reducing the number of failed builds and flaky tests. Additionally, AI uses historical data and recent code changes to prioritize and select the most relevant test cases, saving both time and computing resources.

During deployment, AI enables anomaly detection to spot irregularities that might cause downtime. It also performs auto-tuning of deployment settings, adjusting configurations based on previous performance or incident data to enhance system stability.

For developers, these improvements result in faster feedback cycles, fewer manual interventions, and greater confidence in each release. Overall, AI-driven CI/CD pipelines ensure higher efficiency, reliability, and agility in the software development lifecycle.

The following table summarizes how AI improves various aspects of CI/CD pipeline performance:

AI capability	Impact on CI/CD process
Predictive analysis	Reduces build failures and flaky tests.
Smart test case selection	Improves testing efficiency using code history.
Anomaly detection	Prevents downtime during deployment.
Auto-tuning of deployment settings	Enhances performance and stability post-deployment.

***Table 10.2**: AI contributions to CI/CD optimization*

Smart infrastructure provisioning and management

AI is transforming the way developers manage and provision infrastructure by enhancing the concept of **infrastructure as code** (**IaC**). Traditionally, IaC allows teams to define and manage infrastructure through code-based templates, ensuring consistency and repeatability. However, manual configurations and performance tuning can still be time-consuming and prone to inefficiencies.

AI brings intelligence and automation to this process. By analyzing patterns in infrastructure usage, AI systems can recommend optimal resource configurations that match specific application workloads. It also uses predictive scaling models to automate provisioning, ensuring that resources adjust dynamically based on demand. Moreover, AI can detect underutilized or misconfigured resources, helping organizations reduce costs and improve performance.

For developers, these capabilities translate into a smoother workflow. They can focus more on building and improving applications rather than managing infrastructure details. The result is a self-optimizing environment that minimizes manual intervention, enhances efficiency, and reduces the overall burden on DevOps teams.

The following table gives a brief overview of AI's role in enhancing infrastructure performance:

AI capability	Impact on infrastructure
Resource configuration recommendation	Ensures optimal performance for varying workloads.
Predictive scaling automation	Adjusts resources dynamically based on demand.
Resource utilization detection	Identifies and resolves underuse or misconfiguration.

Table 10.3: *AI contributions to smart infrastructure management*

Enhanced observability and incident response

AI plays an essential role in improving observability, which refers to a system's ability to show what is happening inside it through logs, metrics, and traces. Modern applications generate a huge amount of telemetry data, and manually analyzing this information is time-consuming and complex. AI helps by automatically studying this data, identifying unusual patterns, and pointing out problems before they grow into failures.

AI-powered observability tools can connect related events, understand system behavior, and provide developers with clear, meaningful alerts. This reduces the effort needed to understand the root cause of issues. For example, instead of reading thousands of log entries, developers can receive an AI-generated summary explaining why an error occurred.

AI also supports predictive monitoring. It can identify early warning signs—such as increasing response time or memory usage—and alert developers before users experience any issues. Additionally, AI can create visual dashboards automatically, showing the most important performance trends without manual setup.

Overall, AI makes system monitoring faster, smarter, and more efficient. Developers can troubleshoot problems quickly, avoid performance degradation, and focus more on building new features rather than solving repetitive issues.

The following table explains the key AI features and their benefits:

AI feature	Explanation	Developer benefit
Root cause summaries	AI reads logs and identifies the main reason for an issue.	Saves time and reduces manual effort.
Predictive alerts	AI detects early signs of failures.	Prevents downtime and improves reliability.
Auto-generated dashboards	AI creates useful visual views automatically.	Helps developers understand trends quickly.

Table 10.4: *AI-enhanced observability features and benefits*

Adaptive security and compliance

AI is playing a major role in improving IT operations, especially in the areas of security and compliance. As organizations move toward DevSecOps, where security is integrated into every stage of development, AI helps developers manage threats more efficiently. Traditional security checks are often slow and require manual review, but AI speeds up the process by analyzing large amounts of data and identifying risks automatically.

AI-powered security tools can scan application code, APIs, and container images to detect vulnerabilities before the software is deployed. This helps developers fix issues early, reducing the chances of security flaws reaching production. AI can also monitor real-time network traffic and system activity to identify suspicious or malicious behavior. When unusual patterns are detected, the system alerts the team immediately so that quick action can be taken.

Another important benefit is AI's ability to assist with patch management. It can recommend fixes, prioritize critical patches, and even suggest rollback options if an update causes unexpected issues. For developers, this creates a safer and more predictable environment.

The impact on developers is significant. AI allows vulnerabilities to be resolved faster, reduces the manual work involved in meeting compliance standards, and strengthens the overall security feedback loop. This aligns well with agile development practices, where quick iterations and continuous improvement are essential.

The following table highlights how AI improves security tasks and supports developers:

AI feature	How it works	Benefit for developers
Vulnerability scanning	AI inspects code and container images	Early detection and quick fixes
Real-time threat monitoring	AI analyzes traffic for malicious activity	Immediate alerts and improved safety
Patch management support	AI recommends fixes or rollbacks	Faster updates and reduced manual effort

Table 10.5: AI-driven security features and developer benefits

Personalized developer workflows

AI is increasingly being used to make development tools and workflows more **personalized**, even though this capability is less commonly discussed. Modern AI systems can observe how individual developers work their habits, preferences, and daily patterns and then optimize the tools around them. Instead of developers having to adjust their workflow to match the system, AI reshapes the system to better support each developer's style.

For example, AI can analyze a developer's past activities to understand which tasks they usually complete first, which files they open most often, and what kind of issues they typically work on. Based on this, the system can automatically reorder tasks or highlight the most relevant items, saving time and improving focus.

AI can also recommend useful documentation, code snippets, or solutions related to the developer's current task. This reduces the effort needed to manually search for information and speeds up problem-solving. Another emerging feature is AI-assisted scheduling. By observing productivity patterns, such as peak concentration hours, AI can suggest the ideal times to run builds, tests, or deployments to avoid interruptions in workflow.

Overall, AI makes the development environment more intelligent and supportive. It creates a customized experience that boosts efficiency, reduces context switching, and helps developers stay productive. In this way, tools adapt to the developer instead of forcing the developer to adapt to the tools.

The following table summarizes how AI personalizes the development workspace:

AI feature	How it works	Benefit for developers
Task reordering	AI analyzes work patterns and arranges tasks.	Better focus and reduced workload switching.
Relevant suggestions	AI highlights useful code and documentation.	Faster problem-solving and less searching.
Smart scheduling	AI identifies peak productivity times.	Smoother workflow with fewer disruptions.

Table 10.6: *AI-based personalization features and their developer benefits*

Collaborative AI and team productivity

AI is not only helping individual developers, it is also transforming the way entire teams collaborate. Modern software teams deal with large amounts of communication, documentation, and task coordination. AI reduces this workload by generating clear summaries, organizing tasks, and helping team members stay aligned. This results in a smoother development process and fewer miscommunications.

One major benefit is smart documentation. AI can convert discussions, meeting notes, or even code changes into well-structured design documents. This ensures that important decisions are recorded without requiring extra effort from the team. AI can also analyze team expertise and code ownership to suggest the most appropriate reviewers for a pull request, reducing delays in the review process.

AI also strengthens project management. By studying past data such as task completion time, workload distribution, and issue patterns, it can prioritize backlog items intelligently. This helps product managers and teams focus on what truly matters for upcoming releases.

As development infrastructure becomes more abstract, especially with technologies like Kubernetes, cloud-native platforms, and serverless computing, AI acts as the connecting layer. It ensures that developers, operations teams, and tools work in harmony, even when systems are complex and distributed.

Overall, AI improves teamwork, enhances productivity, and keeps projects on track by providing clarity and coordination.

For better clarity, refer to the following table, which highlights the key AI-powered collaboration features and their benefits:

AI feature	How it works	Team benefit
Smart documentation	AI converts discussions / code changes into documents	Saves time and improves clarity
Reviewer suggestions	AI identifies experts for code review	Faster, more accurate reviews
Backlog prioritization	AI predicts project needs and ranks tasks	Better planning and improved productivity

***Table 10.7**: AI-enhanced team collaboration features and benefits*

Enhanced coding efficiency with AI tools

AI-powered tools such as GitHub Copilot, TabNine, and similar intelligent assistants are changing the way developers write and manage code. These tools work directly inside development environments and provide real-time support, making the entire coding process smoother and more efficient. By analyzing the context of the current file, previous functions, and even project-level patterns, AI can predict what a developer is trying to do and offer accurate suggestions instantly.

One of the biggest advantages of these tools is their ability to generate **context-aware code completions**. As a developer types, the AI understands the logic, the surrounding code, and the intent behind the snippet. It then provides relevant suggestions, which reduce the amount of manual typing and help avoid syntax errors. AI can also automatically generate boilerplate code such as class structures, function templates, and repetitive logic, which normally consumes a lot of developer time.

Beyond suggestions, AI tools offer **smart error detection**. They highlight potential issues, incorrect logic, or missing references even before the program is compiled. This leads to a more proactive debugging experience. Many AI assistants also support multiple programming languages, enabling smooth development across different platforms like web, mobile, and cloud.

For developers, the benefits are significant. These tools reduce repetitive work, minimize mental fatigue, and speed up the entire development cycle. Developers can focus more on creative problem-solving rather than routine tasks. In turn, this results in higher productivity, fewer bugs, and quicker delivery of high-quality applications.

For quick reference, the following table outlines the data that highlights how AI improves the coding experience:

AI feature	How it works	Developer advantage
Context-aware suggestions	AI predicts code based on the surrounding context.	Faster coding with fewer errors.
Boilerplate generation	AI writes repetitive structures automatically.	Saves time and reduces manual effort.
Smart error detection	AI identifies issues while typing.	Early debugging and cleaner code.
Multilingual support	AI works across multiple languages.	Flexibility for different platforms.

***Table 10.8**: AI-driven coding features and developer advantages*

Figure 10.1 shows how AI tools interact with different stages of a developer's workflow:

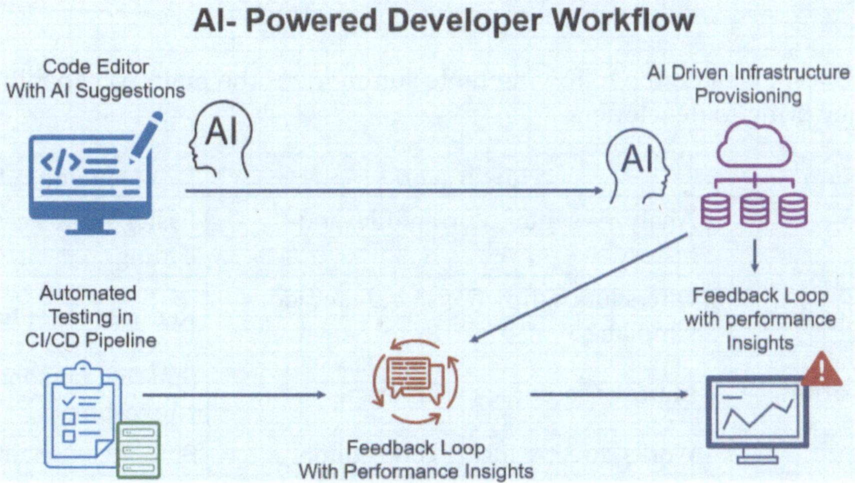

***Figure 10.1**:AI-powered developer workflow*

AI-driven code suggestions and autocompletion

AI-powered autocompletion tools have become an essential part of modern software development. These intelligent assistants help developers by predicting what they want to write next and offering suggestions that match the structure and purpose of the ongoing code. Instead of manually typing every line, developers receive real-time recommendations that fit the project's logic, style, and previous patterns. This not only accelerates coding but also provides guidance when working with unfamiliar frameworks or newly introduced APIs.

These tools work by studying the current file, analyzing syntax, understanding naming conventions, and even learning from the developer's previous work. Over time, the AI becomes more accurate, providing smarter predictions that align closely with the developer's intentions. It can suggest entire methods, loops, conditional blocks, or ready-to-use function calls, reducing the amount of repetitive work involved in writing boilerplate code.

Another major advantage of AI-based autocompletion is its deep integration with modern IDEs. Whether a developer uses VS Code, IntelliJ, PyCharm, or other environments, the AI blends seamlessly into the workflow. This creates a smooth, uninterrupted coding experience where suggestions appear naturally as part of the typing process.

For developers, the benefits are substantial. AI reduces cognitive load by handling routine tasks, lowers the chances of syntax or formatting errors, and ensures consistency with coding standards across a project. It enables faster development cycles and boosts confidence, especially when exploring new technologies or working on complex features. Ultimately, AI autocompletion helps developers become more productive while maintaining high code quality.

To make the concept clearer, the following table summarizes the main AI capabilities and the advantages they bring to developers:

AI feature	How it works	Developer benefit
Context-based predictions	Analyzes syntax, current file, and history.	Faster, more accurate coding.
Full block suggestions	Offers loops, functions, and method templates.	Reduces repetitive tasks.
Continuous learning	Improves accuracy with usage.	Smarter, personalized suggestions.
IDE integration	Works directly inside code editors.	Smooth, efficient workflow.

***Table 10.9**: Key AI autocompletion features and their developer benefits*

Figure 10.2 presents a clear comparison of developer productivity before and after using AI-assisted coding tools. It highlights how AI significantly reduces coding time, error rates, and repetitive effort. This visual summary helps readers quickly understand the impact of AI on the overall development workflow.

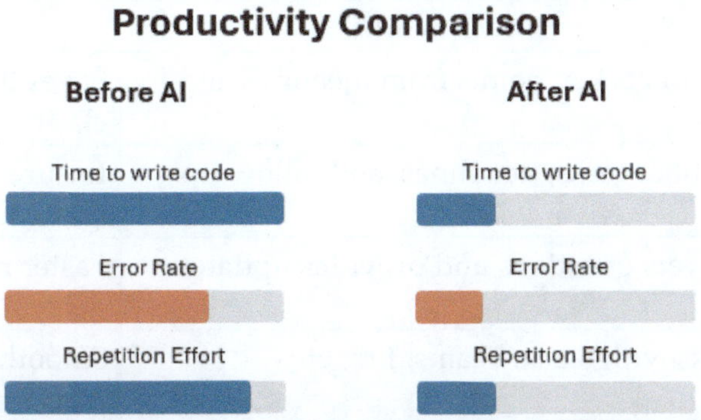

Productivity Comparison

Before AI

Time to write code

Error Rate

Repetition Effort

After AI

Time to write code

Error Rate

Repetition Effort

Figure 10.2*: Productivity comparison: Before AI vs. After AI*

Improved collaboration and communication

AI is rapidly transforming the way software teams collaborate by making communication clearer, faster, and more organized. Modern development teams often work across multiple tools, tasks, and communication channels, which can lead to misunderstandings or missed updates. AI helps solve these challenges by analyzing conversations, summarizing key points, and highlighting the most important actions that team members need to take. This ensures that everyone stays aligned, whether they are developers, testers, or operations personnel.

One of the major advantages of AI in collaboration is its ability to automatically generate concise summaries of meetings, discussions, or chat threads. Instead of re-reading long conversations, team members can simply look at the summarized highlights. AI can also identify potential action items—such as tasks, bugs, follow-ups, or deadlines—and present them in an organized format. This helps teams maintain clarity even during fast-paced development cycles.

Additionally, AI-powered chatbots play a supportive role by answering common coding questions, providing project updates, or reminding team members about pending tasks. When integrated with popular collaboration platforms like Slack, Microsoft Teams, or Jira, AI can prioritize important messages, suggest task scheduling, and ensure that critical information does not get buried.

For developers, the benefits are substantial. AI reduces communication overload, helps teams make faster decisions, and prevents misunderstandings. This leads to smoother workflows, better team coordination, and quicker project delivery.

For better clarity, refer to the following table that highlights the role of AI in improving collaboration:

AI feature	How it works	Team benefit
Automatic summaries	AI extracts key points from meetings and chats.	Saves time and improves clarity.
Action item detection	Identifies tasks, deadlines, and follow-ups.	Ensures nothing important is missed.
AI chatbots	Answers questions and provides updates.	Faster response and reduced delays.
Tool integration	Works with Slack, Teams, Jira, etc.	Smooth coordination across platforms.

Table 10.10: AI-enhanced collaboration features and their team benefits

The following image visually represents how AI integrates into modern software development teams to enhance collaboration and productivity.

It highlights AI-driven features such as smart assistance, automated suggestions, and streamlined communication flows.

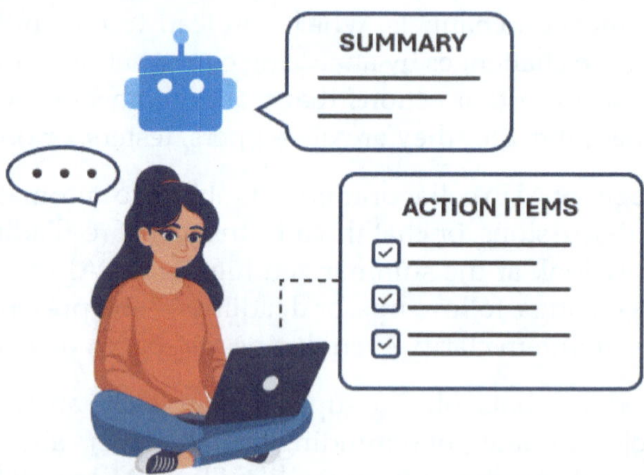

Figure 10.3: AI-powered team collaboration workflow

The illustration shows how AI helps developers, testers, and managers stay aligned through real-time insights and intelligent support.

AI-enhanced debugging and troubleshooting

AI has transformed the way developers debug and monitor software systems. Traditionally, identifying bugs required manually scanning logs, reviewing hundreds of lines of code, and spending hours tracing the source of the issue. AI now makes this process far more efficient by understanding code behavior, detecting unusual patterns, and pinpointing the exact causes of problems much faster than manual methods.

AI-powered tools continuously scan application performance, error logs, runtime data, and system events. When something goes wrong—such as a sudden spike in response time or a function behaving unexpectedly—AI instantly identifies the anomaly and informs the developer. Instead of searching blindly, developers receive clear insights about what went wrong and why.

Another major advantage is that AI provides intelligent suggestions. When a developer encounters an error, AI can recommend the most likely fixes, point to documentation, or show similar bugs resolved in the past. This reduces trial-and-error and speeds up the entire debugging cycle. AI can even simulate the impact of code changes, helping developers verify solutions before deploying them to production.

AI also strengthens system stability. With real-time monitoring, teams receive alerts about potential problems before they escalate. This enables quick incident response and reduces downtime—an essential factor for maintaining smooth operations.

Overall, AI takes over the repetitive and time-consuming parts of debugging so developers can focus on improving features and building better software. It leads to cleaner code, faster issue resolution, and a more reliable production environment.

The following table summarizes how AI contributes to debugging and monitoring while highlighting the key benefits for developers. It provides a clear comparison between AI capabilities and the advantages they offer.

AI contribution	Developer benefit
Automated analysis of logs and errors	Faster identification of bugs
Smart fix suggestions and documentation links	Reduced debugging effort
Simulation of code changes	Safer and more accurate fixes
Real-time anomaly detection	Quick incident response and less downtime

***Table 10.11**: AI in debugging and monitoring, contributions, and developer benefits*

AI-driven continuous learning for developers

AI is transforming the way developers learn and grow in their profession. Instead of following traditional learning methods—like searching for courses, reading through long documents, or attending workshops—AI brings learning directly into the daily workflow. It studies how a developer writes code, what tools they use, and where they face difficulties. Based on these patterns, AI delivers personalized learning support that blends naturally with everyday tasks.

AI systems can identify gaps in a developer's knowledge by observing coding behavior. For example, if someone frequently struggles with a particular library, syntax pattern, or concept, the AI recognizes it and suggests relevant tutorials or documentation. This targeted learning eliminates the need to browse multiple resources and ensures that developers get only the most useful content.

In addition, AI provides interactive learning experiences such as short quizzes, coding challenges, and instant feedback. These features allow developers to practice concepts in real-time and understand mistakes immediately, because the learning content adapts based on progress, and developers receive guidance that matches their skill level and personal goals. Whether someone wants to master a new framework or strengthen fundamentals, AI adjusts the learning journey accordingly.

This approach makes upskilling more efficient. Developers no longer have to pause work or spend hours searching for the right materials. Instead, AI acts as a personal learning assistant—delivering the exact information needed at the right moment. This type of continuous, on-the-job learning not only saves time but also improves confidence and performance in real projects.

The following table presents how AI supports continuous learning and how these contributions directly help developers. It summarizes the connection between AI features and their practical benefits:

AI contribution	Developer benefit
Identifies skill gaps from coding patterns.	Focused learning without guesswork.
Suggests personalized tutorials and documentation.	Saves time searching for resources.
Provides quizzes and real-time feedback.	Faster understanding and improvement.
Adapt learning content to progress.	Learning stays relevant and effective.

***Table 10.12**: AI-powered continuous learning, features, and developer advantages*

Evolving role of developers in the age of AI

AI is reshaping the software development industry, and with it, the role of developers is also undergoing a major transformation. Instead of spending most of their time on repetitive activities like writing boilerplate code, running tests, or fixing minor bugs, developers now work alongside AI tools that automate these tasks. This shift is allowing developers to take on more strategic and creative responsibilities within a project.

AI systems support the development process by generating useful code suggestions, completing functions, and automating many routine activities. However, these AI-generated outputs still require human oversight. Developers are now expected to review, validate, and fine-tune the code that AI produces to ensure it is secure, reliable, and aligned with project goals. This means developers must develop strong analytical and decision-making skills to verify AI contributions.

Additionally, the rise of AI introduces new skill requirements. Developers are increasingly working on tasks related to integrating AI APIs, managing data pipelines, understanding model behavior, and even designing prompts that guide AI tools effectively. This expands the developer's role beyond traditional coding and pushes them toward more advanced responsibilities such as system optimization and architecture planning.

Overall, AI is enhancing the quality of work developers do. With less time spent on repetitive tasks, they can concentrate on solving complex problems, designing innovative features, and ensuring ethical use of AI in software systems. This evolution opens new career paths and positions developers as strategic contributors rather than just implementers of code.

The following table shows how AI is redefining developer responsibilities and the specific advantages this shift brings. It clearly highlights how daily tasks are transforming and what developers gain from this evolution.

AI contribution	How developers benefit
Automation of repetitive coding and testing.	More time for creative and complex tasks.
AI-generated code requiring human validation.	Stronger oversight and quality improvement.
New skills: AI integration, data handling, and prompt design.	Expanded career opportunities.
Support in architecture and system optimization.	More strategic involvement in projects.

***Table 10.13**: How AI is transforming developer responsibilities and benefits*

Challenges and considerations

While AI brings major improvements to the software development process, its integration also comes with several difficulties that organizations and developers must carefully manage. These challenges arise because AI systems are not perfect and often rely on large datasets, automated decision-making, and complex algorithms. As a result, developers need to balance the advantages of AI with an awareness of its limitations. If these issues are not addressed early, they can affect code quality, team efficiency, and overall project reliability.

One of the biggest concerns is that developers may become too dependent on AI-generated suggestions. When this happens, their problem-solving and critical-thinking skills may decline over time because they are not fully engaging with the code. In addition, AI tools are usually trained on publicly available datasets, which may contain biased or faulty examples. This can introduce ethical concerns, security risks, or unexpected behavior in the final software. Another major issue is explainability—AI may recommend a solution without providing clear reasoning. When developers cannot understand why something is suggested, trusting the output becomes difficult, especially for sensitive or high-risk tasks.

Adapting to new AI-powered tools also requires time and effort. Developers must learn how to interpret AI responses, customize tool settings, and evaluate outputs critically. This learning curve can temporarily slow down productivity.

To overcome these challenges, organizations must promote transparency in how AI systems operate, provide training to help teams use AI responsibly, and encourage regular feedback so the tools can improve over time. With the right safeguards, AI can remain a powerful assistant without compromising developer skills or software quality.

The following table summarizes the major challenges developers may face when adopting AI into their workflow. It organizes each concern along with a brief explanation for better clarity.

Challenge	Explanation
Overreliance on AI	Developers may depend too much on AI suggestions, reducing independent skill growth.
Data bias	AI trained on biased datasets can cause ethical, security, or performance issues.
Lack of explainability	AI may provide solutions without context, making validation difficult.
Learning curve	Developers need time to adapt to AI-enhanced tools and workflows.

***Table 10.14**: Key challenges in AI integration*

The shift from traditional development practices to AI-augmented environments has brought significant changes in how developers interact with tools, teams, and infrastructure. The following table presents a side-by-side comparison to clearly show how AI has enhanced the developer experience across different areas of the software lifecycle:

Aspect	Traditional development	AI-enhanced development
Code writing	Manual typing and referencing documentation.	Smart suggestions and auto-completion.
Debugging	Time-consuming and manual.	AI-assisted with quick root cause analysis.
Infrastructure setup	Manual configuration and provisioning.	Automated using AI and **infrastructure as code** (**IaC**).
Collaboration	Based on manual communication and code reviews.	AI suggests reviewers and summarizes discussions.
Learning and skill growth	Developer-driven, with limited personalized resources.	Adaptive and personalized AI-driven learning paths.
Security and compliance	Post-development security checks.	Real-time security feedback integrated into workflow.

***Table 10.15**: Comparison of traditional vs. AI-enhanced developer experience*

The following figure illustrates a side-by-side comparison of traditional development practices and AI-enhanced development, highlighting key differences in efficiency, automation, and intelligence across the software development lifecycle:

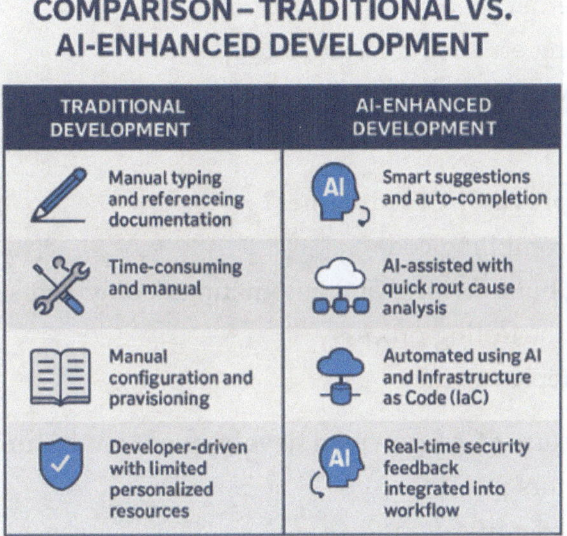

***Figure 10.4**: Traditional vs. AI-enhanced development*

Conclusion

This chapter explains how AI is changing the way developers work, especially in IT infrastructure and operations. AI helps developers write better code faster, fix bugs easily, and manage systems with less effort. It also supports developers by giving smart code suggestions, automating testing, and helping with quick deployment.

AI tools can make work easier by handling routine tasks, personalizing workflows, and offering learning tips based on each developer's needs. Developers can also collaborate better as AI improves communication and team coordination. However, the chapter also discusses challenges, such as over-reliance on AI and the need to understand how AI decisions are made.

Overall, AI is not replacing developers but helping them become more productive and creative. This chapter helps readers understand how to work with AI tools and prepare for the future of software development in smart IT environments. In the next chapter, we will discuss the critical role of well-crafted prompts in unlocking the full potential of **large language models** (**LLMs**) and enabling accurate, efficient task performance, and explore automated prompt engineering techniques that simplify and optimize the process of creating effective prompts.

Multiple choice questions

1. **What is one major benefit of AI in code autocompletion?**
   a. Increased internet speed
   b. Reduced typing errors and faster coding
   c. Longer code writing time
   d. Improved battery life
2. **How does AI improve CI/CD pipelines?**
   a. By manually compiling code
   b. By predicting build failures and automating deployments
   c. By removing the testing process
   d. By blocking deployments
3. **What is a key feature of AI-powered development environments?**
   a. Static text editors
   b. Manual error identification
   c. Real-time code suggestions and formatting
   d. Hardware updates
4. **How does AI help in debugging?**
   a. By hiding bugs
   b. By adding more logs
   c. By analyzing logs and suggesting fixes
   d. By restarting the system
5. **What is the role of AI in smart infrastructure provisioning?**
   a. Preventing server access
   b. Manual configuration of each device
   c. Automating setup and scaling
   d. Increasing code length
6. **AI tools help developers collaborate better by:**
   a. Sending frequent emails
   b. Automatically merging code
   c. Summarizing discussions and recommending reviewers
   d. Limiting access to the codebase

7. **Personalized developer workflows are made possible by**:
   a. Group settings only
   b. Hard-coded workflows
   c. AI learning developer behavior and preferences
   d. Shared server files

8. **Which of the following is not an AI benefit in the developer experience?**
   a. Repetitive task automation
   b. Smart testing
   c. Automatic hardware replacement
   d. Real-time feedback

9. **How does AI enhance security in development?**
   a. By hiding code
   b. By enforcing offline work only
   c. By scanning for vulnerabilities in real-time
   d. By deleting old code

10. **What is a challenge developers may face with AI tools?**
    a. Faster learning
    b. Clear documentation
    c. Overdependence on AI and lack of transparency
    d. Better work-life balance

11. **What does AI offer in personalized learning?**
    a. Same lessons for all developers
    b. Tutorials based on skill gaps and progress
    c. Weekly quizzes only
    d. Team-based workshops only

12. **What kind of tasks can AI tools automate for developers?**
    a. Project planning
    b. Code reviews, syntax formatting, and testing
    c. Team meetings
    d. Business strategy creation

13. **Which of the following is a key change in job roles due to AI in development?**
    a. Developers writing more documentation
    b. Developers becoming passive users
    c. Developers shifting to strategic and design-focused roles
    d. Developers replacing AI systems
14. **What is a benefit of AI-driven observability?**
    a. Slower incident resolution
    b. Anomaly detection and root cause analysis
    c. Manual log review
    d. Ignoring system health
15. **Which table compares developer experience with and without AI?**
    a. Table of programming languages
    b. Table of server specifications
    c. Comparison of traditional vs. AI-enhanced developer experience
    d. Table of software licenses

Answers

1	b
2	b
3	c
4	c
5	c
6	c
7	c
8	c
9	c
10	c
11	b
12	b
13	c
14	b
15	c

CHAPTER 11

Coding to Prompting an Agentic AI Revolution

Introduction

Prompts are natural-language instructions that can effectively empower different language models to perform well on their tasks. Creating and feeding clever, specific prompts is essential to getting more out of LLMs. Prompt engineering is, therefore, an important field of engineering in the agentic AI era. However, prompt engineering has proven to be a complex process, as crafting highly effective prompts is neither simple nor straightforward. However, well-crafted prompts are indispensable, as they can guide LLMs to generate accurate and appropriate results. Thus, for effectively completing language processing, understanding, and generation **natural language processing, understanding, and generation** (**NLP/U/G**) tasks, LLMs, in conjunction with powerful prompts, are the need of the hour. Prompts may include queries, context, examples, and instructions to fully leverage LLMs. In short, carefully and contextually prepared prompts go a long way toward deeply and decisively enriching LLMs so they can perform their tasks precisely and perfectly. Thus, to leverage the astonishing and astronomical power of autoregressive and diffusion language models, the role and responsibility of highly optimized, well-organized prompts become even more significant. This chapter is prepared to elucidate the importance of automated prompt engineering. The latter portion of the chapter explains the evolving automated prompt engineering techniques.

With the widespread adoption of generative AI tools such as **large language models** (**LLMs**), there is a tectonic shift in how software applications and services are built. With the onset of the agentic AI paradigm, software systems are increasingly being built as dynamic collections of AI agents. Due to the overwhelming power of coding assistants propelled by a growing array of language models, there is a fruitful transition from coding to prompting. That is, with optimal prompts, it is possible to create correct software source code. In this chapter, we aim to demystify the need to craft efficient prompts.

Structure

This chapter covers the following topics:

- Recap on agentic AI paradigm
- Illustrating the importance of prompt engineering
- Categorizing prompts

Objectives

The objective of the chapter is to explain the transition from traditional coding to prompt-driven development in the agentic AI era, while highlighting the importance of prompt engineering in enhancing the performance and reliability of language models. It aims to describe the capabilities of agentic AI systems, including reasoning, autonomy, and integration with tools and services, and to outline the structured process of designing, testing, and refining effective prompts. The chapter also focuses on key prompt engineering techniques such as zero-shot, few-shot, and JSON prompting, along with introducing automated prompt engineering methods for improving scalability and efficiency. Overall, it emphasizes the role of well-crafted prompts in enabling accurate, context-aware, and actionable outputs from AI systems.

Recap on agentic AI paradigm

Several years ago, someone famously said that software eats the world. Software solutions are the most significant enabler of business automation. Software has become pervasive and persuasive. For ages, we have been coding in one or more programming languages, such as Python, Java, and Kotlin, to create and deploy robust software solutions for a variety of business, government, and IT problems. There are innumerable software engineering technologies and tools to simplify and speed up software construction.

Today, digital technologies and tools are decisively and deeply impacting every industry vertical and functional domain. Undoubtedly, **artificial intelligence** (**AI**) is a prominent and dominant digitalization technology transforming the business domain. AI thrives as it enables the long-pending goal of data-driven insights and insights-driven decisions and deeds. AI started its transformative innings as a predictive technology. AI facilitates the transition from data to information and to knowledge. That is, the complex task of knowledge discovery and dissemination is being simplified and accelerated by a host of distinct advancements emerging in the AI space. Predictive AI algorithms (**machine learning** (**ML**), **deep learning** (**DL**), and **reinforcement learning** (**RL**)) enable the visualization and implementation of predictive AI models.

Now, from being predictive, AI has transitioned to being generative in its operations and deliveries. Language models (large, small, vision, and multimodal) are blossoming these days to support NLP/U/G use cases. Not only text data, but also visual and audio data are processed, understood, and generated. Thus, generative AI has become pervasive and persuasive with a tremendous adoption of purpose-specific and agnostic language models. Not only NLP but also **computer vision** (**CV**) applications are maturing and becoming more stable as language models advance. Language models are being substantially enhanced by a brew of new techniques and tools, such as **retrieval-augmented generation** (**RAG**) frameworks, knowledge graphs, and vector databases. These advancements help train and feed language models with decision-enabling context details, thereby achieving the goal of producing correct and relevant responses and recommendations.

Now, there is a grandiose leap in the form of agentic AI. We have been fiddling with AI models for a long time. With the ready availability of a dazzling array of competent technologies, there is a strategically sound transition from AI models to AI agents. AI agents are autonomous, meaning they can make decisions and take real-world actions. AI agents internally rely upon AI models and other sources such as data stores (internal and external), microservices, APIs, automated toolkits, enterprise-scale software systems, etc.). Complex activities such as context engineering, user intent understanding, etc., are being elegantly accomplished by AI agents with the help of several innovations being unearthed and articulated in the agentic AI space. AI models are attracting significant attention because they can perform autonomous reasoning, decision-making, and real-world action through internal and external microservices, enterprise-scale software solutions, and automated toolkits. That is, AI agents can collectively complete complex, multi-step tasks with very minimal intervention and instruction from human resources.

With generative AI, we can increasingly express our requirements in natural language. For example, we plan a vacation trip. There are several popular generative AI tools, such as ChatGPT, Gemini, and Llama. All we need to do is describe where we want to go.

As the chosen generative AI tool books the trip, there may be occasions when we need to exit the tool and search for hotel, tourist spot, cab, and airline websites to buy tickets. That is, several decisions and activities should be handled manually. Herein comes the astonishing power of agentic AI. That is, AI agents collaborate to make decisions and perform the identified activities with very minimal human involvement

Without an iota of doubt, agentic AI systems are sufficiently empowered by high-quality AI models, especially language models. How AI agents are game-changing in their functions and deliveries is explained as follows:

- **Reasoning**: LLMs are consistently equipped to be the most prominent and promising reasoning engine. Through reflection, planning, and self-adaptation, the much-vaunted reasoning capabilities are being prepared and made available. The overwhelming success of AI agents lies with this phenomenal upgrade. Thus, language models play a stellar role in shaping the agentic AI phenomenon.
- **Tools, microservices, APIs for enterprise-scale systems**: AI agents can connect to multiple internal and external services, data sources, toolkits, etc., to gain decision-

enabling context. Further, such integration helps AI agents become more autonomous in their decision-making and action-taking.

- **Memory:** There are vector databases, knowledge graphs (graph databases), etc., to store information. AI agents use not only current information but also historical data to make accurate, informed decisions.
- **Goal-oriented autonomy:** AI agents are goal-driven, as they can unambiguously understand the problem at hand by breaking down problem statements into smaller pieces. Through query optimization steps, AI agents could clearly understand the user's Intent.

Thus, with a clear understanding of goals and user intents, AI agents can decide which services and tools to integrate with to become autonomous in their contributions. A seamless and spontaneous integration of many enabling software services, applications, databases, and tools makes AI agents cognitive and complete.

AI agents are being designed and equipped to be trustworthy, transparent, explainable, resilient, and scalable. Agentic AI is being heralded as the transformative paradigm in the long, mesmerizing journey of AI. Multiple AI agents communicate, collaborate, coordinate, negotiate, and compete to build and run sophisticated and autonomous AI systems. A growing array of improvisations and improvements in the agentic AI space can ultimately lead to the realization of the vision of **artificial general intelligence** (**AGI**) or **super intelligence** (**SI**).

Illustrating the importance of prompt engineering

Language models (large, small, vision, and multimodal) are hugely popular in this generative AI era. There are other advances, such as **large-scale reasoning models** (**LRMs**), **large-scale quantitative models** (**LQMs**), **large-scale action models** (**LAMs**), etc. The noteworthy point here is that with LLMs, there is a sound transition from information processing to language processing. There are other advancements, such as RAG frameworks, vector databases, and knowledge graphs, to address the widely reported problem of hallucination. Thus, the use of LLMs for processing and extracting valuable knowledge from multimodal data is skyrocketing. Not only NLP applications but also CV use cases are being developed and implemented as LLMs grow in power.

The adoption rate of language models in our personal, social, and professional lives is simply tremendous. Advanced users also get unique benefits out of language models. However, there are some inhibiting challenges. Moreover, AI researchers, in collaboration with domain experts, are developing sophisticated technology-based solutions to overcome them. As noted, viable solution approaches are being rolled out. However, some limitations persist. There is a multi-pronged approach to resolve those issues. One prominent workaround is to focus intensely on prompt generation. There are pros and cons to manual and automated prompt generation.

A prompt is text-based input for LLMs. Prompting guides and empowers LLMs to generate useful outputs. A prompt can be audio transcribed into text, which is then fed to LLMs to generate output accordingly. Prompts typically consist of instructions and context details. Prompt engineering helps explore and experiment with new applications that utilize LLMs. Well-crafted prompts can yield precise, personalized responses. The hallucination problem gets solved through high-quality prompts. Highly optimized prompts can lead to accurate, appropriate, context-sensitive, and actionable responses from LLMs. Researchers use different prompts to extract new insights from datasets diligently.

Researchers and information seekers can benefit immensely through cognitively formulated prompts. By feeding different prompts, users can gather valuable information, such as a deeper understanding of how an LLM works. With solid experience, users can land on building effective prompts. Prompts come in handy for understanding the limitations of LLMs and for grasping ways to surmount them. With few-shot learning, it is possible to build, release, and run sophisticated, specific LLM applications such as conversational AI chatbots, expert and decision-support systems, and question-and-answer systems. Besides content, source code generation is fast-tracked. Precisely speaking, through carefully designed prompts that are nimbly embedded with context information, it is possible to unlock the full potential of LLMs. The value of LLMs depends squarely on producing and feeding the right prompts. Hence, experts insist on unearthing viable techniques and tools to elicit relevant and rewarding responses and recommendations from LLMs. Therefore, the rise of prompt engineering is phenomenal. Any information seeker has to work smartly to derive high-quality prompts. To obtain varied capabilities from LLMs, the answer is to develop and submit well-crafted prompts.

Prompt engineering in agentic AI concerns the process of designing, structuring, and augmenting prompts that cognitively guide agentic AI systems to fulfil their expectations. Prompt is the brain of any AI agent, containing the details to describe what the agent has to do. Gradually, all the agent's complexity is pushed into the prompt. Therefore, coming up with lean, specific prompts is definitely tough, but technology giants and inspired individuals have developed several enabling tools to simplify prompt creation and tuning. Prompts need to evolve as new use cases and requirements emerge.

Articulating the process of prompt engineering

Here is a list of activities categorized as the way forward to simplify and streamline the complex task of practical prompt engineering:

1. **Defining the goal**: For every serious activity, it is logical to start by defining its goal. For prompt creation, it is also essential to define the prompt's goal. This well-intentioned definition will lay a strong foundation for correct outputs from the LLM.

2. **Understanding the model's capabilities**: There are many language models (large, vision, and multimodal) with varied capabilities. It is essential to have a good

understanding of the model's capabilities. This knowledge helps to synthesize correct prompts.

3. **Choosing the proper prompt format**: Experts insist on forming clear, precise, and concise prompts and feeding them to the model. Such prompts typically comprise all essential context, user intent, constraints, format preferences, and goals. That is, a good prompt comprises a clear user intent, sufficient context, and a specific output format. These well-crafted prompts ultimately enable the language model to produce clear, cogent responses.
4. **Testing and refining**: This is about testing how a prompt works with the chosen language models and refining the generated response to achieve the desired result.

In short, the key tasks in the prompt engineering process are as follows:

1. Define the goal for a prompt formation by illustrating the purpose/task.
2. Deep dive into the task at hand and draft the initial prompt.
3. Turning the prompt by adding structure and context.
4. Verify the output and refine the prompt till getting satisfactory responses.

Key prompt engineering techniques

Prompt engineering pioneers and pundits have proposed several techniques for designing effective prompts. Let us discuss a few:

- **Zero-shot prompting**: providing the language model with an instruction or question without examples.
- **Few-shot prompting**: Here, one or more examples of the desired input/output are embedded in the prompt to guide the language model in its service delivery.
- **Role prompting**: This instructs the language model to represent a specific persona or role. This helps the language model deliver the response accordingly.
- **Contextual prompting**: This is to empower prompts with context information. This helps the language model understand user intent and context. The output will be tailored accordingly.
- **Chain-of-thought (CoT) prompting**: This breaks a complex problem into several easily manageable subtasks, facilitating step-by-step reasoning. The accuracy of the final output through multiple reasoning steps is on the higher side.
- **Tree-of-thoughts (ToT)**: This is to expand CoT by prompting the model to explore many *thought* paths. By treating different reasoning steps as branches of a tree, this technique empowers the language model to backtrack and evaluate its outputs objectively before generating correct responses.

A few more techniques are emerging:

- **Retrieval-augmented prompting**: This is used to attach documents or details to get grounded answers.
- **Instruction chaining**: This is used to break a complex problem into smaller sub-prompts.
- **Prompt templates**: To leverage reusable patterns for specific domains (summarization, coding, etc.).
- **JavaScript Object Notation (JSON) prompting**: This is the technique for structuring prompts (inputs for language models) in JSON format. This is a popular machine-readable and key–value structured mechanism for formally interacting with language models. This prompt structuring helps to send prompts to language models in an unambiguous manner.

JSON prompting is about prompts formatted as JSON objects rather than natural-language text. The JSON contains clearly labelled keys/values that articulate what is expected out of a language model. Instead of a free-form paragraph, we can organize any request using key-value pairs, objects, and arrays within a JSON structure.

Natural language prompt: `Give me study tips for engineering college students.`

The JSON prompt:

```
{
  "task": "study_tips",
  "who_for": "engineering college students",
  "how_many": 4,
  "vibe": "upbeat",
  "output": "list"
```

Another example is as follows:

```
{
  "task": "write a story",
  "topic": "redemption",
  "style": "viral",
  "length": "under 580 characters"
}
```

This is just a contrast to the traditional way of forming prompts, such as `Write a viral-style story about redemption under 580 characters`.

Example 1: JSON as input prompt

The following example illustrates JSON as input prompt:

```
{
  "task": "Create a summary of this research paper",
  "language": "English",
  "text": "Agentic AI is the latest phenomenon in the mesmerizing AI journey. Agentic AI, a collection of collaborative AI agents, is being explored and tested across industry verticals. AI agents can collectively produce and sustain autonomous systems capable of mimicking human brain-like capabilities … "
}
```

Prompt instruction (to the language model):

Read the following JSON and perform the task specified under the task key.

Example 2: JSON output prompt

It is also possible to instruct the language model to respond in JSON format.

Prompt:

```
Summarize the following text in 3 sentences.
Respond only in valid JSON with keys summary and keywords.
The model output will be as per the prompt instruction.
```

Example 3: JSON for multi-step reasoning

The following presents a JSON for reasoning:

```
{
  "question": "What are the benefits of LLM observability platforms?",
  "steps": [
    "Define observability",
    "List a couple of LLM observability platforms.",
    "Provide two real-world examples."
    "Articulate a few key benefits of LLM observability."
   ]
}
```

Example 4: Enforcing JSON schema

Here is a sample:

```
{
  "type": "object",
  "properties": {
    "summary": {"type": "string"},
    "keywords": {"type": "array", "items": {"type": "string"}}
  },
  "required": ["summary"]
}
```

This makes the language model guarantee a specific JSON structure in its output.

The following are the JSON prompting advantages:

- Keys unambiguously specify various parts (task, topic, audience, style, etc.) of the prompt.
- It is possible to tell language models to produce outputs in a preferred format.
- Structured prompts can extract values, integrate with APIs, and automatically validate output, etc.

LLMs can be trained on a lot of JSON-structured data (APIs, configuration files, etc.) to respond accordingly to any JSON-like prompts.

In summary, JSON prompting involves formatting user inputs/prompts/instructions for language models as structured JSON data rather than natural language text. Such a format is intended to ensure greater precision, less ambiguity, and consistent, machine-readable outputs. This technique is suitable for complex tasks and for integrating AI into software applications.

Trends and transition in prompt engineering

Conversational AI chatbots are increasingly prominent across business domains these days. The tremendous success of language models, especially large, small, vision, and multimodal models, has laid a stimulating and sparkling foundation for envisioning and implementing conversational AI systems. To reap all the initially expressed benefits of such advanced systems, it is essential to develop the competency to create and optimize prompts. This need has inspired researchers to focus on prompt engineering, aiming to develop sophisticated techniques for prompt tuning and optimization. Other initiatives include the development of domain-specific prompt engineering tools that can relevantly and rewardingly interface with LLMs. Another popular approach is to leverage ML, DL, and RL algorithms to automate the production of optimized prompts for accomplishing specific tasks. Researchers are exploring advanced techniques, such as transfer learning. As is well known, knowledge distillation is a mature and well-established method that enables transfer learning.

Another research opportunity is to uncover effective ways to responsibly deploy prompt engineering to empower language models to produce highly reliable results. It is important to develop methods that can proactively detect and minimize potential flaws and biases in language models' inputs and outputs. All these equip and ensure that language models deliver traceable, transparent, and trustworthy responses and recommendations. Language models are being keenly and exemplarily experimented with across multiple industry verticals. As prompts are considered the brains of language models, producing effective prompts attracts much attention.

Typically, DL models derived from **deep neural networks** (**DNNs**) are black-box systems. Hence, there are clarion calls to add an explainability/interpretability layer to DL models. Experts say that prompts can enable language models to function and deliver their services in an interpretable, explainable, and reliable manner. The primary focus is on the adroit use of prompt engineering to build efficient, scalable language models.

Importance of well-prepared prompts

As the use of LLMs is trendsetting and tremendous, the use of prompt creation and optimization techniques and tools is rising significantly. Such a tuning is meant to help properly reap all the distinct improvisations being unearthed and articulated in the LLM space. That is, LLMs require expert guidance to generate highly relevant and personalized results. It is not an exaggeration to say that unlocking the growing power of LLMs requires efficient prompts. To substantially improve the accuracy and reliability of LLMs' outputs, it is insisted that high-quality prompts are the need of the hour.

Key aspects of prompt engineering

Prompts are supposed to provide unambiguous instructions to LLMs. Prompts also carry context and prior interaction information, enabling LLMs to generate contextually relevant responses. Further on, prompts can have examples. Positive examples will be associated with the desired output, and negative examples with the undesired output. Different prompts are checked and refined iteratively to arrive at efficient prompts. Prompts can clearly define the task and specify that the response must be in the preferred format.

In short, prompt engineering is being pronounced as the most important ingredient for realizing the astounding success of LLMs. With intelligently crafted prompts, the LLMs' outputs become highly useful and readily actionable. In the agentic AI era, AI agents directly consume LLMs' outputs. Moreover, it is indispensable for LLMs to emit trustworthy recommendations. By methodically incorporating all necessary elements into prompts, it is possible to obtain accurate outputs from LLMs. Besides examples and clear-cut instructions, context and intent must be impeccably embedded in prompts to elicit accurate responses.

As worldwide business behemoths and start-ups embrace LLMs to deliver premium, path-breaking services and applications to their customers and consumers, the importance of highly optimized prompts becomes even more pronounced. Also, experts claim that prompts can easily pinpoint the limitations and capabilities of LLMs. Besides generating responses, LLMs are poised to become orchestration engines and reasoning models. Prompts can enhance LLMs' ability to solve complex tasks, such as real-world conversational AI chatbots and arithmetic reasoning. With RAG becoming the mainstream technology for advancing LLMs, robust prompts can interface not only with LLMs but also with other tools.

Prompts for LLM applications

LLMs are the most recent and advanced AI systems, methodically trained on large corpora of text data to generate relevant responses to user prompts. LLMs are DL models built on the game-changing transformer architecture, which uses the popular multi-head attention mechanism. A transformer is a DNN capable of systematically processing and understanding any hidden relationships between words. Such a more profound understanding empowers LLMs to provide contextually relevant answers to users' queries. There is a growing array of everyday applications for enigmatic LLMs. Natural language processing, understanding, and generation are the top use cases of LLMs.

Prompts play a vital role in shaping tasks such as text summarization, question answering, text classification, conversation, content and code generation, etc. Expert and decision-support systems, language translation, digital assistants, etc., are the renowned applications of LLMs. To obtain robust results from these state-of-the-art AI systems, crafting well-intentioned prompts is essential. It is mandatory to insert appropriate phrases, words, etc., to empower LLMs to correctly understand user intent and maintain a firm grasp of context. This technological empowerment of LLMs enables higher-accuracy, more relevant results. LLMs are becoming multimodal. That is, multimodal LLMs can receive and recognize multimodal data, and on the other side, these powerful LLMs can generate new multimodal content (textual, visual, and audio). Prompt tuning is strongly encouraged to leverage the distinct contributions of multimodal language models. Precisely speaking, **prompt engineering and enhancement (PE2)** techniques make a significant contribution to the design and implementation of sophisticated AI systems.

Distinctions of optimized prompts

Experts have identified several unique advantages of intelligent prompting, as outlined in the following list:

- **Subject matter expertise**: A well-crafted prompt can guide language models to delve into a particular subject of study and research, yielding appropriate answers along with correct source details. For example, take the medicine field. Herein, doctors, surgeons, scholars, nurses, and specialists can formulate well-defined prompts comprising patient history and physiological symptoms into the query field. Thus, language models (large, small, vision, and multimodal) equipped with clever prompts can decisively aid subject matter experts in their everyday assignments and obligations. Well-crafted prompts with many innovations and disruptions (language models, retrieval-augmented generation, vector databases and knowledge graphs, enabling libraries and frameworks, etc.) in the generative AI space can guarantee breakthrough improvements for studying and researching in science and technology domains.

- **Critical thinking**: Numerous noteworthy developments are emerging in the LM space. Reasoning and quantitative models are emerging and evolving rapidly. As problem complexity steadily increases, the power of language models must be enhanced to tackle new challenges. Experts say that language models can analyse information from different perspectives. The language model can then evaluate the credibility of the extracted information to make correct decisions. If there are multiple solutions to a problem, the language model can arrive at and articulate the best-in-class solution. These complex tasks are being greatly simplified and streamlined through the use of mature prompts.
- **Creativity**: It is all about articulating fresh concepts and product proposals. Artificial prompting and prompt tuning can be used insightfully to strengthen language models and generate patentable ideas. Thus, the leverage of effective prompts yields several advantages for LLM users. As far as the benefits of prompt engineering are concerned, there are a few noteworthy ones: improved model performance, reduced bias and hallucination, increased control, consistency, and predictability, fair and personalized responses, enhanced user experience, etc.

The prominent use cases include creative writing, summarization, translation, conversation, **question-answer** (**Q/A**), code generation, optimization and completion, image generation, etc.

Prompt engineering meets agentic AI

Through natural language, we can interact with the agentic AI, which works with us to plan and book travel. A prompt can invoke many AI agents. If the prompt is incorrect, unnecessary AI agents may be invoked. Alternatively, right AI agents may be left out. Thus, prompt generation is a vital task to be done with utmost care. Increasingly, for complex, long-running problems, **multi-agent systems** (**MAS**) are being recommended. Thus, as prompts are to call different agents, prompt building is a difficult task. Experts have recommended two approaches:

- **Driver's seat**: We need to identify and specify which AI agents ought to be called in our prompts. Besides indicating AI agents, the sequence of calling has to be specified. If prompts are not appropriately crafted, we cannot fully leverage the power of AI agents. As we specify everything explicitly, we end up minimizing the risk too much.
- **Passenger's seat**: As LLMs are increasingly intelligent, we can articulate the task or tasks. We do not need to specify which AI agents to invoke or the sequence in which to invoke them. LLMs decide which AI agents to call. LLMs also decide the sequence.

The second approach is like declarative programming, whereas the first one is imperative programming.

Here is an example of a multi-agent system. Let us choose the famous software engineering domain, and let five AI agents handle different activities:

- **CodeReviewer**: This AI agent reviews and checks whether the source code fully complies with best practices and is easily maintainable.
- **BugHunter**: This AI agent is to meticulously traverse through the code to bring forth any security holes or vulnerabilities.
- **CodeFixer**: This AI agent can debug and optimize the source code.
- **PerformanceAnalyzer**: This agent analyses code performance and, based on its findings, recommends relevant code optimizations.
- **DocumentWriter**: This automatically generates documentation for codebases.

For the first case, we need to indicate everything precisely through our prompts. These AI agents do not automatically invoke one another. In the prompt, we can instruct generative AI which of the agent AIs ought to be invoked. We also have to specify the invocation sequence.

Here is the initial prompt:

```
My Python code runs slowly, and I feel there might be some performance bottlenecks. Please run the PerformanceAnalyser AI agent and run the CodeFixer AI agent to fix any performance bottlenecks. Then check whether the code runs faster. Finally, let me know once all the actions are done.
```

The generative AI tool parses the prompt and calls each agent it contains. The generative AI tool may provide one or more clarifications, and once everything is over, we will receive an accomplishment reply.

In the second case, we let the generative AI tool determine which AI agents to invoke and in what sequence. In this case, the initial prompt can be as follows:

```
My Python code runs slowly. I presume it might have some bugs. Please use the relevant AI agents to correct the issues.
```

When this prompt is fed, the generative AI tool can go through the appropriate AI agents, identify issues with the assistance of CodeReviewer and BugHunter, and finally resolve them with CodeFixer.

Thus, AI agents emerge as the next-generation powerhouse for producing sophisticated AI systems. MASs are also getting much attention these days. There are research works that can insightfully recommend which AI agents to call upon to accomplish a task. MAS is the future of AI agents for tackling complex, long-running business problems.

In a nutshell, the generative AI paradigm can succeed or fail based on the prompt crafted and supplied. Any poorly crafted prompts can confuse language models. That is, language models may misinterpret prompts, leading to incorrect results. Thus, with the emergence of MAS, the importance of efficiently generating and feeding prompts is increasingly emphasized.

Prompt engineering gives an important and productive edge. As widely reported, hallucination is being presented as a significant problem of language models. Moreover, experts recommend ways and means of hallucination avoidance prompting. This is all about designing prompts that empower language models to avoid producing incorrect, irrelevant, or inaccurate information. The core principles of hallucination-avoidance prompting are as follows:

- **Grounding**: This is the process of anchoring the language model's reasoning to specific, verifiable sources or context. A prompt example is as follows:

  ```
  Use only the content in the text below, and summarize the author's argument in 2 bullet points.
  ```

- **Instructional clarity**: This is to avoid vague instructions. That is, we need to explicitly tell the language model what to include and exclude.
- **Stepwise reasoning**: This is to encourage transparent reasoning rather than one-shot answers.
- **Role framing**: This enables the language model to deliver its response as a fact-checker, researcher, or summarizer rather than a creative generator.
- **Verification loop**: This asks the language model to double-check its own answer for factual accuracy.

The following are the different techniques of prompt engineering:

- **Chain-of-feedback (CoF) prompting**: This is a powerful prompt engineering technique that can improve the quality of language model outputs. This improvement is being achieved by incorporating structured feedback loops into the generation process. Feedback is used to evaluate and fine-tune.
- **CoT prompting**: This technique is used to improve reasoning, problem-solving, and multi-step inference performance. This is to encourage the language model to generate intermediate reasoning steps before arriving at a final answer.
- **CoT factored decomposition prompting**: This is to enhance the conventional CoT prompting with an additional instruction that tells language models to produce one or more queries and answers while generating responses.
- **Chain-of-verification (CoV) prompting**: This technique extends the traditional CoT approach by adding a verification phase. Here, the language model checks its own reasoning and outputs before arriving at the answer.
- **TrueFakes prompting**: It refers to using structured, ethical prompt engineering to ensure that generative AI outputs are synthetic in authenticity rather than synthetic in deceit.

- **Directional stimulus prompting (DSP)**: This technique is a steerable prompting method that guides model outputs toward desired behaviors without requiring explicit fine-tuning. It sits at the intersection of prompt engineering and implicit model control.

- **Disinformation detection and removal prompting**: Use generative AI as the preferred filter to detect and mitigate disinformation and misinformation across text, images, and multimedia sources. It is recommended to use linguistic, semantic, and contextual cues to distinguish truthful reporting from manipulated content.

- **Emotionally expressed prompting (EEP)**: It refers to the intentional use of emotional language, sentiment, or context in prompts to shape the style, tone, and quality of model-generated responses.

  End-goal prompting: It describes what we ultimately want the language model to produce or achieve. Then it is to ask the language model to generate or plan steps that directly serve that goal.

- **Generating prompts via generative AI**: It involves automatically generating prompts. This is to generate writing, image, or chat prompts.

Demystifying recursive prompt engineering

Recursive prompt engineering (**RPE**) represents a paradigm shift in generative AI. That is, RPE redefines how machines interact with and clearly comprehend human language. RPE is a fresh approach enabling language models to dynamically adapt and refine prompts iteratively. RPE is to substantially enhance language models' capabilities of contextual understanding and response generation.

Traditional prompts are static. That is, a fixed instruction guides the language model's behavior. However, RPE differs in that it introduces a dynamic prompt-generation process. This allows language models to evolve their prompts in real-time by responding to varying contexts and user interactions. The following are various prompts:

- **Traditional prompt**: `Translate the following English text to French: 'The cat is on the mat.'`

- **RPE prompt (After iteration 1)**: `Translate the English text into French.`

- **RPE prompt (After iteration 2)**: `Translate this text to French.`

The following list outlines RPE framework:

- **Initial prompt generation**: The RPE process begins with a generic prompt. This prompt serves as a starting point for the interaction between the user and the language model.

- **User interaction and tuning**: As the user interacts with the language model, practical context details are likely to arise. The additional information serves as decision-enabling cues for effective prompt refinement. The prompt tuning involves removing unnecessary details and adding precision.

- **Response generation**: With the finetuned prompt, the language model can generate responses that are closely aligned with the user's intent and context.
- **Continuous feedback loop**: RPE excels because it uses a continuous feedback loop. User feedback, model performance evaluation, and contextual updates, collectively and iteratively, help tune prompts so that the language model ultimately produces accurate results, recommendations, and responses.

Delineating the RPE techniques

RPE achieves its intended goal by leveraging iterative finetuning to empower language models:

- **Dynamic prompt adaptation**: This enables language models to flexibly adjust their prompts based on user input and context. The noteworthy point here is that dynamic adaptation ensures the prompt is contextually accurate, so the model's response is appropriate.
- **Contextual prompt generation**: This is to generate prompts that are fully and finely aligned to the user interaction.

  User: `Tell me about the weather in Bangalore.`

  Iteration 1: `Provide Bangalore's weather forecast.`

  User: `What about this weekend?`

  Iteration 2: `Give me the weather forecast for Bangalore this weekend.`

  Here, the prompt evolves to capture better the user's context, an evolution and subsequent adaptation yield a precise and concise response.

- **Intent recognition and disambiguation**: As articulated, user intent recognition is vital for language models to respond reliably and confidently.

  User: `Find articles about Chips.`

  Iteration 1: `Search for articles about banana chips.`

  User: `No, I meant articles about the microchips.`

  Iteration 2: `Retrieve articles about the microchips.`

- **Hybrid approaches**: This involves combining multiple RPE methods to achieve good performance. For example, a Q/A system can use dynamic prompt adaptation, contextual prompt generation, and user intent recognition concurrently.

  User: `Who wrote 'War and Peace'?`

  Iteration 1: `Find the author of 'War and Peace'.`

  Iteration 2: `Tell me the author of 'War and Peace'.`

RPE represents a dynamic, iterative approach to significantly enhancing language models. Iteratively adapting prompts and capturing context through user interactions helps language models produce accurate, relevant results. There will be continuous improvements in the RPE space to unlock the full potential of language models. Not only text but also visual and audio prompts will be powered by RPE in the years to unfold.

Prompt engineering for code generation

Diffusion-driven prompt tuning (**DDPT**) for code generation—as is widely known, large language models excel in content and code generation. However, the output quality of LLMs depends squarely on the quality of the prompts crafted and supplied. However, producing high-quality prompts is beset with many practical challenges. There is a need for considerable knowledge and expertise for prompt engineering. In short, valid prompts are essential for information seekers, software developers, and researchers to benefit from language models. Having taken the necessity of crafting sagacious prompts into acute consideration, a team of researchers *(Jinyang Li and his team)* has proposed a novel solution (Diffusion-Driven Prompt Tuning). DDPT can generate optimal prompt embedding from Gaussian Noise. This is to automate the generation of quality prompts for code generation.

The DDPT method uses the diffusion-based optimization and abstracts the optimal prompt embedding as a directional vector. Further, the authors have used code-generation losses provided by the LLMs to help the diffusion model capture the distribution of optimal prompt embeddings during training. The trained diffusion model can build a path from the noise distribution to the optimal distribution. The research paper shows that DDPT improves prompt optimization for code generation.

Experts recommend that creating high-quality code-generation prompts involves variant testing, prompt chaining, versioning, integration with development flows, and output evaluation.

Understanding automated prompt engineering

Prompt engineering has become a critical aspect for extracting and articulating the unique capabilities of LLMs. To draw LLMs' fullest potential, prompt tuning is important. Manual prompt creation can be highly time-consuming, error-prone, and yield suboptimal results. Automating this process is a game-changer for the LLM era. **Automated prompt engineering** (**APE**) is a novel method for systematically and sagaciously generating prompts that can deliver significant performance improvements in LLM workloads. APE helps in reducing trial and error. APE optimizes LLM responses and scales across different domains and use cases.

Automated prompt engineering approaches

Automated prompt generation for LLMs involves using software, models, templates, or workflows to automatically create and refine prompts. Automated prompt engineering is important because prompts must incorporate context and personal details. The business problems to be solved through prompting are also becoming complex and involving multiple steps. Producing prompts manually is a slow, error-prone process; automated generation uniformly applies rules and styles to produce consistent, convincing prompts. Automation involves experimentation and explores several variations; hence, prompt accuracy is bound to improve significantly.

There are a few concrete approaches towards automated prompt generation:

- **Template-based prompt construction**: Use predefined templates with variables filled dynamically.
- **Self-refining**: This enables language models to generate and improve their own prompts iteratively to satisfy user requirements.
- **Prompt optimization using grid search**: The grid searches through many prompt variations.
- **Programmatic prompt assembly in RAG pipelines**: This retrieves relevant knowledge chunks and inserts them into a structured prompt.

```
PROMPT = SYSTEM + RETRIEVED_CONTEXT + EXAMPLE_PAIRS + USER_INPUT
```

APE can augment manual prompt creation with intelligent automation. There are a few automation approaches, which are outlined in the following list:

- **Breakthrough algorithms for automated prompt engineering**: APE uses powerful algorithms to generate many prompts for a given task, test them, and iteratively refine them to enhance their ultimate performance. This automation is intended to significantly reduce users' cognitive load. Also, APE can produce better results compared to manual prompt creation and enhancement.

- **Dynamic adaptation**: Prompts for a particular task are continuously checked and refined in real-time with feedback from the LLM, making this adaptation especially effective in production environments.

- **Exemplar selection**: By choosing appropriate example prompts, the response-generating LLM can solidly enhance its understanding of the task at hand. With a deeper understanding, the LLM can generate accurate responses. Exemplar selection is touted as a promising APE technique, referring to the dynamic selection of example prompts from a dataset. The selected example prompts are the most relevant to the query at hand.

This is to select a subset of examples that guide the LLM to generate an accurate response. By automating this selection process, it is possible to set up and sustain a system that can artistically choose the best exemplars. The following list outlines a few implementation methods:

- **Clustering input queries**: This proposes the proven clustering approach. That is, all input queries must be grouped by semantic similarity. Semantic similarity helps with advanced context understanding.
- **Metric-driven selection**: Here, the recommended approach is to use performance metrics, such as accuracy, relevance, and confidence scores, to inform exemplar selection. The selection process can be automated by training a classifier to predict which exemplars are most likely to yield the best results.
- **Contextual embeddings**: It uses embedding models to represent both the input and possible exemplars and then calculates the cosine similarity between them to select the closest match.
- **Feedback loop**: This technique facilitates continuous evaluation of the LLM's performance based on the prompts it generates. Then, the prompt parameters are accordingly adjusted to achieve better results.
- **Prompt diversity generation**: Here is a tool to automate the generation of a diverse set of prompts. This can empower the language model to generalize. Therefore, the widely talked-about problem of overfitting can be substantially minimized:
    - **Synonym substitution**: The words in the prompt get replaced with their synonyms while not damaging the prompt semantics.
    - **Paraphrasing models**: There are paraphrasing models that can help generate multiple variations of a prompt. Then test the language model's performance with the paraphrased prompts. This opens the door to increased performance.

Prompt diversity generation is about creating multiple varied prompts to accomplish the task at hand with all the astuteness. This is to improve the robustness of language model outputs.

Reinforcement learning for prompt optimization

RL algorithms are popular because they can produce and deploy advanced AI models to tackle complex tasks. In recent years, researchers have explored leveraging the distinct advances in the RL space to optimize prompts. Using RL algorithms, the goal is to automatically improve prompts. This is to equip language models to produce better outputs that meet objectives such as creativity, correctness, and conciseness.

RL provides a systematic feedback loop. It starts with generating an output using the initial prompt. Then, the output score must be computed using a reward function. Then the next logical step is to update the prompt to increase the reward value. Higher rewards correspond to better prompts. This is getting repeated till the required performance is achieved. Thus, RL algorithms are tuned to expedite the automatic generation of prompts. That is, the idea is to integrate RL into APE. Some works illustrate how to use policy gradient methods in RL to train a model that generates optimal prompts. The policy is iteratively improved by using the reward signal. Another option is to start with simple prompts and gradually introduce more complex ones. Such an approach helps the model to learn to be perfect.

Active learning for automated prompt engineering

Active learning can be used to refine any automatically generated prompts. The key idea here is that the system first learns which examples are the most informative ones and then generates prompts accordingly:

- **Uncertainty sampling**: The APE system can request human feedback or additional data if the language model's output is not up to the mark. This feedback loop is to enhance the language model's performance.
- **Iterative finetuning**: It combines the outputs of the language model with human-labeled data, making it easy and fast to refine the prompt-generation system.

Integration with MLOps pipelines

It is shown that APE tools can be fit seamlessly into MLOps pipelines. Integrating APE with MLOps is essential as businesses worldwide increasingly adopt different language models across their processes/workflows. Previously, MLOps pipelines were created and used for static models trained on structured data and static parameters. There are several open-source and commercial-grade MLOps platforms and tools. MLflow is one of the popular MLOps tools. However, LMs primarily depend upon well-prepared prompts. Prompts are typically dynamic instructions for language models. Due to this dynamism, prompts ought to be versioned, optimized, verified, and monitored.

Integration of APE with MLOps

Once language models are deployed, prompts are getting changed frequently, business requirements continuously evolve to cope with the market sentiments, data and performance drifts can occur, and even language models' versions may also advance. So, it is essential that prompts be version-controlled, their performance minutely monitored, and they be retrained automatically, etc. That is, prompts are the first-class MLOps artifacts.

The benefits of automated prompt engineering are clear: improved accuracy, lower latency, and scalability for any LLM workloads. By integrating APE into our existing workflow, we can achieve consistent and reliable performance improvements.

In summary, APE is a powerful approach to optimizing LLM performance, delivering significant improvements in accuracy, latency, and output quality.

Prompt optimization through the hyperparameter optimization technique

As discussed, prompt engineering has proven indispensable in the language model era. The goal of prompt engineering is to carefully design and fine-tune a language model to elicit actionable, trustworthy responses. To enhance model performance, hyperparameter optimization is one of the widely recommended approaches. That is, in addition to optimizing parameters, hyperparameters (learning rates, number of epochs, batch sizes, etc.) are also identified and tuned.

In the traditional case, different strategies (E.g., Random search, grid search, Bayesian search) are used to explore combinations of hyperparameter values systematically. These proven, pivotal strategies and principles can also be applied to APE. Here, hyperparameters are numerical, so selecting values for them is easy and fast. Prompt is a different type of hyperparameter, as prompts are primarily text-based. Therefore, generating prompts is not easy. However, language models are increasingly being considered as tools for continuously generating prompts.

There are three key ingredients for initiating and implementing the APE workflow:

- A labelled dataset representative of the task for which an optimized prompt has to be generated.
- An initial prompt
- An evaluation metric

The APE workflow commences with the initial prompt and the dataset being fed into the target language model. The language model generates responses based on the dataset and the initial prompt. Now, an evaluator language model is used to evaluate the language model's response. Then, an optimizer language model is invoked to generate a new prompt. These generation, evaluation, and optimization steps are repeated until the prompt is sufficiently refined. Finally, it is all about choosing the best-in-class prompt. This automated process generates many prompts quickly.

Strategies for prompt optimization

Random prompt optimization, such as hyperparameter optimization via random search, also takes a brute-force approach. Here, the optimizer LLM generates a series of random prompts without considering previous prompts or their results.

Optimization by PROmpting (OPRO), as mentioned, the method of random prompt optimization is analogous to random search in hyperparameter optimization. OPRO, on the other hand, is the same as the Bayesian search. In OPRO, we actively hill-climb using results from previous iterations to minimize the evaluation metric. OPRO meticulously keeps track of the scores for all previous prompts and sorts this set of prompts by a performance metric along an optimization trajectory. This guides the optimizer LLM to pinpoint effective prompts.

The key aspect in OPRO is the meta-prompt, which guides the optimizer LLM. With this prompt, the optimizer LLM can analyze patterns in the optimization trajectory. This helps identify the elements of successful prompts and eliminate unsuccessful ones. This learning process iteratively empowers the optimizer to generate increasingly better prompts.

Moving beyond prompt optimization with exemplar selection

There are a few other approaches to optimizing prompt generation. Instead of just providing instructions, it is recommended to give a few examples of the ultimate output. This is typically termed as few-shot prompting. Such embedded examples adroitly enhance the power of LLMs in generative optimized prompts. The examples incorporated go a long way toward enhancing LLMs' generative power by improving understanding.

Few-shot prompting can be added to APE via exemplar selection, which helps in selecting the best few-shot examples for a given task. By incorporating a few examples, it is possible to generate optimized prompts. If an optimized prompt is identified via OPRO, a few examples can significantly improve the target LLM's performance. The aspect of exemplar selection systematically tests different sets of examples and tracks the performance of the prompts.

Delineating APE frameworks and tools

There are several tools and frameworks for enabling automated prompt engineering. These come in handy in generating, evaluating, and optimizing ng prompts for different language models. APE extends the manually crafted prompts by adding competent tools:

- Generating many prompt variants instead of hand-crafting each.
- Evaluating prompts systematically through performance metrics.
- Versioning, tracking, and managing prompts as first-class artifacts in your workflow.
- Integrating feedback loops to refine prompts further.

The prominent APE tools are as follows:

- **PromptLayer**: It is a popular tool for prompt version control, logging, and capturing prompt-model interactions and model-agnostic templates.
- **LangSmith**: It is another tool built for LLM application workflows. Supports debugging, structured output, and prompt evaluation.
- **PromptPerfect**: It is for automated prompt optimization. It takes a prompt and refines it to get better outputs for various LLMs.
- **PromptAppGPT**: It is a low code framework for building applications via prompts. This includes automatic user interface generation and related features.
- **Humanloop**: It lets real user feedback drive prompt improvement.

Libraries like *DSPy*[1] provide ready-made solutions for implementing prompt optimization and exemplar selection techniques. These libraries handle the complex algorithms behind the scenes, so we can focus on using APE without getting bogged down in the technical details. However, while these libraries are undoubtedly helpful, they often operate as black boxes, hiding the inner workings of the optimization process.

Categorizing prompts

There are various types of prompts used for activating LLMs:

- **Direct prompts (Zero-shot)**: This involves providing the model with a direct instruction or question without any additional context or examples. An example is to request the generation of an essay on deforestation.
- **One, few, and multi-shot prompts**: This involves providing the model with one or more examples of the desired input-output pairs before presenting the actual prompt.
- **CoT prompting**: It is a powerful technique widely recommended for subdividing a complex question into a few easily manageable, logical parts. This empowers the language model to solve problems through several steps rather than a direct and single step. Such an approach can produce correct and cognitive results.
- **Zero-shot CoT prompts**: This combines CoT prompting with zero-shot prompting by asking the model to perform reasoning steps, which may often produce better output.
- **Tree-of-thought prompting**: This is another popular technique that generalizes the chain-of-thought prompting method. This prompts the model to generate one or more possible solution steps. Then the proven tree search method is applied to determine the best-in-class steps that yield the most competent answers.
- **Generated knowledge prompting**: Firstly, it prompts the model to generate relevant facts necessary to arrive at a competent and complete prompt. For example, a user prompts the model to create an essay on the negative impacts of deforestation. The model might first generate facts like deforestation contributes to climate change and deforestation leads to loss of biodiversity. The model will then generate the final output.
- **Least-to-most prompting**: The model is first prompted to list the subproblems of a problem, then to solve them in sequence.
- **Self-refine prompting**: The model is prompted to solve the problem, critique its own solution, and then resolve the problem, considering the problem, solution, and critique. This refinement process gets repeated till a satisfactory answer is reached.

1 https://dspy.ai/

- **Directional-stimulus prompting**: This technique includes a hint or cue, such as desired keywords, to guide the language model toward the desired output.
- **JSON prompting**: JSON prompting is the process of structuring LLM queries using the JSON data format. Such a formulation of queries is to increase clarity, consistency, and precision in LLMs' outputs. Instead of an ambiguous text prompt, users' queries are structured as key-value pairs, arrays, and objects.

All the mentioned techniques support practical prompt engineering.

Conclusion

Manual prompt engineering is time-consuming and error-prone. Prompt generation requires a good understanding of prompt structures and how they behave with and activate the language model. It is always challenging to give language models clear, concise instructions for specific tasks. Also, manually trying out different prompts is time-consuming. That is why there is an insistence on unearthing technology-powered solutions to automate prompt generation and tuning. In this chapter, we have discussed the challenges of manual prompting, the need for automated prompting, techniques and tips for accelerated, accurate prompt generation, and key approaches to simplifying and streamlining automated prompt engineering. Finally, some automated tools for APE are described. This chapter provides detailed guidance on engineering optimal prompts in an automated manner, thereby unlocking the hidden capabilities of language models.

Multiple choice questions

1. **What is the primary focus of accelerated software engineering in the agentic AI era?**
   a. Writing long manual codes
   b. Managing hardware devices
   c. Using AI agents to automate development tasks
   d. Avoiding software testing
2. **In the transition from coding to prompting, the developer's role mainly shifts towards:**
   a. Debugging hardware circuits
   b. Writing detailed assembly language
   c. Designing effective prompts for AI systems
   d. Replacing databases manually

3. **Agentic AI systems are characterized by their ability to:**
   a. Act autonomously to complete tasks
   b. Store only static data
   c. Operate without algorithms
   d. Eliminate user interaction completely

4. **Prompt engineering primarily involves:**
   a. Configuring network cables
   b. Structuring inputs to obtain desired AI outputs
   c. Writing machine code
   d. Designing computer chips

5. **One major advantage of AI-assisted software development is:**
   a. Increased manual workload
   b. Slower development cycles
   c. Faster prototyping and deployment
   d. Reduced collaboration

Answers

1	c
2	c
3	a
4	b
5	c

Index

B

C

H

I

J

K

L

M

N

O

P

W

Z